TEACHING THE TEXT

TEACHING THE TEXT

EDITED BY

Susanne Kappeler
and
Norman Bryson

Routledge & Kegan Paul
London, Boston, Melbourne and Henley

First published in 1983
by Routledge & Kegan Paul plc
39 Store Street, London WC1E 7DD,
9 Park Street, Boston, Mass. 02108, USA,
296 Beaconsfield Parade, Middle Park,
Melbourne, 3206, Australia, and
Broadway House, Newtown Road,
Henley-on-Thames, Oxon RG9 1EN

Set in 10 on 12 point Baskerville by
Inforum Ltd, Portsmouth
and printed in Great Britain by
Redwood Burn Ltd,
Trowbridge, Wiltshire

ISBN 0-7100-9412-4

Contents

Preface

In the spring of 1981, when the problems and contradictions concerning the study of English at university became temporarily topical in the eyes of the national press, one particular issue, central to our minds, received little or no explicit comment. This was the issue of teaching (as opposed to the issue of keeping or losing a university teaching post), and the issue of theory and its relation to practice. Pronouncements on individual teachers were made on the basis of their research and publications, and there was much talk of cramming students' heads with high-level theories and abstruse research interests. Teaching and research, however, are two different aspects of an academic's activities, and it is one of the foremost tasks of the job to bring them into satisfactory interaction. It is presumably rare for any academic to 'teach' research straight and unmediated to students, i.e., without consideration of the needs and requirements of the students, the curriculum and the departmental structure.

It is a particular feature of English 'literary' criticism, as opposed to continental modes of criticism, that it has rarely concerned itself with 'pure' theory. The strength of English criticism lies in its practice; its potential weakness, in unreflected practice. It is thus neither surprising nor uncharacteristic that a commitment to theory among English critics reflects itself in practice, and that the emphasis is on *approach* – which is approach *to* – rather than on pure methodology and theorising.

The contributors to this volume, all of whom taught for the English faculty during the academic year 1980/1, are committed to teaching through practice, to demonstrating their approaches in use. At present, curriculum determines to a large extent the literary texts to be taught and studied. Students interested in different approaches will learn about them through seeing them in use, applied to the texts they are studying. They may attend a particular lecture because of the set text it deals with, or because of the specific approach used by the lecturer, or both. The question 'Should we teach theory and methodology, or should we teach "literature"/"the literary canon"?' seems the wrong question to ask. Whatever we are teaching, it seems legitimate to ask how.

Academic publishing has largely aligned itself with the category 'research', which is an essential vehicle in the career structure of academics, while textbooks, essential for the students, are a special sub-category. Research publishing has developed its own conventions of genre, emphasising unification through 'theme', 'subject' or 'material', where there is not already unification through single authorship (see casebooks, readers).

It seemed important to us to reflect the reality of teaching in a university English department not only through a variety of teachers/authors and a pluralism of approach, but also through the range of different texts and subjects offered to students: 'canonical' English texts, American studies, European writing, genres, periods, critical issues. Each contribution is taken, of course, from a larger teaching context determined by lists of set texts and lecture courses offered by the faculty. For instance, Frank Kermode's lecture on *Troilus and Cressida* is not just one of eight lectures on Shakespeare, but one of eight lectures on *Troilus*, a set text; John Barrell's piece documents one of a series of classes on eighteenth-century poetry, while Lisa Jardine's lecture was part of a course on 'The literary representation of women'. The criteria of delineating the subject of a lecture or class are markedly different from those of a research paper or learned article for a journal. It is these criteria of teaching that we wish to make visible with this volume.

ı The public figure and the private eye: William Collins' 'Ode to Evening'

John Barrell

This piece is a reconstruction of some remarks made *ex tempore*, punctuated by questions and observations from students and followed by discussion, in one of a series of classes on eighteenth-century poetry.

> If ought of Oaten Stop, or Pastoral Song,
> May hope, chaste *Eve*, to sooth thy modest Ear,
>   Like thy own solemn Springs,
>   Thy Springs, and dying Gales,
> O *Nymph* reserv'd, while now the bright-hair'd Sun   5
> Sits in yon western Tent, whose cloudy Skirts,
>   With Brede ethereal wove,
>   O'erhang his wavy Bed:
> Now Air is hush'd, save where the weak-ey'd Bat,
> With short shrill Shriek flits by on leathern Wing,   10
>   Or where the Beetle winds
>   His small but sullen Horn,
> As oft he rises 'midst the twilight Path,
> Against the Pilgrim born in heedless Hum:
>   Now teach me, *Maid* compos'd,   15
>   To breathe some soften'd Strain,
> Whose Numbers stealing thro' thy darkning Vale,
> May not unseemly with its Stillness suit,
>   As musing slow, I hail
>   Thy genial lov'd Return!   20
> For when thy folding Star arising shews
> His paly Circlet, at his warning Lamp

1

The fragrant *Hours*, and *Elves*
Who slept in Flow'rs the Day,
And many a *Nymph* who wreaths her Brows with Sedge, 25
And sheds the fresh'ning Dew, and lovelier still,
  The *Pensive Pleasures* sweet
  Prepare thy shadowy Car.
Then lead, calm *Vot'ress*, where some sheety Lake
Cheers the lone Heath, or some time-hallow'd Pile,   30
  Or up-land Fallows grey
  Reflect it's last cool Gleam.
But when chill blustring Winds, or driving Rain,
Forbid my willing Feet, be mine the Hut,
  That from the Mountain's Side,   35
  Views Wilds, and swelling Floods,
And Hamlets brown, and dim-discover'd Spires,
And hears their simple Bell, and marks o'er all
  Thy Dewy Fingers draw
  The gradual dusky Veil.   40
While *Spring* shall pour his Show'rs, as oft he wont,
And bathe thy breathing Tresses, meekest *Eve*!
  While *Summer* loves to sport,
  Beneath thy ling'ring Light:
While sallow *Autumn* fills thy Lap with Leaves,   45
Or *Winter* yelling thro' the troublous Air,
  Affrights thy shrinking Train,
  And rudely rends thy Robes.
So long, sure-found beneath the Sylvan Shed,
Shall *Fancy, Friendship, Science,* rose-lip'd *Health,*   50
  Thy gentlest Influence own,
  And hymn thy fav'rite Name![1]

    The 'Ode to Evening', by William Collins, first appeared in 1746, in his *Odes on Several Descriptive and Allegoric Subjects*; though the text I have reproduced incorporates some later revisions presumed to be Collins' own.[2] Exactly what Collins meant by the title of his volume has been the subject of some discussion; in particular, it isn't clear what sort of a distinction he assumed between the allegorical and the descriptive – whether, for example, he thought of them as mutually exclusive, or whether an allegorical subject might also be a descriptive one. What agree-

ment there has been among critics of Collins about his intentions
as a poet has usually been based on those announced by his friend
Joseph Warton, whose odes were at one time intended to be
printed alongside Collins' but in the event appeared separately,
also in 1746. Warton prefaced his collection with an advertisement in which he claimed for them an intention usually taken to
correspond pretty much with Collins' own:

> The Public has been so much accustom'd of late to didactic
> Poetry alone, and Essays on moral Subjects, that any work
> where the imagination is much indulged, will perhaps not
> be relished or regarded. The author therefore of these
> pieces is in some pain least certain austere critics should think
> them too fanciful or descriptive. But as he is convinced that
> the fashion of moralizing in verse has been carried too far,
> and as he looks upon Invention and Imagination to be the
> chief faculties of a Poet, so he will be happy if the following
> Odes may be look'd upon as an attempt to bring back Poetry
> into its right channel.[3]

The emphasis Warton wished to place on invention and imagination, at the expense of the didactic and moral, can be understood
in terms of the process whereby poetry becomes, in the mid-
eighteenth century, more concerned with the direct representation of nature – what I mean there by 'direct' will become evident
later; for you will notice that Warton seems to assume a close
relation between description and the inventions of fancy. It seems
to me that Collins' ode also invites itself to be read as partaking in
that process, but not in such a way as to endorse Warton's preference for the descriptive over whatever it is – the moral, the
didactic, or it may be the allegorical – that we might take to be
inhospitable to description. Whatever Collins meant by the title of
his volume, and I don't think that can be determined, I see this
poem as one which enables a transition, back and forth, between
an understanding of its subject as 'allegorical' and as 'descriptive';
so that if we were to construct a history of eighteenth-century
poetry as a body of writing in which is effected a transition,
among other things, from allegorical to more directly descriptive
representation, I would like this ode to be understood as one
which makes us aware of the value of both procedures, and which
produces some sort of accommodation between them. To make

this point, I shall have to discuss in some detail the syntax of the ode, for it is, I shall argue, largely by the structure of its sentences that the accommodation is effected. I shall not demand of you, however, any understanding of sentence structure beyond what you might have picked up, had you been candidates for English language at O level twenty years ago. Let me begin by asking a few of you to read aloud the first sentence of the poem, or its first five stanzas.

(Two members of the class then read the sentence, in such a way as to divide it up into three separate sentences, treating each colon as a full stop. A third read it most of the way through very tentatively, in a way that committed her to no decision about its overall structure, then stopped, and re-read it so as to indicate her understanding that the clause beginning 'Now teach me . . .' (line 15) was what answered the conditional clause in the first stanza.)

I'll try and frame what I have to say as a commentary on those readings, suggesting also some alternative possibilities which none of you came up with. As you'll have realised from the last reading we heard, the first five stanzas of the poem can be read so as to form one extended sentence of some complexity; so that if, on a first reading, we are concerned to understand the meanings of the sentence in terms of the relations proposed by its syntax, we are likely to pick our way through it with considerable care, as we search for a main clause to answer the opening conditional; and that main clause is held back, apparently, until the fifteenth line of a sentence of twenty lines. When we reach it, the structure we will have discovered could be summarised like this: 'If there's any music that will soothe you, while the sun sets and silence reigns, teach it to me now; or 'If there's any music that will soothe you, now, while the sun sets and silence reigns, teach it to me.' But those summaries, while they can indicate rather baldly the shapes we have found for the sentence, conceal what the last reader evidently felt to be the problem of reading the passage; for in whittling down to four the seven clauses which precede the main clause (and for the sake of my argument I'll be content with a grammar which finds clauses only where it finds finite verbs), we largely get rid of the difficulty she experienced; that the main clause, on which the preceding seven are all directly or indirectly dependent, continually, as it were, fails to appear.

When she discovered a structure for the sentence, and read it again, she found herself continually prompted to indicate, by a succession of imperfect cadences at the end of each clause, that she was still waiting for the main clause, for the element in the structure that will answer the opening 'if '. The continual need to indicate, at the end of each clause, that the structure is still open, incomplete, is facilitated of course by the absence of rhyme, but still it makes the experience of reading or listening to the poem a much less placid experience than the vocabulary of the sentence – 'sooth', 'reserv'd', 'hush'd', and so on – suggests it should be. Now perhaps we could understand it as being precisely to the point that this anxious syntax is all that the poet can manage, unless Eve comes to his aid. But his description of himself, as 'musing slow', suggests that he is not at all anxious, and that Eve may have answered his request, to be taught 'some soften'd Strain', by the very manner in which he is inspired to make it; and this notion is not, we may feel, best communicated by being involved in such a long, elaborate and suspenseful opening structure of dependent clauses, so inappropriate to the hushed atmosphere of the evening. There are however a number of other ways of reading the sentence which may *seem*, at least, to reduce this difficulty, by treating the words in the ninth line, 'Now Air is hush'd', as a main clause or something like it. The first of these seems perfectly acceptable in terms of grammar, but is most unlikely to be opted for by any reader of the poem; the second is justifiable grammatically but not particularly intelligible; the third produces a sentence not well-formed, but it was the reading adopted, and with good reason, in two of the versions we've just heard.

We can summarise the first of these readings as follows: 'If there's any pastoral music that will soothe you, Eve, now's a quiet time (except for the sounds of bat and beetle), teach it to me now.' That summary reveals the advantage and conceals the implausibility of this way of reading the sentence in a way that's fairly instructive. For, by it, we allow the clause 'Now Air is hush'd' to stand in briefly as a main clause; to fulfil, temporarily, our desire to put an early end to the succession of dependent clauses, before we come to the main clause proper – proper, in the sense that only it will satisfactorily answer the conditional clause at the start of the sentence. But it's most unlikely that we'll find ourselves choosing this reading, and I've never heard the sentence read this way;

5

partly, no doubt, because this structure is too informal for the solemnity of the poem, partly because the success of such a structure as this depends almost entirely on the brevity of the expression which stands in as a main clause. 'Now's a quiet time' is sufficiently brief; 'now's a quiet time (except for the sounds of bat and beetle)' is already uncomfortably extended; and the full six lines, from 'Now Air is hush'd' to 'heedless Hum', reintroduce into the sentence all the suspense that this reading, if we were to choose it, would have been chosen to allay.

The next two alternatives I wish to consider seem to make much less sense, at least in terms of syntactical relation, and yet both of them seem in some degree to be invited by the text. I can best introduce them by looking again at the clause 'Now Air is hush'd', and pointing out that, according to our third reader's understanding of the structure of this sentence, that clause was, as it were, co-ordinate with the earlier clause, 'while now the bright-hair'd Sun/Sits in yon western Tent'; so that the two clauses could (for our immediate purposes) be summarised like this: 'While now the sun sets' and 'while now', or 'now that', 'silence reigns'. But of the two words that introduce the clause about the sun, the poem picks up – if you'll forgive me putting it this way – the wrong one, one which conceals instead of indicating the relation between the two clauses: not 'While Air is hush'd', or even 'Now that Air is hush'd', but, simply, 'Now'. That there is something at stake here – how importantly at stake we'll be able to consider in a moment – is clear from the fact that, when the poem appeared in a 1758 edition of Robert Dodsley's *Collection of Poems by Several Hands*, 'Now Air' became 'While Air'. The emendation was made in Collins' lifetime, but not necessarily at his suggestion; and it has the advantage, or the disadvantage, of removing all the alternative readings of the sentence I am examining, and leaving us only the thoroughly well-formed and thoroughly complex structure we looked at first, and one other possibility, which we'll glance at in a while.

Clauses introduced by the word 'while' can only be depen-dent, but 'now' can also introduce a main clause, and it is as a main clause that our first two readers of the poem seemed to find themselves taking the words 'Now Air is hush'd'. If we read the sentence like this, we can do so in such a way as to produce two possible structures for it – the one we choose will be indicated by the cadence we employ in our reading of the last lines of the second stanza. We can produce, to begin with, a structure that can be summarised like this: 'If there's any pastoral music that will soothe you, Eve, while the sun is setting, now is a quiet time, except for the sounds of bat and beetle'; a reading which goes on to treat 'Now teach me . . .' as effectively introducing a new sentence. This is, I suppose, a perfectly grammatical reading – we have something that behaves like the apodosis of a conditional sentence, but which, though it does something, does very little indeed to reveal how the opening conditional is imagined as being fulfilled. But what is lost to the sense of the lines is a gain to our sense of the propriety of this structure to the words of the text, for there is now much less of the suspense which, in our original reading of the sentence, seemed so much at odds with its semantic content. We can, however, reduce the sense of deferment, of suspense, still more, by treating the first eight lines as themselves a complete sentence, though an ill-formed one – and if this seems an unlikely reading it is exactly the one produced by our first two readers, as it often is by those I can persuade to read the poem aloud. This is a version which is impossible to summarise, but which, by reading the lines 'With Brede ethereal wove,/O'erhang his wavy Bed' in the tone of a perfect cadence, behaves as though the opening conditional has been answered, the sentence is already complete, and then goes on to treat the next two sections of the sentence, 'Now Air is hush'd . . .' and 'Now teach me . . .', as each of them separate and complete sentences. The complex twenty-line sentence has now been divided into three short ones, allowing a far more measured, more hushed and solemn reading, than will any structure which attempts at once to be properly grammatical and wholly intelligible.

Both of these readings which treat 'Now Air is hush'd' as a main clause seem to be invited by the colon at the end of the eighth line. I make that point tentatively, for we can never be sure how much control over the accidentals of the text a pre-nineteenth-century poet would have had; and there are anyway many reasons why poets may choose to ignore the conventions for the use of punctuation marks, or to invent their own. The conventions for the use of the colon were not much more clear in the eighteenth century than they are today; but one rule, at least, was pretty well established, if only to the satisfaction of grammarians. Here are three versions of it, from the beginning, middle and end of the century:

'The Colon or two points comprehend indeed an entire sense by it self; but yet such a one as depends upon, and is joined to another'; 'A Colon . . . marks a perfect Sense; yet so, as to leave the Mind in Suspense and Expectation of what is to follow'; and, finally, 'When a member of a sentence forms complete sense, and does not excite expectation of what follows; though it consists but of a simple member, it may be marked with a colon.'[4]

These three specimen rules don't agree on whether a colon should be used so as to excite expectation, at the end of 'a perfect Sense', of what follows; but they do agree that the clauses preceding the colon *should* make 'perfect' or 'complete' sense, by which phrase, as their examples make clear, they mean a well-formed sentence. Now, according to any reading of this sentence which seeks to represent it as well-formed, this rule is not observed by this text – no consideration of syntax will persuade us that the first two stanzas could thus stand on their own – and this is only one of a considerable number of occasions in the early texts of Collins' poems where the punctuation is so extremely rhetorical that the colon is used, with little regard for the conventions of grammarians, to mark pauses, or structural divisions within the stanza; indeed, before the final stanza of this poem, we find even a full stop before the completion of 'a perfect sense'.

But these considerations don't dispose of the problem entirely; for the combination of the colon, and the fact that we cannot *predict*, certainly not on a first reading, the grammatical relation of the clauses before it and those that follow, may persuade us to do what our first two readers did, and to treat the first eight lines *as if* they made 'complete sense', and the lines which follow as starting a quite new sense-unit. For this seemed to be exactly what happened to our first reader, whose tone of voice suggested that he was, almost until the end of the second stanza, expecting and looking for a clause to answer 'if'; but, apparently seeing the colon ahead of him, and seeing no obvious relation between what he was reading and what he was about to read, he dropped his voice on the phrase 'wavy Bed', to indicate that the sense-unit was, for him, somehow at an end. And if this colon persuades us that a perfect sense has been made, the next one may do so as well, though as we'll see there is another alternative. But if we do read 'Now teach me . . .' as introducing a third unit of complete sense, then by dividing the sentence into three separate sentences we have managed, as I say, to slow it down, and to produce a concord between its syntax and the reticent vocabulary it employs. In doing so, we produce a syntax that is more musical than logical, whose function is to mark the speed of our reading, and to produce formal relations in the sequence of words which are not always consequential relations.

If, by one or the other of the readings I've just outlined, we do take 'Now Air is hush'd' as a main clause, whether as the apodosis to the 'if' clause, or as starting a new sentence, we quite change the nature of the poem as it was interpreted by our third reader, who read all twenty lines as one sentence with one main clause only. This ode, as I've said, comes from a collection of odes 'on several descriptive and allegoric subjects'; and I want to suggest that our third reader placed her emphasis on the poem as an allegorical ode, as an ode of address, that is, to a personification imagined as a figure of allegory; and that our first two readers, who divided that opening sentence into three, shifted the emphasis towards the poem as a descriptive one. Let me explain what I mean. If we treat these twenty lines as together forming one well-formed sentence, then it is the opening conditional clause, and the main clause, that carry most of the weight of our reading, and are ushered into the foreground: 'If there's any pastoral music that will soothe you, Eve, teach it to me.' 'If' excites expectation, 'Now teach me' fulfils it, and all that intervenes between them, as it defers the appearance of the main verb, is treated as secondary, as material to be *got through* on the way to that fulfilment. And if this is true, then the effect is intensified as we read down the page, approaching nearer to the main clause but, in terms of the structure of dependence among the clauses, getting further away from it. Thus the clause 'Or where the Beetle winds/His small but sullen Horn' is dependent upon 'Now Air is hush'd', which can perfectly well be taken as dependent upon the conditional clause, which in its turn is dependent upon the main clause; and 'As oft he rises . . .' is still further removed from the main clause.

The longer the sentence is extended, the more the content of the dependent clauses, to be managed at all, must be pushed into the background of our attention, to enable the conditional and its answering main clause to reveal the structure as well-formed, and so to allow us to experience it as complete. The rest becomes the background, as it were, against which the transaction between

Eve and the poet takes place; and it is the background clauses and phrases which hold the directly descriptive content of the sentence. In front of, and above them, rides the rococo personification of Evening – to whom, if we have read the poem before, we can attribute a good deal of identifying paraphernalia: the evening star which is the lamp she carries, the chariot in which she will ride, together of course with the vaguely classical draperies, and the wreath of sedge, myrtle or some other appropriately dusky vegetation which, as Donald Davie has pointed out of eighteenth-century personification in general, we may be sure a contemporary reader would have visualised as the accoutrements of such a figure as this without having to be invited to do so.[5] We are offered an image of evening as an image of Eve – in a manner we may compare with these reproductions, which I'll circulate, of William Kent's frontispieces to James Thomson's *Seasons*, where the main focus of attention is less the seasonal landscape than the sky, in which float a host of attendants to a tutelary deity,[6] who are clearly far more responsible for conveying the meaning of the landscape, and of the poem, than is the landscape itself. In just this way, these twenty lines, read as one sentence, offer an image of Eve as the tutelary goddess of a landscape which is much less attended to than she is herself; and prepare us for the next sentence, the next two stanzas, where we are invited to imagine Eve's attendants preparing the 'shadowy car' in which she rides across the sky.

By dividing the sentence into three, however, we shift all that background into foreground, and come to attend to the images of the evening itself at least as much as to the image of Eve. The effect is initiated in the first of the three sentences we produce, the ill-formed one, where the need to finish the second stanza in the tone of a perfect cadence gives an emphasis to the details of the sunset far greater than in the other reading; and it is secured in the second sentence, where no reference to Eve appears. Here the topic is simply the silence of the evening landscape, as it is at once broken by the sounds of bat and beetle and reinforced by the fact that, at evening, such sounds can make themselves heard. In this sentence the main clause is offered us straightaway, so that we read through the clauses in which the bat and beetle are referred to with no sense (however pleasurable it might be) of deferment, and are able to allow them much more of our attention. And the effect of these images of bat and beetle becoming more salient is now less evident to us than it would have been to mid-eighteenth-century readers, for such 'mean' images would then have called attention to themselves the more by the fact of their meanness, by the discomfort such objects could threaten to a sense of propriety. Such images had an appropriate place in satire, for example, but a less secure one, still, in the diction of some other *genres* of poetry – even in Georgic, thought Joseph Warton, such words as 'horse', 'cow', 'ashes', and 'wheat' would 'unconquerably disgust many a delicate reader'.[7] If their appearance in poetry neither satirical nor burlesque could be justified – and a beetle finds its way into Gray's 'Elegy', for example – it could be so most easily by a knowledge of their provenance in the works of Shakespeare and Milton, but only there in passages which might similarly have disturbed a mid-eighteenth-century sense of propriety, by suggesting that there might be an inverse relation between genius and taste. By one reading of the poem, such images are more easily admissible, as descriptive divagations from the main topic of the sentence; by another, they are pulled almost as uncomfortably close to the reader as the beetle is to the pilgrim, the evening rambler, into whom the beetle crashes in mid-flight.

By the first of those readings, then, the poem introduces itself by its first sentence as primarily an ode of address to an allegorical personification; by the second, as a descriptive poem at least as much as an allegorical one; and in the mind of a reader concerned to discover a 'correct' structure for the sentence, and so aware also of the obstacles to its discovery, these readings will both be present, each able to be played off against the other.

At this point let me introduce one further possible reading of these lines which is relevant to the issue of what kind of poem we think we are reading. For if we find ourselves reading the first two stanzas as if they formed a complete sentence, we then have the option of reading the whole of the next three stanzas as a second complete sentence, of which 'Now teach me . . .' is the main clause: 'Now' that 'Air is hush'd' (except for, and so on), 'Now teach me . . .'. That reading seems to me to offer an intermediate understanding of these stanzas, between a version of them as primarily allegorical, and one in which the descriptive content is foregrounded; for it does not push the clauses in which the evening itself is described as far into the background, or pull

11

them as far into the foreground, as do the other readings we're currently considering. And that will be particularly the case if, as might well happen, we launch ourselves into lines 9–14 without a clear understanding of their syntactical function, but then indicate by an imperfect cadence before the second colon that we have now discovered a function for them, as dependent upon the clause which follows.

I want now to suggest that, in thus negotiating between an allegorical mode and a descriptive one, the poem also negotiates between a conception of poetry as public statement, and as the expression of private, 'individual', or 'particular' experience. That this issue was an important one in the poetry of the mid-eighteenth century I hope has already been sufficiently established by earlier classes in this course, but perhaps I can remind you briefly of what the issue is. I have in mind, for example, the sense we often find evinced in the poetry of the mid-century, that the range of poetry had been unduly contracted during the career and by the influence of Pope; that poetry, in becoming more concerned with public themes, and more didactic, had developed a range of concerns which excluded, and a language by which it was not possible to express, private, or individual, feelings and experiences, and by which the epigrammatic statement of a conventional social wisdom had come to seem of more value than the inventions of a poet imagined as a man of a particularly refined and sensitive nature. The justice of these criticisms of Pope and of his influence is not at issue here; what I am pointing to is an explicit or implicit criticism of him – you can find it, for example, in the remarks I quoted at the start of this lecture by Joseph Warton, regretting the prevalence of 'Essays on moral Subjects' – which prompts the experimentation with forms other than the heroic couplet, and with poetic languages other than Augustan – with blank verse, the ode, the elegy, the Spenserian stanza, the sonnet and the ballad, and with versions of the language of Milton, Spenser or Shakespeare, of middle-English poetry or the liturgy, of Celtic or popular poetry; all of which could be argued as attempts to recover the range that had been lost to poetry, and even to propose versions of an ideal, less complex society for the poet to operate in, where private experience was not separable from public, or not suppressed in favour of an abstract idea of the typical, the representative, the common.

In terms of this concern, personification can be understood as a figure which encourages an awareness of what is common in our experience, to the exclusion of what is private or individual; the personification of Eve, for example, has as its function to unite, stand for and replace the various images and ideas that as individuals we have of evenings here and there, in such a way as to produce a statement about Evening which we all recognise as corresponding with our own, or rather, perhaps, which is not so specific as evidently *not* to do so. It is, like the notion of what will appeal to our 'common humanity' propounded by Johnson, or like the abstract image of beauty argued for by Reynolds in his *Discourses*, a general idea which unites us as a public; and the more it can make the personification capable of being visualised, by the attribution, say, of lamp and chariot, the more it can satisfy our hunger for the concrete in such a way as successfully to efface the vividness of our individual and different experiences of evening. It is a figure which demands that we attribute no value to whatever we do experience as individuals which does not correspond with common experience; and to this generalised image, the particular and the specific are enemies, just because they proceed from individual experience.

It is in these terms that the 'Ode to Evening' seems to negotiate between a public and a private image; as far as it preserves, and emphasises, the conventions of an address to an allegorical figure, it addresses us as a public, or as readers it seeks to unify into a public; as far as it invites us also to read it as something like the opposite of that, it offers us images of evening itself too particular – for example in the image of the beetle colliding with the evening rambler – to be regarded as parts of a common experience, and too mean to form part of an idea of evening represented as 'above' the specifics of our experience as individuals. In doing so, it does not attempt to displace the public in favour of the private, but instead makes room for individual experience, as the experience of the particular, within the procedures of art, in a way more comparable with the practices of Romantic poetry. We could take as an example Keats' 'To Autumn', which also preserves the proper form of an address, while describing with a persuasive degree of particularity the figures to be encountered in an autumnal landscape; and it achieves this by treating the personification of Autumn as if it were continually migrating, and were thus able to be discovered in each of the figures in turn: the winnower, the reaper, the gleaner and the cider-maker.

This negotiation continues throughout the 'Ode to Evening': the next sentence, in stanzas 6 and 7, works to make more visible the figure of Eve which had been in danger, earlier, of being submerged by the details of the landscape, and it does this by attracting attention to the attributes and attendance of the deity; while the eighth stanza invites us, by images of considerable specificity, to attend to the evening more than to Eve – most notably in the image of the grey 'up-land Fallows' reflecting the 'last cool Gleam' of the 'sheety Lake'.[8] The next two stanzas seem to offer to do the same, but instead find a way of uniting the experience of the poet as he imagines himself observing the landscape, with the image of Eve as its tutelary goddess. The effect is perhaps best described by attending again to the structure of the sentence that makes up these two stanzas, though I shall do so this time, you will be glad to hear, rather less minutely. I can introduce the issue by looking at how the transition is managed, across the stanza-break, from images of a rain-swept wilderness with 'swelling Floods', to the calm images which follow, 'Hamlets brown, and dim-discover'd Spires'. The contrast between these images would have struck an eighteenth-century reader, much more than it will us, as a contrast between images of sublimity, with the power to resist our ability to grasp the world as order, and others, which do not seem to threaten that ability at all. By some means or other, a transition is made between them in such a way as to comprehend the images of a disorder within a landscape we finally experience as composed and harmonious.

In the first place, these images of differing power and tractability are held together by the innocent copula, 'and', which accords them all more or less equal weight within a simple list of the objects of the poet's vision, or of the vision available from the 'Hut'. But the list of words and phrases linked by 'and' then seems to expand, apparently to include the clauses 'And hears . . .', 'and marks . . .', which are not a part of that list at all, but separate activities of the hut, which 'views', 'hears' and 'marks' the various aspects of the landscape. The last of these clauses re-introduces Eve, both as an object of vision, part of what the hut observes and organises, and also as herself an active agent harmonising the

14

landscape; for the 'gradual dusky Veil' that Eve draws across the images of the landscape, by harmonising them to the neutral tones of a painted landscape of evening, blurs the distinctions between them. The property of evening becomes the ability to harmonise what, in the full light of day, seems discordant; that property is observed by the poet himself, as he organises by means of syntax the objects imagined as seen from the hut; but the inclusion of the 'Dewy Fingers' of Eve, among the images observed, works to validate, on the basis of his own imagined observation, the representative power of the personification, and the harmonising property by which it discovers similarity in difference.

The remaining three stanzas can therefore return the poem to one which is unequivocally an ode of address, and of address to a personification no longer in danger of excluding individual experience, because acknowledged by it. The handling of the personification becomes no less remarkable, however, for being thus, as it were, stabilised; for as Eve herself is now an appropriate subject for the descriptive powers of the poet, she is described, in a series of images strikingly specific, as successively transformed by the different actions of the four personified seasons. And the characteristics of the seasons, violent as well as mild, can now by this means be fully emphasised, precisely because they also can now be understood as offering no threat to our sense of harmony which Eve cannot fully contain. For just as the wild landscape could be perceived as harmonious from within the security of the hut, so the seasons can be from within the 'Sylvan Shed', where activities and virtues which themselves promote harmony wor-ship Eve as their tutelary goddess: in the original of line 49 (*Odes*, 1746), these personifications were described as 'regardful of thy quiet rule' – acknowledging themselves as subject to Eve's sway, and as bound to observe her (as it were, monastic) code of dis-cipline and conduct.

By this move, evening becomes more than a time of day: it comes to represent that position, conscientiously sought for by a number of eighteenth-century poets, from which, withdrawn from the world, we can experience as concord whatever, within the world, we experienced as discord. The attainment of this position is of course a means of recovering, by an internal com-posure of mind, the harmony which was lost at the Fall, when

John Barrell

perpetual Spring ceased to reign throughout the year, and the
seasons began – a notion which may entitle us to understand Eve,
our universal mother, as also redeemed, as become no longer the
'old' but the 'new Eve' in the view composed by her namesake.[9]
But there was a social as well as a moral Fall recognised by writers
of the eighteenth century, by which were introduced, among
other things, money, the differentiation of members of society by
rank and occupation, and a form of society in which public and
private life were divorced; and the 'Ode to Evening' offers us the
model of a poetic procedure by which it came to be believed that
that breach, also, could be healed.

NOTES

1 The text of the ode is taken from *The Works of William Collins*,
   ed. Richard Wendorf and Charles Ryskamp, Oxford
   University Press, 1979.
2 'Collins' *Ode* . . . was published by Andrew Millar on
   20 December 1746 (but was dated 1747, as was common with
   publications late in the year)' – Wendorf and Ryskamp, op cit.,
   p. 123. The notes to the poem in this volume, and in Roger
   Londsdale (ed.), *The Poems of Gray, Collins and Goldsmith*,
   London, Longman's, 1969, contain, among other valuable
   information, useful bibliographies of critical discussions of the
   'Ode'.
3 Joseph Warton, *Odes on Various Subjects*, 1746, 'Advertisement'.
4 Michael Maittaire, *The English Grammar; or, An Essay on the Art of
   Grammar Applied to and Exemplified in the English Tongue*,
   London, 1712, p. 191; James Buchanan, *The British Grammar*,
   London, 1762, p. 51; John Walker, *A Rhetorical Grammar, or
   Course of Lessons in Elocution*, London, 1785, p. 35.
5 Donald Davie, *Purity of Diction in English Verse*, London,
   Routledge & Kegan Paul, 1952, p. 40.
6 A facsimile copy of *The Seasons*, London, 1730, was circulated.
   An excellent account of Tardieu's engravings of Kent's designs
   will be found in Ralph Cohen, *The Art of Discrimination:
   Thomson's The Seasons and the Language of Criticism*, London,
   Routledge & Kegan Paul, 1964, esp. pp. 269ff. Cohen however
   sees in these illustrations more of a unity than I do between sky

and landscape, supernatural and natural, which Kent may certainly have intended but which I do not find achieved. Those who agree with Cohen may find a similarity between Kent's accommodation of the allegorical and the natural descriptive and Collins', as I see it in the 'Ode to Evening'.

7 Joseph Warton, 'Reflections on Didactic Poetry', in his *Works of Virgil*, London, 1753, vol. I, P. 294.

8 For a discussion of to what or whom these 'gleams' are to be attributed, see Lonsdale, op. cit., p. 465.

9 I am thinking of I Corinthians 15: 44–5: 'It is sown a natural body: it is raised a spiritual body. There is a natural body, and there is a spiritual body. And so it is written, The first man Adam was made a living soul; the last Adam *was made* a quickening spirit.'

2 'So truth be in the field': Milton's use of language

Colin MacCabe

In this lecture I want to investigate some of the terms in which Milton's language has been discussed in the twentieth century. This important debate, which touches on the very nature of poetic language, is generally considered to be closed with Milton triumphantly vindicated. What I hope to show is that this vindication depends on ignoring some of the most valuable aspects of Milton's language; on abstracting Milton's writing from its historical conditions. I begin with a quotation from the *Four Quartets* from the section in 'Little Gidding', when the persona of the poem meets in a dream another poet, partly a younger version of himself, partly a composite of other poets, and they discuss their earlier projects. The discussion between the two is characterised in terms of language:

> For last year's words belong to last year's language
> And next year's words await another voice.
> But, as the passage now presents no hindrance
> To the spirit unappeased and peregrine
> Between two worlds become much like each other,
> So I find words I never thought to speak
> In streets I never thought I should revisit
> When I left my body on a distant shore.
> Since our concern was speech, and speech impelled us
> To purify the dialect of the tribe
> And urge the mind to aftersight and foresight . . .[1]

What we notice is that for Eliot the concern with language is above all a concern with speech, and that this speech is what urges the mind to aftersight and foresight. 'Aftersight' is an unusual word

18

to use here, in that it is to all intents and purposes a coinage and replaces a word we might expect to find coupled with foresight, namely hindsight. But on reflection this is unsurprising because in 'aftersight' Eliot articulates his whole theory of tradition in which the past is ever present but changed by the present, so it is not simply a question of hindsight – of seeing how it really was – but, exactly, *aftersight* – seeing from our position in the present a new configuration in the past.

Eliot's definition of language in terms of speech and above all in terms of sight is one that I might return to in another lecture. What I want to draw out for our particular purposes today is that it is in these terms of speech and sight that Eliot condemns Milton's language in his two famous lectures of 1936 and 1947. It is Milton's refusal to concern himself with colloquial speech (and in this he is opposed to Dryden) which is the crucial term of Eliot's reproach, and it is the term that dominates Leavis' criticism as well, although one of the points I want to make is that Eliot's understanding of the relation between speech and writing and Leavis' are very different indeed.

In his second lecture on Milton, Eliot makes the following comments:

> His style is not a *classic* style, in that it is not the elevation of *common* style, by the final touch of genius, to greatness. It is, from the foundation, and in every particular, a personal style, not based upon common speech, or common prose, or direct communication of meaning. Of some great poetry one has difficulty in pronouncing just what it is, what infinitesimal touch, that has made all the difference from a plain statement which anyone could make; the slight transformation which, while it leaves a plain statement a plain statement, has made it at the same time great poetry. In Milton there is always the maximal, never the minimal, alteration of ordinary language. Every distortion of construction, the foreign idiom, the use of a word in a foreign way or with the meaning of the foreign word from which it is derived rather than the accepted meaning in English, every idiosyncrasy is a particular act of violence which Milton has been the first to commit.[2]

What one reads in this passage is Eliot's recognition of a very different practice from his own. The terms in which Leavis elaborates such criticism is much more evaluative:

> The extreme and consistent remoteness of Milton's medium from any English that was ever spoken is an immediately relevant consideration. It became, of course, habitual to him; but habituation could not sensitize a medium so cut off from speech – speech that belongs to the emotional and sensory texture of actual living and is in resonance with the nervous system; it could only confirm an impoverishment of sensibility.[3]

Where Eliot opposes two attitudes to speech, Leavis simply poses an opposition between the correct way to write and the way that will impoverish the sensibility, the way that will, as it were, literally (and at this point the physiological metaphor becomes absolutely dominant) devitalise speech. And Leavis explains how the rot goes much further when he continues:

> We remain predominantly aware of elegance and declamation; our sense of words as words, things for the mouth and ear, is not transcended in any vision – or (to avoid the visualist fallacy) any *realization* – they convey.[4]

Now this critique of Milton's language was held to apply to the level of the most simple use of language – that is to say, the level of the construction of sense. A great deal of the force of the attack originally derived from this analysis, and it is also, in some sense, a force which has since been deflected – primarily by Christopher Ricks' book, *Milton's Grand Style*, but also by a whole host of other studies which have followed. I can point to the way in which that particular criticism has been deflected just by taking an example from Book II of *Paradise Lost*:

> For while they sit contriving, shall the rest,
> Millions that stand in Arms, and longing wait
> The Signal to ascend, sit lingring here
> Heav'ns fugitives . . .   [II, 54–7][5]

This was picked on by Eliot in a footnote, and then taken up by Leavis, as a supreme example of Miltonic rhetoric, in which sense was totally sacrificed to an artificial and poetic use of language. The analysis insisted on the verbal contradiction of 'sit' and

20

'stand'. How could these millions both sit and stand at the same time? This was clear evidence of a lack of attention to precise use of language. What Ricks pointed out, brilliantly and devastatingly, was that of course they weren't sitting and standing at the same time; the 'sit lingring here' is related to 'shall the rest', that is to say, it's a future 'shall the rest sit lingering here/Heav'ns fugitives' that is opposed to the present of 'millions that stand in Arms'. Now the point about this particular kind of criticism is that, although it is extremely effective and points out a straightforward misreading in both Eliot's and Leavis' criticism, it reduces the interest in what Eliot had originally pointed out. Above all, it conflates Leavis' and Eliot's accounts of Milton. But while the accusation of a lack of sense was central to Leavis' argument, I would argue that it was not much more than a footnote to Eliot's. Christopher Ricks rescues Milton at the level of grammar but fails to consider the discursive effects that Eliot had pointed to. Eliot's careful delineation of a particular attitude to poetic language is aligned with Leavis' simple condemnation, and when that condemnation is correctly refuted, the interest of what Eliot said passes unnoticed. Much recent criticism of Milton's language has defended it in terms of a mimetic use of syntax. The formal patterns of language are held to be at the service of the meaning. But Milton's syntax is much more interesting than that. To see how Milton is defended in terms which foreclose much of the interest of his practice, let us look in detail at another famous passage of Milton's verse which Leavis comments on at the beginning of his essay on Milton in *Revaluations*:

> The hasty multitude
> Admiring enter'd, and the work some praise
> And some the Architect: his hand was known
> In Heav'n by many a Towred structure high,
> Where Scepter'd Angels held thir residence,
> And sat as Princes, whom the supreme King
> Exalted to such power, and gave to rule,
> Each in his Hierarchie, the Orders bright.
> Nor was his name unheard or unador'd
> In ancient Greece; and in Ausonian land
> Men called him Mulciber; and how he fell
> From Heav'n, they fabl'd, thrown by angry Jove

21

> Sheer o're the Chrystal Battlements: from Morn
> To Noon he fell, from Noon to dewy Eve,
> A Summers day; and with the setting Sun
> Dropt from the Zenith like a falling Star,
> On Lemnos th'Aegaean Ile: thus they relate,
> Erring . . .   [*Revaluations*, p. 44]

Leavis' comments are worth quoting at length to see how the objection to a certain use of language is tied to a particular view of subjectivity, and, further, that the objection is substantiated by an account of linguistic efforts at the local level which is demonstrably wrong. Because, as we go through this passage, we can see the way in which the whole attack on Milton is related to particular ways in which language and subjectivity are held to go together. Leavis comments on this first passage as follows:

> The opening exhibits the usual heavy rhythmic pattern, the hieratic stylization, the swaying ritual movement back and forth, the steep cadences. . . . But from 'Nor was his name unheard' onwards the effect changes. One no longer feels oneself carried along, resigned or protesting, by an automatic ritual, . . . the verse seems suddenly to have come to life. Yet the pattern remains the same; there are the same heavy stresses, the same rhythmic gestures and the same cadences, and if one thought a graph of the verse-movement worth drawing it would not show the difference. The change of feeling cannot at first be related to any point of form; it comes in with 'ancient Greece' and 'Ausonian land', and seems to be immediately due to the evocation of that serene, clear, ideally remote classical world so potent upon Milton's sensibility. But what is most important to note is that the heavy stresses, the characteristic cadences, turns and returns of the verse, have here a particular felicity. What would elsewhere have been the routine thump of 'Sheer' and 'Dropt' is here, in either case, obviously functional, and the other rhythmic features of the verse are correspondingly appropriate. The stress given by the end-position to the first 'fell', with the accompanying pause, in what looks like a common, limply pompous Miltonicism –

> and how he fell
> From Heav'n, they fabl'd, thrown . . .

is here uncommonly right; the heavy 'thrown' is right, and
so are the following rise and fall, the slopes and curves, of
the verse.   [*Revaluations*, pp. 45–6]

Now what Leavis is arguing is that this particular use of language,
which is divorced from speech, is only redeemed at a moment
when some notion of a full subjectivity can be called into account.
That is to say, it's the moment when Milton becomes really
involved, when he is talking of the classics, which, on this account,
is the only moment when the poetry becomes 'right'. Indeed, one
could remark in passing that this passage indicates how far Leavis'
attack on Milton is an attack on a poet who is not held to be
English enough – whose interest in the classics conflicts with his
nationality. But more importantly, the accuracy of the language is
determined entirely by Milton's subjective interests: when he is
really interested, the language becomes clear.

Leavis says that if one draws a verse diagram, this will show no
changes. Well, Anne Cluysenaar, in a book called *Introduction to
Literary Stylistics*, actually did draw a verse diagram and discovered
that there were in fact a great number of differences to be pointed
out:

> /// The hasty multitude ⟨
> Admiring·⟩ enter'd, // and / the work / some / praise //
> And / some / the Architect: // his hand / was known / →
> In Heav'n / by many a Towred structure high, //
> Where / Scepter'd Angels / held / their residence, //
> And / sat / as Princes, // whom / the supreme King / →
> Exalted / to such power, // and / gave / to rule, ⟨
> Each / in his Hierarchie, ⟩ the Orders bright. ///
> Nor / was / his name / unheard or unador'd / →
> In ancient Greece; // and / in Ausonian land /⇒
> Men / called / him / Mulciber; // and [[how / he / fell /⇒
> From Heav'n,]] they / fabl'd, // thrown / by angry Jove /
> Sheer o'er the Chrystal Battlements: /// from Morn →
> To Noon / he / fell, / from Noon to dewy Eve, ⇒
> A Summers day; // and / with the setting Sun / ⇒
> Dropt / from the Zenith / like a falling Star, / →
> On Lemnos th' Aegaean Ile: /// thus / they / relate, //
> Erring. . . .[6]

23

The fundamental point of Cluysenaar's analysis (for the exact notation see note 6) is that, whereas in the first part of the passage the grammatical and prosodic closures are congruent and the verse thus gives an impression of stasis, in the second part the line endings and the grammatical pauses do not coincide, thus carrying us through the syntax in a mimesis of Mulciber's fall. The effects that Leavis notices in the second part of the passage are not to be explained by any simple reference to Milton's attachment to the world of classical mythology, but by the structure of the verse. However, Cluysenaar's analysis, although valuably correct in its demonstration of how the second part of the passage functions, gives a very inadequate account of the use of language in the opening eight lines. For the language that describes the angels entering Pandemonium escapes both the form of Cluysenaar's analysis and any justification in terms of mimetic syntax. The reader is introduced to fundamental questions of language and interpretation which cannot be captured by reference to the decoding of the correct syntax or by the praising of Milton for the imitative felicity of some grammatical effect. Look, for example, at the syntax of the proposed clause boundary at line 2: 'and the work some praise / And some the Architect'. The point about this clause boundary is that it becomes clear only as we read into line 3. That is to say, to start with, 'some' may appear to be of the class of determiners like 'the', 'my', 'that', etc., which limits the noun it precedes, but unlike 'the' or 'my' doesn't specify it. If we read line 2 like this, with 'praise' as a noun of which we are told that some limited but not specified amount was lavished on the buildings, we would then expect to be dealing with the sentence of the subject-verb-object type (with the order of object and verb inverted), and would wait for the verb to complete it (as in 'the work some praise received', for example). Instead of the verb, however, we find a conjunction followed by 'some the Architect'. At this point it becomes clear that 'some' is not functioning as a determiner but as a proform which anaphorically relates back to 'multitude' and which can be spelt out as 'some (of them)'. And so we recognise that 'praise' is not a noun but a verb and that the sentence is of the object-subject-verb order.

My point is not very complicated. It's simply that Cluysenaar's firm boundary becomes a firm boundary only at the point when we have read on to line 3 *and back*. This syntactic complexity continues with a series of subordinate clauses initiated by 'where', 'whom', 'while'; whereas in the second part of the passage conjunction becomes the dominant grammatical relationship.

This kind of inherent ambiguity can be analysed even more clearly if you look at what Cluysenaar calls 'interrupting clauses'. I'm not sure exactly what she means by that phrase, but I imagine that she has in mind the kind of sentence, common enough in speech, in which one clause interrupts another without entering into any specific syntactic relation with it: 'That man, now I'm speaking frankly, is a real pain'; 'Then Jane, I introduced you to her last week, left the party.' It should be obvious even from these examples that to use an interrupting clause in writing without any of the intonation markers that disentangle the two sentences in speech immediately involves one in a complicated decoding process. If we look at the example, 'Each in his Hierarchie', we may well agree that 'each' is functioning as a quantifier referring back elliptically to the princes; we will understand it as a sentence such as 'each of the princes ruled in his particular hierarchy', in which the spelling out of the clause involves nothing that cannot be recovered from the sentence in which it is embedded. However, the process of decoding suggests anything but a firm boundary between lines and this is even clearer in the case of 'admiring'. Cluysenaar's analysis would seem to understand 'admiring' as a participle functioning elliptically, so that the sentence can be spelt out as 'the hasty multitude, who were admiring, entered'. The sense here is obviously that now obsolete sense much closer to the Latin derivation from the verb *mirari*: to wonder, in which the strong emotion of 'wondering' is intended, rather than our contemporary and weaker sense of 'regarding with pleased surprise'. This older sense took a prepositional complement – 'King Ahab stood admiring at the miracle' – and its absence requires a reference back to previous lines in the text. In fact it would seem much more plausible to analyse admiring as a participle functioning adjectivally which Milton has placed after the noun it qualifies. Presumably Cluysenaar does not wish to adopt this analysis because, even more clearly than in her reading, the line ending would not act as a firm syntactic boundary.

So, Cluysenaar is certainly correct to say that the movement of the verse is very different in the two sections. But it is not simply a question of the relation between syntax and prosody. I want now

25

to move on to another passage, this time chosen for my own purposes, and to attempt to show how these difficulties occur not simply at the level of syntax, but also at other levels in the verse. They indicate a use of language which cannot simply be explained by an appeal to a mimetic syntax, but which must find its explanation in the position offered to the reader by the poem. These discursive effects can be further explained by the attitudes to language and interpretation forced on Milton both by the contradictions of Protestantism and by his particular position as one of the last representatives of a Renaissance attitude to language – an attitude which, in the years that *Paradise Lost* was being written and published, was fast disappearing under the pressure of a set of political and ideological strategies.

Consider the passage in which Milton describes Satan moving to the shore to address the fallen angels:

> He scarce had ceas't when the superior Fiend
> Was moving toward the shore; his ponderous shield
> Ethereal temper, massy, large and round,
> Behind him cast; the broad circumference
> Hung on his shoulders like the Moon, whose Orb
> Through Optic Glass the *Tuscan* Artist views
> At Ev'ning from the top of *Fesole*,
> Or in *Valdarno*, to descry new Lands,
> Rivers or Mountains in her spotty Globe.
> His Spear, to equal which the tallest Pine
> Hewn on *Norwegian* hills, to be the Mast
> Of some great Ammiral, were but a wand,
> He walkd with, to support uneasie steps
> Over the burning Marle, not like those steps
> On Heavens Azure; and the torrid Clime
> Smote on him sore besides, vaulted with Fire;
> Nathless he so endur'd, till on the Beach
> Of that inflamed Sea, he stood and calld
> His Legions, Angel Forms, who lay intranst
> Thick as Autumnal Leaves that strow the Brooks
> In *Vallombrosa*, where th' *Etrurian* shades
> High overarcht imbowr; or scatterd sedge
> Afloat, when with fierce Winds *Orion* armd
> Hath vext the Red-Sea Coast, whose waves orethrew

Busiris and his *Memphian* Chivalrie,
While with perfidious hatred they persu'd
The Sojourners of *Goshen*, who beheld
From the safe shore thir floating Carcasses
And brok'n Chariot Wheels. So thick bestrown
Abject and lost lay these, covering the Flood,
Under amazement of thir hideous change.   [I, 283–313]

Now the entire sequence produces a constant change in perspective in which similes follow one another so quickly that there
is no question of a basic description which the comparisons and
equivalences elaborate. Rather, the description simply becomes
the passage through these comparisons, a veritable transport of
language (to give *metaphor* its original and etymological form). As
we follow the comparisons of 'his Legions, Angel Forms', what we
notice is the constant change of viewpoint, a change motivated by
the passage through a seemingly infinite number of subordinate
clauses, and by the variety of literary references that Milton calls
upon within the one comparison. The simile that Milton is using
here is one hallowed by the epic tradition in which *Paradise Lost* is
contradictorily inscribed. It is first used by Virgil in Book Six of
the *Aeneid*, when Aeneas enters the Underworld and sees the
numerous dead 'thick as the leaves of the forest that at Autumn's
first dropping fall, and thick as birds that from the seething deep
flock shoreward, when the chill of the year drives them overseas
and sends them into sunny lands'. The two elements of Virgil's
simile are unified by the reference to autumn and this unity is
preserved by both Dante and Tasso. Milton's use is very different.
There is no such conceptual unity which binds together the leaves
in the brook at Vallombrosa and the ruins of the Pharaoh's army
in the Red Sea. More importantly, the simile is heterogeneous in
its range of literary reference. The worlds of pastoral, evoked by
the brooks and bowers of Vallombrosa, and of the Bible are
harshly discordant, and the mention of Orion merely complicates
the picture further. The reader has no generic or narrative order
in which to harmonise these literary references.

As a syntactic analogue to the difficulty of literary reference,
we can note that the initial disjunction is followed by a further
adverbial clause of time before we reach a relative clause which
supplies us with a point of rest: 'While with perfidious hatred they

persu'd/The Sojourners of *Goshen*, who beheld/From the safe shore thir floating Carcasses'. There is a sense in which it is not only the sojourners of Goshen who've been delayed until then, but also the reader: a point of identification from which now finally to stand and look back over this multitude of similes. In the delay of a moment of identification, in this refusal of a standard world of literary reference, Milton forces the reader to refuse any of the particular representations of the fallen angels in order that he may construct the truth of their situation.

For Milton to engage in such activity it was necessary to have a theory of language which allowed truth to be produced through an activity in language. We perhaps are familiar with such a theory in psychoanalysis, with its notion that through repetition certain truths can be produced in language. But I think it is important to remember that this notion is really very foreign to England and also to Europe in the period from 1660 to the Romantics and beyond. Yet the Renaissance did have equivalent theories concerning the creative power of language. On the one hand there was a hermetic theory, an understanding of the world and language as articulated together within 'correspondences', which ensured that one was as likely to find the relations between things in words as in the world of the senses. And on the other hand, and perhaps more importantly, there was an Augustinian theory of language in which God's redeeming of Man entailed that, although normal uses of language were false and mis-leading, certain figurative uses of language could provide glimpses of divine truth.

It is in the light of Milton's practice of writing that we can consider the earlier reference in this passage to Galileo – 'the Tuscan Artist'. If we remember that Galileo is the only contemporary other than Milton himself to figure in *Paradise Lost*, then we may suspect that the standard gloss which reads 'scientist' for 'artist' is potentially misleading. It is perfectly true that a meaning which covers every intellectual activity is still current, but the word 'artist' is already beginning to lose that sense and to acquire some of the senses more familiar to us, most particularly the sense in which it is opposed to science. Now it is quite important to be clear what the question is here. There is no question in the late seventeenth or eighteenth century of a notion of art as that supreme product of the creative imagination which is our contemporary notion. That awaits the Romantics and particularly Coleridge. Neither is there our contemporary meaning of science which primarily refers to the natural sciences: it is again much later, during the 1840s or 1850s, that this meaning is developed. But there is a distinction which runs throughout the eighteenth century, an opposition between art and science which has something of the terms familiar to us. Indeed, the first mention of such a meaning in the *Oxford English Dictionary* is in 1668, just a year after *Paradise Lost*'s publication, when a manual on making sun-dials records: 'though we may justly account Dyalling originally a Science, yet it is now become to many of the ingenious no more than an art' (no more difficult than an art). This example is dangerous if we think it asserts our modern opposition of natural science to art. But it is important as an index of emergence of a realm of enquiry which can produce Truth – Science – as opposed to the mere practice of art, which has no epistemological status (is mere technique). In other words, Milton is writing at a time when conceptions that allow his writing to function are themselves dying out. Whether the use of 'artist' is here intentional, whether it lays a deliberately polemical claim to truth, is not at issue here. What is important is that this established use, which is so central to Milton's project in *Paradise Lost*, is itself in the process of being displaced.

It is in this context that we can understand why Galileo is the only other contemporary figure besides Milton himself to be included in the poem. The paradigmatic figure of the new forms of knowledge is included by Milton to indicate that his own work is on the same epistemological footing – a search for truth which is as valid as Galileo's.

The complexity of the patterns of subordination of the verse, and the difficulty in which they place the reader, can perhaps be highlighted by reference to the modern linguistic distinction first elaborated by Chomsky between 'competence' and 'performance'. 'Competence' is understood as the subject's knowledge of the language, as opposed to the actual use of the language, which is described by the term 'performance'. Competence refers to the ability of the speaker to judge as grammatical or as non-grammatical sentences that he or she might never dream of actually producing, i.e., performing. Part of the usefulness of the distinction is that it allows for further discrimination between

29

Colin MacCabe

grammatical and acceptable sentences. There are certain examples, such as the centre embedding of relative clauses: 'the man who the boys pointed out is a friend of mine' is all right, but certainly not 'the man who the boys who the students who came down from London recognised pointed out is a friend of mine'. A particular sentence can be grammatical (recursive addition of relative clauses) but unacceptable: we are unable to perform it. Whatever the strength or weakness of these concepts in terms of linguistic theory, they do seem to me to offer one way of understanding the difficulty of Milton: how his use of language constantly pits our performance against our competence, constantly insists on those limits where syntactic patterns can no longer be held together. The precise point of this forcing I shall come back to, but it should be noted that it cannot simply be escaped by an appeal to the argument that Milton's – and his readers' – practice of reading classical texts enabled them to hold syntactic connections with much greater ease than we do.

I hope that at this point some of the terms in which we should consider Milton's use of language have become clearer, in particular the specific discursive effects of his poetry: where by discursive I mean those features of the articulation of the language which determine a certain address; determine the place, often plural and contradictory, to which the reader is called. I now want to return to what Eliot said about Milton and see how clear Eliot himself is about Milton's practice. Eliot says, right at the beginning of his first study of Milton, that the most important fact about Milton for his purposes is his blindness, and he goes on to spell out what he means in an illuminating comparison between Milton and Joyce. He says:

> I think that it is not unprofitable to compare Milton's development with that of James Joyce. The initial similarities are musical taste and abilities, followed by musical training, wide and curious knowledge, gift for acquiring languages, and remarkable powers of memory perhaps fortified by defective vision.   [I, pp. 142–3]

The crucial feature that accompanies the lack of vision is distance from any spoken language, and I hope that we can now return to the later essay and see how Eliot's characterisation of Milton's practice is not in contradiction with the analyses we have been considering:

> In Milton there is always the maximal, never the minimal, alteration of ordinary language. Every distortion of construction, the foreign idiom, the use of a word in a foreign way or with the meaning of a foreign word from which it is derived rather than the accepted meaning in English, every idiosyncrasy is a particular act of violence which Milton has been the first to commit. There is no cliché, no poetic diction in the derogatory sense but a perpetual sequence of original acts of lawlessness. Of all the modern writers of verse, the nearest analogy seems to me to be Mallarmé, a much smaller poet, though still a great one. [II, p. 154]

Joyce and Mallarmé, blindness rather than sight, writing rather than speech. I hope that this makes clear that Eliot's Milton is not Leavis': that what Eliot is presenting in his discussion of Milton is not a simple criticism, but the delineation of a position very far from his own, a position which in many ways he finds abhorrent, but in which he recognises an endeavour fundamentally different from his own writing. And in fact, if you look at the essays it is quite clear that Eliot does recognise that what he is writing about is what he calls the Civil War and what I would call the English Revolution, and that as an Anglo-Catholic, a monarchist, and a classicist, he is writing in active opposition to Milton. And it's quite clear that what gets buried in the taking up by Leavis or Eliot, and what gets even further submerged by someone like Ricks, is the political element, the way in which Eliot is saying that the Civil War is still an active issue in English society.

What is the conclusion one might draw from this? I certainly do not want to imply some sense in which Milton suddenly becomes a modernist writer. It is not the case that I simply want to read back into Milton, in some ahistorical way, features one can discover in modernism. For, the most important thing to remember is that Milton's introduction of the reader to the contradictions of language is not in any sense devoted to getting away from the final meaning: it is rather a preparation for that final meaning, that final meaning being available only in relation to God, and that relation is not linguistic.

31

It is not possible for me to offer a definitive explanation to end this lecture. I want instead to suggest some of the texts and contexts in which we might begin to understand Milton's practice without simply reducing it to modernism. Above all, this would be in terms of the way in which the logical problems of Protestantism became a terrifying actuality for many in England in the period 1642–5 and perhaps for no one more than John Milton.

If Catholicism proposes an institutional control of meaning, whereby a social institution, the Church, determines the possible interpretations of Holy Scripture, Protestantism refuses such mediation and presumes to build its social institutions on the individual's reading of the Bible. Of course the problem, and one that is always present as a logical structure within Protestantism, is that it is assumed an honest reading of vernacular Bibles by committed Christians will produce an agreed form for a Church. But as meanings proliferate, as individuals cannot agree about what they read in the Bible, Protestantism is faced with the dilemma of choosing between interpretations, of privileging one reading over another. But so to do is to accept the social mediation of meanings. If one is to take Protestantism to its logical conclusion – as Milton did in *De Doctrina Christiana* – then one will have to admit that a church can be composed of one person, that you may have as many social institutions as individuals. Already in the *Areopagitica*, Milton has pushed his Protestantism to the point where he argues that a man can be a heretic in the truth. Because if you simply accept a meaning because it is provided for you (by a church), even if it is the correct meaning, the truth, you will have failed in your duty to discover it for yourself. The process of interpretation is the guarantee of Christian virtue, not the possession of some unchanging meanings. Between the Presbyterian pamphlets of 1641–2 and the *Areopagitica* of 1644, Milton completely changes his understanding of meaning and truth. In the early pamphlets he accepts what one might call a 'naive Protestantism', in which the honest reading of the scriptures will produce universally agreed truths; for the Milton of the *Areopagitica*, however, truth can be only searched for, not found. What separates the *Areopagitica* from the early pamphlets is the early years of the English Revolution, when these logical problems of Protestantism became daily matters of dispute, particularly around the question of Presbyterianism and the imposition of a new discipline. And these disputes touched Milton very personally because of the divorce pamphlets that he wrote in 1643 and 1644. Here is the man who is perhaps more convinced than anyone in Europe has ever been of his ability to speak the truth of the Bible. He publishes the divorce pamphlets. They are considered immoral; they have an enormous amount of ridicule and obloquy heaped on them. The Bible is no longer the source of obvious truth, and instead the whole process of interpretation, both for Milton himself and for the English Revolution, becomes extremely difficult. A constant search. I think that Milton's whole life is, in some sense, from then onwards, an ever more painful recognition of this difficulty; a despair which through the years of the English Revolution becomes ever more desperate. It is this despair which we can perhaps read in one of the most astonishing documents that Milton ever wrote, *The Readie and Easie Way to Establish a Free Commonwealth*. The visceral irony of that title is still quite unsettling. Here is a man who has spent twenty years of his life devoted to exactly the establishing of a free Commonwealth. Shortly before the King returns, he writes a text called 'The Readie and Easie Way to Establish a Free Commonwealth'. It is also the period when scholars now think he starts *Paradise Lost*, and, in fact, he ends the pamphlet with a statement which I think should be borne in mind as we read *Paradise Lost*:

> What I have spoken, is the language of that which is not call'd amiss *the good old Cause*: if it seems strange to any, it will not seem more strange, I hope, than convincing to back-sliders. Thus much I should perhaps have said though I were sure I should have spoken only to trees and stones; and had none to cry to, but with the Prophet, *O earth, earth, earth!* to tell the very soil itself what her perverse inhabitants are deaf to. Nay though what I have spoke, should happ'n (. . .) to be the last words of our expiring libertie. But I trust I shall have spoken perswasion to abundance of sensible and ingenuous men: to som perhaps whom God may raise of these stones to become children of reviving libertie . . .[7]

Here is Milton's recognition of the loss of an audience. *Paradise Lost* has, I think, been written in that loss of an audience, trying to introduce the reader to a whole work of language in which it might be possible to discern the seeds of, among other things, a reviving liberty.

NOTES

1 T.S. Eliot, *Four Quartets*, London, Faber and Faber, 1972, p. 54, II, 118–28.
2 T.S. Eliot, 'Milton I, II', in *On Poetry and Poets*, London, Faber and Faber, 1971, II, p. 154.
3 F.R. Leavis, 'Milton's Verse', in *Revaluations: Traditions and Development in English Poetry*, London, Chatto and Windus, 1969, p. 51.
4 F.R. Leavis, 'Mr Eliot and Milton', in *The Common Pursuit*, London, Chatto and Windus, 1972, p. 18.
5 References to *Paradise Lost* are to *The Poetical Works of John Milton*, vol. I, *Paradise Lost*, ed. Helen Darbishire, Oxford University Press, 1952, unless cited from other works.
6 Anne Cluysenaar, *Introduction to Literary Stylistics: A Discussion of Dominant Structures in Verse and Prose*, London, Batsford, 1976, p. 55. / = phrase boundary; // = clause boundary; /// = sentence boundary; [[ ]] = rank shifted clause; ⟨ ⟩ = interrupting clause; → = run on; ⇥ = strong run on; ⇥ = strongest run on.
7 'The Readie and Easie Way to Establish a Free Commonwealth', in *Complete Prose Works of John Milton*, vol. VII, ed. Robert W. Ayers, rev. edn, New Haven and London, Yale University Press, 1980, pp. 462–3.

3 History in Robert Musil's *Törless*

J.P. Stern

Young Törless, published in 1906, is Musil's first book.[1] Robert Musil was born in the Austrian provincial capital of Klagenfurt in 1880, spent three years at a military academy in Moravia (1894–7), studied engineering in Brno (the capital of Moravia) where his father was a professor, served in the Austro-Hungarian army (1901–2), and then took a post as university assistant in the engineering department at the Technical High School in Stuttgart. Here, with time on his hands, he began to write sketches for his first novel (1902–3), relating its action and location to his own experiences at the military academy in Mährisch-Weisskirchen (Hranice, referred to in the text as 'W'); nightmare memories of this notoriously severe institution, in which the scions of the Austrian aristocracy were educated, continued to haunt Musil throughout his life, as they haunted the poet Rainer Maria Rilke, who had been there three years earlier.

The book is the opening move in the battle with recalcitrant narrative form which Musil fought throughout his life. Törless, its hero, is a first portrayal of Ulrich, the 'Man Without Qualities' of Musil's *magnum opus*, which he began writing in 1905 and left unfinished at his death in exile and great poverty in Lausanne in 1942.

The book is called *Die Verwirrungen des Zöglings Törless*. 'Zögling' is a slightly old-fashioned and rather formal word meaning 'scholar' or 'boarder' at an educational establishment; it has strong overtones of the Austrian military and civil service establishment; it is upper-class and closely connected with church and court.[2]

J.P. Stern

'Verwirrungen' are dark confusions, chaotic states of the mind. The word has no immediate moral connotations. Since the novel is cast in the narrative imperfect of an episode that is finished and done with, 'Verwirrungen' suggests the possibility that what was confused has been superseded by a state of adult clarity. The word is used several times throughout the novel; at the end, when Törless (we are not given his first name) looks back on the turmoil he has caused, the embarrassments and the mental conflicts he has undergone, 'But what were these things?', we read in the report of his stream of conscious and half-conscious thoughts, 'He had no time to think about it now and brood over the events. All he felt was a passionate longing to escape from this confused, whirling state of things . . .', 'aus diesen wirren, trubelnden Verhältnissen heraus zu kommen' (p. 128).

The historicity of Musil's first book (unlike the historicity of his later novel) has to be pieced together from the scantiest of indications. The location is given in the first sentence of the book: 'A small station on the railroad that leads to Russia', at the outer edge of Central Europe; the subsequent description is permeated by indications of remoteness, alienness, of an inhospitable and outlandish atmosphere. We are placed at the point where the outposts of Occidental (that is, German) culture meet the mysterious Slavonic East – this is the feeling that is to be communicated in the opening sections of the book. The events into which we are drawn are confined to a dominant German-speaking class, soon to call itself 'das deutsche Herrenvolk' and eventually to form the spearhead of the German/Austrian 'Drang nach Osten'; we are within a hundred kilometres of Trebljanka and Auschwitz. Living in a sea of Slav (Moravian) labourers and peasants, the elite group depends on them materially and sexually, but through the sexual link insecurity is carried into its ranks.

On the foundations of an ancient monastery 'a famous boarding school' has been established. The young gentlemen of the Academy carry the light swords of future officers and civil servants; the rural Slav proletariat live in the stews and are dirty, drunken, foul-mouthed and darkly threatening. Contact with them is seen as a contamination, yet life inside the citadel of learning, too, is heavy with sensuality, disaffection and vice. The school was put there (we are told) 'doubtless in order to safeguard the young generation, in its years of awakening, from the cor-

36

rupting influence of the big cities' (p. 8). Thereupon we are introduced to Törless, aged sixteen, and von Reiting, his senior by two years. The young gentlemen are walking back from the railway station, where they have just been seeing off their parents and receiving their blessings and pocket money. Predictably, their first port of call on their way back to school is an inn which also serves as a whore-house. Equally predictably, the peasant woman they meet on their way and the prostitute into whose room we follow Törless and his companion are coarse and licentious, and Slavonic. The visit is remembered later on in the story but not followed up in any direct way – Božena, the prostitute, is introduced partly as an object of Törless' awakening sexuality, partly (her coarseness being contrasted with recollections of his refined mother) in order to indicate the chaos and divisions in Törless' mind.

But are we justified in drawing those – latter-day – nationalist implications from the novel? After all, the only explicit ethnic indications we are given are the geographical setting (the mention of Russia in the first sentence) and Božena's name.[3] To speak of a German elite and a Slav rural proletariat may therefore seem like an historicising indiscretion – the sort of gratuitous hindsight that is typical of interpreters with an historical or political axe to grind. And so it is – a hindsight, occasioned by certain similarities of the novel with an outlook whose most virulent manifestations did not occur until a decade later. But it is not only hindsight. What confirms our reading is the contemporary topicality of the novel; is the fact that it is only one of a whole series embodying the theme of German superiority and the Slav–German conflict in a variety of fictional forms and disguises. Arthur Schnitzler, Rilke, Kafka and Franz Werfel, as well as Joseph Roth, 'Roda-Roda' and Felix Salten, are among those who explore this topos within the context of Austrian *fin de siècle* literature and sub-literature. Paradoxically, the historicity of *Young Törless* is confirmed most strikingly by a work which critics have almost invariably placed beyond concrete location and historical time: Kafka's *The Castle* (written in 1922) shows the same sort of topography and, associated with it, the same distribution of power and social status.

To give the action and location of *Törless* their national dimension and all that it connotes is thus to give them the meaning they had for Musil's first readers and fellow authors. Our interpretation of the novel is confirmed by its reception: history in the work coincides with the work in history.

In outlining the events of the novel – in assessing the importance of the events *for* the novel – we may as well be guided by Musil's own indication of how he saw his undertaking. Some ten years later (1913) he looks back on his first work and defends it against the critics' accusation that it is lacking in action and plot and even perhaps in individual characterisation, and that he is a poor story-teller: 'The reality one is describing is always only a pretext ["ein Vorwand"]', he writes.[4] Once upon a time (he continues) the purpose of story-telling may have been simply to enable a non-intellectual narrator – a person of a weak intellectual and reflective disposition ('eines begriffsarmen Menschen') – to touch again the good and terrible ghosts of his past experiences – ghosts under whose impact his memory is still cringing – and to render the spell of these experiences harmless by repeating them and talking about them. Nowadays, however (Musil continues), and in *his* narrative practice, the description of 'reality' must address itself to men of a strong intellectual disposition, powerfully reflective men ('begriffsstarke Menschen'). *Its* purpose is to enable them to come closer to 'an understanding of their feelings and of the stirrings of their minds'; and this new purpose is to be achieved not by the use of concepts but through the glimmer of, the radiation emanating from, the single case. So, either way, 'The reality which one is describing is always only a pretext.' At the same time we notice that, even though the action and plot (because they are constantly encroached upon by Törless' fantasies as well as by his and the narrator's comments on these fantasies) do not have the status they would have in a realistic novel, yet Törless' eventual repudiation of what is happening around him is an indispensable part – is the realistic component – of his journey out of the 'confusion'.

This is the programme we must keep in mind when assessing the importance of the events for the novel. And we should also note that in outlining this programme Musil is using the word 'reality' to mean precisely the opposite of what he means by it in the novel itself.

The events of the novel's 'reality', then, all take place inside the boarding school. Reiting (a tyrant who loves manipulating others in order, so he says, to train for life in the adult world) and

Beineberg (a sadist with an interest in Indian mysticism) observe
the boy Basini (pretty, effeminate and weak) stealing money from
the other boys' lockers in order to pay off a debt to Reiting.
Beineberg and Reiting decide not to report Basini to the school
authorities, but to use their knowledge of his felony in order
to blackmail him. Törless, who is curious, bemu ;ed, expectant,
avidly yet uneasily waiting for some act of 'terrible animal sensuality' to happen, is initiated into their plan, and takes part in its
execution.

The acts of torture and buggery to which Basini is subjected
take place in a secret room, draped in red flag cloth and furnished
with whips, lamps and a revolver, a hide-out which Beineberg and
Reiting have discovered under the rafters of the old monastic
building in which the school is housed. While Beineberg and
Reiting confine their treatment of the hapless Basini to physical
torture, Törless is increasingly sickened by such acts and takes
pleasure – or at least follows his bent – in torturing Basini mentally, by insisting on having the boy describe to him as minutely as
he can what is being done to him and what his reactions are. This
verbal voyeurism is chief among Törless' conflicting character
traits.

During a brief school vacation (one hesitates to call it anything
so straightforward and Anglo-Saxon as a 'half-term') Törless
and Basini are left alone in the school, and Basini (mainly, one
gathers, as an act of self-defence and in the hope of getting him
on his side) seduces Törless; at this stage Törless' reaction is
shown to be simply sexual. In the absence of Beineberg and
Reiting both the sadistic and the voyeur elements recede behind
the gratification of a pent-up sexual urge; the homosexual nature
of the act is accidental, determined merely by the circumstances
in which it occurs.

The events of the story come to a head when Basini, unable to
bear things any longer, decides to denounce his tormentors. As
soon as the Headmaster starts an investigation, Törless runs away
to a neighbouring town, though it is made clear that he has not
been denounced. Beineberg and Reiting convince the school
authorities that in beating up Basini (whose body is heavily
bruised) they merely gave vent to their righteous indignation
when they discovered that he was a thief. Basini is expelled, and
Törless, on being recaptured, tries in a confused and incoherent

way to explain his involvement in the affair. His speech is unintelligible to others because it is cast in the allusive language of his interior monologue. There was a point when Beineberg and Reiting, in their fear that Törless might betray them, were ready to treat him in the same way as they treated Basini, but when Törless returns from his brief flight they decide to make common cause with him. Törless is not being accused of any misdemeanour and is not trying to excuse himself. The confusion of his account derives from his attempts to convey to the Headmaster and the other masters present an apparently mystical state of mind, during which and for the sake of which he joined Beineberg and Reiting in the persecution of Basini. It is made clear that the mysticism at issue is not to be seen as a religious experience, but as a necessary supersession of reason by the irrational. The irrational, we are told, is at the root of the world; any experience of the world that fails to take issue with it is inadequate. The Headmaster, however, takes Törless' confused account of his involvement to be indicative of great sensitivity and mental stress, and the story ends with Törless being allowed to withdraw from the school in order to follow a course of private education likely to be more appropriate to his distraught state of mind.

It should be clear from this brief account that any resemblance to Kipling's *Stalky and Co.* is purely coincidental, if only because (worse luck) Musil's story has not a funny line in it; what humour there is comes from the presentation of the Headmaster and the clergyman who teaches divinity, as well as the maths master, as simpletons who are not only wrong about Törless' true motives (whatever *they* may be), but also pompous and heavy-handed in their misapprehension. But if any conventional public school story fails to provide an appropriate parallel, the powerful autobiographical element which pervades the book relates it not only to the actual episodes taken from Musil's own life in the military academy, but above all to the mental states he himself experienced there. The portrait is of a budding intellectual with strong aesthetic leanings and 'moments of an almost poetic inspiration' (p. 138) who, it is suggested, may eventually turn out to be a writer. But what sort of a writer? A carefully composed letter the boy writes to his parents, a set of notes in which he is attempting to find words for the 'unsayable', a secret diary – these are among the signs that have led numerous critics to interpret the book as a portrait of the artist as a young man. Perhaps so – but this only raises the question of the kind of writer Musil really was. What is claimed for Törless throughout the book is the aesthete's attitude and privileges; and although it is a moot point whether Törless' creator was – then or thereafter – aware of the difference, 'the aesthetic' is not, after all, the same as the artistically creative.

The book marks a journey into the 'confusions' and out of them, a development or progress such as one might associate with the adolescence and late puberty of a creative mind. This is the time-hallowed theme of the *Bildungs-* or *Entwicklungsroman*, the novel of acculturation, initiation and development, which has been a characteristic feature of German literature since the second half of the eighteenth century and the chief specifically German contribution to European fiction. Now although Musil claims that by the time he wrote Törless, when he was twenty-two, he had 'read very little and knew no model' he might follow (like Törless, Musil received a predominantly scientific education), the family likeness which connects the book with other examples of this genre is obvious. Moreover, an intellectual, an artist, a writer in the making is often the main subject of the classical *Bildungsroman*.

Development – *Entwicklung* – means an unbroken sequence of events, a continuity without jumps, whereas *Verwirrungen*, confusions, means single, possibly catastrophic, mental events; discontinuities. This is not a contradiction but the paradox in which the book is grounded; and in this respect it resembles several other *Bildungsromane*. For it is characteristic of this kind of novel that the existential and intellectual continuities are insisted on, often by formally unconvincing means, all the more strongly as the experiences described are felt to be discontinuous, not readily amenable to orderly presentation. 'The work of art', Musil writes in his diary some twelve years later, 'is not like a single curved line, but like a line that is drawn with ever fresh starts. It is not continuous, but contains cracks ["Sprünge"] which remain below the threshold of observation or irradiate its [the work's] specific character' (T, p. 201). The language of order, coherence and continuity is thus seen to be inadequate, to be at odds with the true nature of experience. But in saying this we are not only characterising Musil's view of language and therefore the way he writes in this book, we are at the same time approaching one of the book's main preoccupations. Both in reporting the content of his consciousness and in reproducing his encounters with the school authorities and his school companions, Törless is shown to be struggling to find words with which to convey the confused experiences within – struggling and failing. Language, in the form of his introspection and inner discourse, is presented in the narrative as a dark medium, discontinuous, as mere lungings at uncertain targets; here 'each venture / Is a new beginning, a raid on the inarticulate / With shabby equipment always deteriorating / In the general mess of imprecision of feeling'.[5]

The inadequacy of language to convey the kind of inner experiences young Törless undergoes becomes a theme of the novel. And what is implied in that thematisation – implied and in no way criticised – is a view of language as a system of labels or names for things which are in themselves wordless, silent. The novel is thus grounded in a dichotomy with language on one side and experience or (to use the novel's own terminology) *Wirklichkeit, reality*, on the other; or again, language, being confined to the process of naming and describing things, and apparently incapable of truly explaining them, is felt, and presented, as being somehow *unreal, unwirklich*, or at least as less real than events, or experiences, or feelings – or indeed 'reality'. This is not the place to show the inadequacy and incoherence of this kind of metaphysics. (In the diary note I quoted earlier Musil had used 'reality' as a pretext 'for the presentation of inner states', and therefore as meaning the opposite of what it means here.) Instead, two historical points should be noted. First, this language/'reality' dichotomy is characteristic of all or almost all important fiction written in German in the first half of this century, and in this sense (as well as in several other senses) the book belongs emphatically and unproblematically to the highly problematic age in which it was composed. Secondly, the authorial reliance on the language/'reality' dichotomy leads to a curious escalation of what is felt and said to be 'real', so that 'reality' comes to consist of what is felt and said to be 'indescribable' (*unsagbar* and similar words occur throughout the text), and the 'indescribable' is apt to be confined to the marginal, the sensational and the catastrophic, to that which results (literally) in an overturning of the ordered and the orderly; and again, this

42

becomes common practice for a whole generation of novelists.

'Reality', in its antithesis to language, means significant, weighty experience, and such experience is said to be found only on the margins of the ordinary world; hence Musil's frequent insistence on *Grenzsituationen, Grenzfälle, Grenzwerte*[6] – marginal situations, marginal cases and marginal values. Hence, too, the significance of the secret red room. While the entire action of the novel takes place in the school, a domain that is deliberately separated from the everyday world, the revelations (such as they are), or – to use a word given a certain vogue by Joyce's Stephen Dedalus and used by several critics – the secular 'epiphanies' Törless experiences, or (to use yet a third fashionable term) his 'privileged moments', come to him at a double remove from the ordinary world, in that star chamber in which Basini is tortured and abused. Similarly, in Thomas Mann's *Magic Mountain* and Franz Kafka's *The Trial* (to choose two out of a very large number of examples), insight and revelation, an understanding of existential truth (however enigmatic and inconclusive) come to the heroes of those novels in *Grenzsituationen*, in such exceptional locations and marginal planes of experience. 'Reality', in the sense which it is given in these marginal situations (and in the sense in which T.S. Eliot says, 'Human kind cannot bear very much reality'), is where there is no 'reality' in the sense of the ordinary and everyday world. 'True reality', we may say, is where there is no reality. And this formula, we may add, provides a key to a good deal that is characteristic and significant in German literature in the first half of this century.

The core of the book before us, then, lies not in its actions and events but (to repeat Musil's own characterisation) in 'the coming closer to the feelings and stirrings of mind . . . of the single case'. And in this sense the single case is representative. These are 'die Verwirrungen', the inward dream-like adventures of a confused adolescent mind. And just as the words which describe this state of mind are searched for with great difficulty and said to be fundamentally arbitrary and imprecise, lungings in the darkness, so the outward events, too, which set the search in train and which are presented with no other purpose in mind than to provide the occasion for and the way into these searchings – so these events too are presented as arbitrary. We shall have to see whether, and with what qualifications, we as readers of the novel can really accept them as such. But first, we must try to indicate the nature of these 'feelings and stirrings of the mind', the nature of what it is that Törless is said to be seeking.

Törless is intent on understanding other minds not on their own terms and for their sake, but only to the extent that they should enable him to understand and grasp the content of his own mind. The understanding he is seeking is solipsistic. Other minds and the world itself are there only as the objects of a series of avowedly arbitrary experiments, experiments designed to reveal a mind that is a puzzle and a problem to itself, a mind that is presented as having no other puzzles and problems save those that are parts of its inscape. The world that is presented as the object of such an enquiry is made up of radical discontinuities or, rather, contradictions. Let me enumerate some of them. The acts of extreme, sordid cruelty in which Törless takes part are juxtaposed to a mind of extreme fastidiousness and sensitivity; Törless' radical estrangement from all around him is juxtaposed to the utmost intimacy and surrender of the sexual act; the extreme closeness to the sentient self of events *experienced* is juxtaposed to the radical distancing of the events when formulated ('when I am formulated, sprawling on a pin'[7]); his willingness to share in the sado-masochistic acts of tyranny and total domination over another is juxtaposed to moments of complete indifference and aloofness – personal aloofness from the events that are happening in his presence in the red chamber, and indifference as to the consequences of those actions – and exacting attempts at a rational account of his psychic life are juxtaposed to mystical intimations. The deep confusion Törless experiences in refusing to contemplate the thought that there is a link between his mother and the prostitute Božena, and between himself and the thief Basini, are further indications of the dual world he inhabits.[8] All these things he experiences as 'breaks', juxtapositions without connecting links. For all these extremes of hot and cold no authorial synthesis is offered. Törless *is* each of these in turn (we have here an opening on to Musil's later work, the portrait of a hero 'with indeterminate qualities'). True, the novel contains, somewhat inadvertently and with only the weakest traces of irony, a brief observation to the effect that 'Later, when he had got over his adolescent experiences, Törless became a young man whose mind was both subtle and sensitive . . . one of those aesthetically inclined intellectuals . . . [whose] needs were acutely and single-mindedly focused on an aesthetic–intellectual approach' to everything around him, especially to moral problems (pp. 111–12). But this attempt at a synthesis (the eventual result of the warring extremes of which Törless' 'confusions' are composed) is encompassed neither by the events of the novel nor by the reported stream of conscious and half-conscious thoughts pertaining to those events.

Alongside attempts at describing these extremes in analytical language, a good many highly charged images are used; and given the avowedly ineffable nature of these 'feelings and stirrings of the mind', it is difficult to assess how successful these images are in conveying 'the mystical'. Some of them offer immediate illumination. Thus, the way to Božena's house at the beginning of the novel leads through a dark and sinister wood, but at the end it is seen to be a mere 'dusty tangle of willows and alders'. But then again Musil takes recourse to a sort of 'naturalistic fallacy', offering to convey darkness by darkness, and leaving us with the impression that the clearer these images are, the less appropriate for the purpose of conveying the unclarity that encompasses the novel's central theme, Törless' 'confusions'.

The most interesting of Musil's images, in which clarity and obscurity are combined, is mentioned for the first time by Törless during the torture scene; the incongruity of image and scene is significant. Basini has just been hit by Beineberg ('now, across his upper lip, mouth and chin, slowly, drops of blood were making a red wriggling line, like a worm' (p. 62)), and Törless compounds Basini's debasement by ordering him to confess: 'Go on, say you're a thief.' As soon as he has said this, Törless is sickened by the scene – he recognises it as a caricature of the illumination he is seeking, and he withdraws his mind from it. There follows an instant act of self-absorption (the English translation places a break here, as though for a new chapter; in the German there are no chapters and no major breaks anywhere): Törless goes back in his mind to a thought he had during a maths lesson, when he found himself puzzled by the meaning and function of the square root of -1. It had been demonstrated to the class that the square of any number can have a square root; but now he is told that the square root of -1, even though it can never be a 'real' number, may nevertheless be needed in certain mathematical operations in order to make possible (or, as Törless puts it, to 'connect') a calculation cast in 'rational' numbers, numbers designating tangible quantities like metres or pounds. In the 'real' calculation (Törless infers) there is a break ('ein Sprung') which only the 'unreal' can bridge. This contrasting of 'the real' and 'the unreal' is seen by him as an illustration of juxtaposing maximum precision (calculation with 'real' numbers) and maximum arbitrariness (calculation with imaginary or 'unreal' numbers); and this in turn serves as an analogy of all the other juxtapositions of extremes, the totality of which is Törless' mind.

It is the sadist, Beineberg, who draws the necessary analogy. Imitating the voice of the divinity master, Beineberg says: 'You see an apple – that's the action of light waves and of the eye and so forth – and you stretch out your hand to steal it – that's the muscles and the nerves that set them in action – but between these two there lies something else that makes one emanate from the other, and that's the immortal soul, which in doing so has committed sin' (p. 74). The fact that Beineberg the sadist has produced this explanation has the same significance as the fact that Törless' recollection of these matters of high intellectual abstraction is occasioned by a scene of degradation and sordid violence; both are intended to illustrate the puzzle itself.

Leaving aside the question whether the discussion of imaginary numbers is set out in terms acceptable to a mathematician, we must ask whether the analogical explanation which Beineberg offers (and which is repeated in different terms elsewhere) provides a valid account of Törless' 'confusions'. The answer is, yes, up to a point. Beineberg's explanation is of course given in a vein of mockery – that's precisely the sort of thing the divinity master *would* say; and for good measure one part of the explanation is repeated at the end (during the Headmaster's investigation) in the most deflating terms by the clergyman himself. In the course of the novel the specifically *religious* part of the clergyman's explanation is denied both explicitly and by implication; throughout, we are moving in an era that lies in the shadow of what Nietzsche called 'the death of God'. Yet stripped of its religious connotations (of all that is said, in Christian terminology, about sin and the immortal soul), the analogy from the discontinuity of imaginary numbers is valid: experience *is* to be seen as discontinuous, toppling over from one extreme to its opposite, from (for instance) the extreme of rationality and scientific accuracy to its opposite, irrationalism and arbitrariness. And (we are meant to infer) if even mathematics hides such 'mystical' contradictions at its core, how hopeless must be all attempts designed to keep contradictions and thus the irrational out of more mundane and scientifically indeterminable areas of experience.

While the strenuousness of this search for 'the mystical' receives a good deal of positive emphasis, the unstable, apparently 'amoral' value of what is accepted at the end of the search is bound to strike us as problematic. For we can see (as Musil did not) that in modern, post-Nietzschean Europe there are only two kinds of mysticism. One is a mysticism directed towards God, such as Simone Weil practised; while the other, which is that of the book before us, finds its consummation in fascism. Again the question of anachronism arises. Insight into the full political implications of the 'mystical' attitude could not be available to Musil any more than insight into the political implications of Josef K.'s and K.'s attitudes to power could be for Kafka, if for no other reason than that each was too much of a *writer* to be a true prophet of what was to come.[9] And if Musil (and Kafka) had confined their novels to psychological portraiture, the relationship between private conduct and its political significance could hardly be more than one of remote implication. But in novels whose settings are as heavily institutionalised as theirs, the political implications are anything but remote, and any critical account that lays some claim to completeness is bound to take issue with them: the political ramifications of what is given in the private sphere cannot be avoided except by an act of omission.

And the same is true of the moral implications of Törless' search for a way out of his 'confusions'. Inevitably, a good deal of our account so far was cast in terms connoting extreme cruelty, sadism, squalid violence – terms heavily loaded with moral values. Musil tries to avoid such terms. He resorts to them only once or twice, briefly, and then they are overshadowed by other expressions of disapproval, of a predominantly aesthetic kind, chief among them the word *Ekel*, 'disgust'. And (we read), as soon as 'this disgust and a certain indistinct, hidden fear' are aroused in Törless, 'the subtle voluptuousness that lay in his acts of degradation became ever rarer' (p. 114). To the extent, then, that disapproval of the torture scenes is shown at all, it is because, at some point or other, they disgust Törless; and they disgust him because they do not fulfil the promise they offered: they promised erotic gratification and looked like leading towards insight into the duality of things, but when he recognises that they are brought about by agents whom he despises – he despises Reiting and Beineberg no less than Basini, in whom at least he could assuage his sexual desire – they turn out to lead only to the feeble beginnings of insight. Musil is thus caught in the same cleft stick as his young hero: in spite of the declared narrative intention to treat action, plot and even the psychology of individual characters as arbitrary, the fact that they are what they are turns out to be an indispensable part of conveying those 'feelings and stirrings of the mind' in the bearing they have on morality. Moral judgments, in the European novel, are not an option.

We are, as I have said, moving within the shadow cast by 'the death of God'. And in this era, Nietzsche also wrote, 'Everything is possible, everything is permitted'. This is the moral space in which the events of the novel are enacted. When Törless tells his two companions that he is bored by the whole conspiracy and will no longer take part in it (the boredom being a mask for 'the disgust and the indistinct fear' I mentioned), Reiting threatens to subject him to the same treatment as that meted out to Basini. Törless repeats his decision to quit:

> 'I'm not going to have any more to do with it. I am sick of the whole thing.'
> 'All of a sudden?' [Reiting retorts]
> 'Yes, all of a sudden. Before, I was searching for something behind it all . . .'. Why did this keep on forcing itself back into his mind . . .?!
> 'Aha, second sight!'

Again, although this is said by Reiting mockingly, the word is an appropriate lead into Törless' searchings and confusions:

> 'Yes [he replies]. But now I can see only one thing – how vulgar and brutal you and Beineberg are.'
> 'But you shall also see Basini eating dirt,' Reiting sneered.
> 'I'm not interested any more.'
> 'But you certainly used to be!'

'I've already told you: only as long as Basini's state of mind was a riddle to me.'

'And now?'

'Now I don't know anything about riddles. Everything happens: that's all the wisdom there is.' [p. 167]

'Everything is possible, everything is permitted', wrote Nietzsche; and, Musil/Törless adds, 'Everything happens: that's all the wisdom there is.'

I don't know whether there are literary genres that can bypass all moral considerations, but I very much doubt whether it is possible to write an amoral novel. It is in the nature of the writing and reading of novels (at least to the extent that they are about human beings, and perhaps even when they are not) that they give rise to moral questions of one kind or another; that they cannot fail to give rise to questions of good and evil, however defined. The reason why I have left such considerations to the end is because they are never an explicit part of this novel, and because even when they occur, always in conjunction with an aesthetic judgment of disapproval, such considerations are unsustained and incidental – incidental to the insights for which the central character searches, and through him the author. And the reason for this defectiveness – whether we see it as a defectiveness in the presentation of a moral censure or of an aesthetic–moral distaste – is very simple. It lies in the solipsism in which the novel is cast: all that happens is presented as happening ultimately in terms of Törless' mind, and at no point is the effect on other minds seriously considered.

Beineberg and Reiting are presented as bullies (there is an obvious moral–aesthetic judgment in that), but their main function is to provide Törless with a spectacle in which he also becomes an agent, and which is to offer him opportunities for gratification and insight – for the gratification of insight. Basini's baseness – Italian names, in the Austrian stereotype, connote cowardice and treachery – is not confined to Törless' view of him; it is, astonishingly, the author himself who speaks of Basini's 'moral inferiority and stupidity' (p. 51). Hence neither Törless nor his creator have any compunction in treating him as a mere object, a means to Törless' end.[10] This is made abundantly clear in that brief and inadvertent page of recollection when, in the course of describing the kind of aesthetically minded intellectual Törless became in later years, the author tells us that '[Törless] never felt remorse for what had happened at that [earlier] time' (p. 148). Through these experiences, we are told, he became 'one of those people who regard the things that make demands only on their moral rectitude with the utmost indifference'. And when asked whether, looking back on this episode of his adolescence, he did not after all have a feeling of shame,

> he answered, with a smile, 'Of course, I don't deny that it was a degrading affair. And why not? The degradation passed off. And yet it left something behind – that small admixture of poison which is needed to rid the soul of its over-confident, complacent healthiness, and to give it instead a sort of health that is more acute, and subtler, and more understanding.' [p. 148]

(The argument is pure Nietzsche.) And lovers too, the not-so-young Törless goes on to ruminate, share such journeys 'through all the circles of hell' – the tone of the recollection has suddenly changed – 'and just as such lovers go that way together, so I at that time went through all those things, but on my own ["so bin ich damals mit mir selbst durch all dies hindurchgegangen"]'.

However, Törless' recollection is playing him false: he was not alone and could not be alone. And it is no irrelevant insight – though it is a judgment not contained in the text of the novel – to say, emphatically, that what was done to Basini at all events cannot be described as 'a small admixture of poison', as a homeopathic cure against over-confidence and complacent healthiness. If ever one looks for a recipe of how to ruin a schoolboy for life, it is given, unintentionally but surely, in the fate of Basini.

If, then, the novel is not (and cannot be) amoral, what sort of a moral scheme does it show forth? The morality in terms of which Törless' 'confusions' are to be justified is put into words in at least three passages, each time by a different character; and again it must be added that, whether or not these passages represent the author's own belief, they are not subjected to any criticism. Rather, the author gives the impression of one who has got his central character into a complicated mess and is quite pleased – in a suitably serious way, of course – that he has found a way of getting him out of it, without bothering too much about the rights and wrongs of it.

1   Early in the novel Beineberg explains his interest in Basini. Having expounded an obscure bit of some Indian mystical clap-trap, – a recipe for bending the external world, including other people, to his will, even if it means destroying them in the process – Beineberg concludes his harangue:

> 'Well, you can see what my interest is. The impulse I have to let Basini off comes from outside me and arises from base motives. You can obey it if you like. For me it's a prejudice, and I have to cut myself loose from it as from everything else that would distract me from my inner ways. The very fact that I find it hard to torture Basini – I mean, to humiliate him, to debase him, to cast him away from me – is good. It requires a sacrifice. It will have a purifying effect. . . .' [p. 60]

2   Immediately before the seduction scene Basini reports to the avid Törless how he was abused and tortured by Reiting:

> 'First of all he gives me long talks about my soul. He says I've sullied it, but as it were only the outermost forecourt of it. In relation to the innermost ["Im Verhältnis zum Innersten"], he says, this doesn't matter at all, it's only external. But one must kill it. In that way sinners have turned into saints. So from a higher point of view sin isn't so bad: only one must take it to its extreme point, so that it breaks off of its own accord.' [p. 101]

3   And here, finally, is Törless himself, becoming conscious of what distinguishes him from his two companions:

> . . . He believed that he could see no trace of shame in them. He did not think that they suffered as he knew he did. The crown of thorns that his tormenting conscience set on his brow seemed to be missing from theirs. . . . He knew that he would debase himself again, but he gave it a new meaning. The uglier and unworthier everything was that Basini offered him, the greater was the contrast with that feeling of suffering sensibility which would set in afterwards. [p. 80]

From a whole variety of sources, including a notorious speech of Heinrich Himmler of October 1943,[11] we know that arguments of this kind were propagated among the SS and believed by some of them. Elisabeth Stopp, in her illuminating essay on *Törless*, says that Musil himself (presumably in his later diaries) had 'a mediumistic premonition of the SS officers who run concentration camps'.[12] The parallel is certainly there, but not the premonition. After all, nowhere in the novel is there a statement to dissociate it from this ethos; nowhere is it said or shown that Törless' development, his journey through his confusions and out of them, is the worse for having been achieved in this way, or that it could have been achieved in any other way. There is as little warning in this portrayal with which Musil opens his literary career as there is in Franz Kafka's novels, which are full of similar anticipations.

Let me recapitulate the three passages. Humiliation entails sacrifice, we read, though (given the ambiguity of the German word, *Opfer*, which means both 'sacrifice' and 'victim') *whose* sacrifice is intended we are not told. And we also read: sinfulness must be taken to its extreme point, and only then will it turn into sainthood. And finally, in terms of explicit blasphemy: the 'thorny crown' of tormenting conscience is a proof of a suffering *aesthetic* sensibility, 'eine leidende Feinheit'.

Törless stands at the threshold of modern German literature. All these ideas, which constitute the moral horizon of the novel, are central to that literature. Its major theme is the search for redemption, validation and an encompassing meaning of life, and these are invariably said to be attainable at the margins of experience – it is the hardness and harshness, the difficulty in the way of attaining the goal, and indeed on occasion its radical unattainability that are offered, in this literature, as a proof of the value of the goal. The greater the sacrifice, the greater what once used to be called 'sin', the harsher the torment of conscience – the finer, the subtler the experience and its validation. What this early novel offers us is an unalloyed, uncritical – indeed, crude – version of the ethos, soon to become an ideology, of the literature of the subsequent age.

To say this is not to say that Robert Musil was some sort of proto-Nazi, any more than that the majority of latter-day critics of the novel, with less excuse than he had for failing to see its moral and political implications, are to be seen as some sort of *NS-Sympathisanten*. (Musil was a difficult, tetchy and deeply honourable man; when Hitler assumed power in Germany, he instantly went into exile, although he was neither a Jew nor in the least politically involved.) History in literary criticism is irrelevant if it does not throw a light on the text, illuminating its excellences and flaws. And so here too our concern must be not with the novel's wrong politics, but with the lack of perceptiveness disclosed by the historical view; or (to put it bluntly) with the authorial failure to make out the sinister but coherent whole that looms up behind the solipsistic self, the self on its indiscriminate quest for 'reality' and experience.

The National Socialists did not descend on Germany and central Europe like some Pizarro and his *conquistadores* on unsuspecting Peru; and national socialism, the dominant ethos and ideology of the subsequent era, was not an isolated phenomenon that came down suddenly, like a thunderbolt from a blue sky; it arose out of an existing, as yet non-dominant ethos, representing its absolute radicalisation. *Törless* and the works whose family likeness it bears present the unsuspecting beginnings of this ethos – an ethos which is not exclusively German or Austrian, though it is at its most concentrated in the literature of those countries. Its literary manifestations in Musil's time remained relatively harmless because they were prevented from attaining any social and political consequences. What prevented their translation into ideology and practical politics was partly the dominant political order of their day, and partly their status as fictions, poetry, literature, in a society that was still capable of distinguishing literature from politics, fiction from fact, though less and less so as time went by. National socialism, on the other hand, is the wholly nihilistic and destructive aspect and consummation of this ethos, born at the point where social anarchy made possible the translation of novels into practical politics; fiction into fact.

Musil's fragmentary masterpiece, *The Man Without Qualities*, was begun the year before *Törless* was published. Its relation to the book before us is a matter of radical transposition into another key. Ulrich too (unlike Törless, he has no surname) is seeking enlightenment and a way out of his unclarities, he too is immensely determinable, a receptacle rather than a fully formed character, experimenting with experience. But two radical changes – transpositions – occur: the experience with which he experiments is Ulrich's own; and other people are involved in it on equal terms – they are not reduced to being mere means to an end. Moreover, the entire scenario of *The Man Without Qualities* – Ulrich and the curious world of Vienna 1913 around him – is itself heavily historicised, and suffused with the light of radical irony. Ulrich calls himself a 'possibilitarian' – one who, while seeking, like Törless, some profound mystical 'reality' behind all things, is content to see the world around him ironically, as a provisional abode on the way to the mystery, a spectrum of changing hues and mere possibilities. The transposition of the search into a new key confronted Musil with formal narrative problems which some critics (including this critic) think he failed to solve. However that may be, to see *Törless* as a first step on the road to *The Man Without Qualities* is only partly valid. One can see nothing in the early novel which would point to that transposition, nothing that would modify that spirit of clammy passion, heaviness and ritual sacrifice which informs Musil's first published work.

NOTES

1 Page numbers in the text refer to the *rororo* paperback, *Die Verwirrungen des Zöglings Törless*, Reinbek bei Hamburg, Rowohlt Taschenbuch Verlag, 1980. I have also used, and occasionally adapted, *Young Törless*, trans. Eithne Wilkings and Ernst Kaiser, London, Panther Paperback, 1979.
2 For this and several other points I am indebted to Elisabeth Stopp's 'Musil's *Törless*: Content and Form', *Modern Language Review*, January 1969, pp. 94–118.
3 And also Basini's name; see below, p. 49.
4 Robert Musil, *Tagebücher, Aphorismen, Essays und Reden*, ed. A. Frisé, Hamburg, Rowohlt Verlag, 1955, p. 776; referred to as T; cf. also Stopp, op cit., p. 94.
5 T.S. Eliot, 'East Coker', *Four Quartets*, London, Faber and Faber, 1972, pp. 30–1, II, 178–81.
6 Gerhart Baumann, *Robert Musil: zur Erkenntnis der Dichtung*, Bern and Munich, Francke Verlag, 1965, passim.
7 T.S. Eliot, 'The Love Song of J. Alfred Prufrock', *Collected Poems 1909–1962*, London, Faber and Faber, 1974, p. 15.
8 See F.G. Peters, *Robert Musil: Master of the Hovering Life*, New York, Columbia University Press, 1978, p. 35.

9 By a (true) prophet I mean one who foresees *and* warns.
10 This is the main tenor of David Turner's 'The Evasions of the Aesthete Törless', in *Forum for Modern Language Studies*, January 1974, vol. X, pp. 19–44. Although the aim of this illuminating and thoughtful study is 'to forge a link . . . between the private world of Törless and the social and political implications of the novel' (p. 20), it seems as if, on the point of analysing the politics of the novel, the author got frightened and shut the door on the perspective opening up before him.
11 See J.P. Stern, *Hitler: der Führer und das Volk*, Munich, Hanser Verlag, 1978, pp. 203–4.
12 Stopp, op. cit., p. 99; the reference is to T, p. 441; cf. also Stopp, op. cit., p. 112: 'Beineberg's cold and lifeless lectures . . . Reiting's smooth, slick accounts . . . would have fitted well into the pages of the *Völkische Beobachter*' (the party newspaper).

4 Of stones and stories: Sartre's *La Nausée*

Christopher Prendergast

Shrove Tuesday (Mardi gras) is the heading of one of the entries in Roquentin's diary. It begins with a nightmare in which Roquentin and two friends do something decidedly vulgar with a bunch of violets to the ultra-right-wing French writer, Maurice Barrès. From this somewhat flamboyant beginning the episode shifts to more mundane matters: the receipt of a letter from his former mistress Anny, lunch at the restaurant in the rue des Horloges, leaving the restaurant to walk the streets of Bouville. The entry closes with the following passage. I shall quote it first of all from the English translation (as I shall most of the other passages for discussion), and then from the French, since the connotations of the key term of the original are not adequately caught by the translation.[1]

> The rain has stopped, the air is mild, the sky is slowly rolling along beautiful black pictures: this is more than enough to make a frame for the perfect moment; to reflect these pictures, Anny would cause dark little tides to be born in our hearts. But I don't know how to take advantage of this opportunity: I wander along at random, calm and empty, under this wasted sky. [p. 104]

> La pluie a cessé, l'air est doux, le ciel roula lentement de belles images noires: c'est plus qu'il n'en faut pour faire le cadre d'un moment parfait; pour refléter ces images, Anny ferait naître dans nos cœurs de sombres petites marées. Moi, je ne sais pas profiter de l'occasion: je vais au hasard, vide et calme, sous ce ciel inutilisé. [p. 103]

The passage contrasts two attitudes to the sky, that of Anny and that of Roquentin. Anny's gesture, as imagined by Roquentin, would be of an appropriating sort, appropriating the natural world in the attempt to make it conform to a literary model – the model of the 'moment parfait', which is taken over wholesale from Proust's *A la recherche du temps perdu*. Anny's transformed sky is a literary sky; it is infested with metaphor, the verbal equivalents of an attempted pictorial framing, not unlike the Proustian sky filtered through the forms of Elstir's paintings, for which in turn – in a closed circular movement – the narrator seeks to provide a literary version. Roquentin's sky is utterly different: it is merely vacant, it does not lend itself to metaphorical appropriations. It remains – this is the key term which the English 'wasted' does not adequately render – it remains 'inutilisé'. There is however a difficulty here. The phrase 'ciel inutilisé' is itself metaphorical. The negative prefix is, of course, designed to refuse the consoling, emotionally utilitarian orderings of the natural world made available by metaphor. There is nevertheless a paradox: the paradox whereby Roquentin deploys metaphor to reject metaphor. I shall return at a later point, and in greater detail, to the particular question of metaphor in *La nausée* (it is, by the way, the main theme of Robbe-Grillet's criticism of Sartre's novel). For the moment I simply want to use the example as an illustration of a more general paradox, for it is around this paradox that most of the interesting questions of *La nausée* revolve. *La nausée* is a book which affirms the valuelessness of books, on the grounds that they furnish the stereotyped formulae of inauthentic living; they give the forms and alibis of ways of living that, in the terms of Sartre's existentialist morality, are manifestations of 'bad faith'. 'It seems to me as if everything I know about life I have learnt from books', remarks Roquentin, with the implication that the 'knowledge' in question is entirely specious and, therefore, that which we would do better to dispense with altogether. Yet we, as readers, know about this claim only because Roquentin has noted it in his diary, or, more pertinently, because it appears in a book by Jean-Paul Sartre. Moreover, it is perhaps one of the nicer ironies of the subsequent destiny of *La nausée* that this book, which loudly proclaims that we should not live our lives through books, was to become both myth and model for a whole post-war generation; the frequency with which intellectuals, and not only on the boulevards and in the cafés of Paris, were seized with bouts of contingency-sickness must certainly be ascribed in part to their having read *La nausée*. (This aspect of the matter is, incidentally, parodied in Boris Vian's very funny novel, *L'Écume des jours*, where one of the characters displays a morbid enthusiasm for the writer Jean-Sol Partre, author of the influential novel, *Le Vomi*, and philosophical essay, *Paradoxe sur le Dégeulis*.)

The paradoxes thus proliferate in a variety of directions, and I shall come back at a later juncture to a few more. Their general form should however be clear, and indeed already familiar as one of the sign-posts in the landscape of the modern novel as a whole: they point to that paradoxical disposition of modern narrative to query or repudiate the genre of which it is itself a member. In this respect it is worth recalling the date of *La nausée*'s publication: 1938. The significance of that date can be construed in a number of different ways. Perhaps the most familiar – although in many respects unsatisfactory – is the line of enquiry which seeks to relate *La nausée* to the philosophical themes (largely of the phenomenological and existentialist sort) engaging Sartre's attention at the time, and which were to issue in what for many is Sartre's *magnum opus*, *L'Être et le néant*. There is here in fact a set of potentially interesting questions. They have to do with whether or not the central emphases of the philosophical endeavour are of a kind that actively command, or conversely militate against, a literary mode of expression: for example, what we might call the drive towards 'narrative' in L'Être et le néant arising from the detailed phenomenological descriptions of behaviour which Sartre explicitly posits as methodologically crucial to the enterprise of philosophy as such. On the other hand, there is the argument that there is a fundamental tension, or 'dissonance', between the claims of existentialist doctrine and the basic generic requirements of narrative: broadly, the incompatibility of, on the one hand, the existentialist proposition that the world is wholly contingent and the individual wholly free, and, on the other, the anticipatory and foreclosing operations vital to anything we might plausibly recognise as a *narrative* structure. These again are matters to which I shall return. The point I want to make here is a far more limited one: that it does not seem a particularly profitable exercise to discuss *La nausée*, as it is so often discussed, as a fictionalised version of a series of philosophical themes; the terms of such discussion effectively reduce the text of *La nausée* to purely instrumental status – to being, as it were, the handmaiden of another order of discourse – and hence give no framework for addressing the far more important question: its status as a work of fiction.

From this latter point of view the date 1938 is of some interest in terms of twentieth-century literary history. *La nausée* stands roughly half-way between those forms of narrative experiment which, in France, we associate largely with the names of Proust and Gide, and those which later emerged under the collective if essentially polemical heading of the *nouveau roman*. Although I am not here concerned with tracing lines of influence, either backwards or forwards, the date of publication of *La nausée* perhaps indicates its place as a point of transition in the developing entry of the novel into what Nathalie Sarraute has called its 'age of suspicion'. That is, *La nausée* is mapped out on an experience of what we might term a generalised epistemic anxiety, a loss of certainty in familiar paradigms of knowledge and understanding, and within which the novel itself, and the models of intelligibility it characteristically sustains, become a privileged object of 'suspicion'. The novel can no longer be taken for granted as an instrument of discovery. Its hermeneutic credentials are no longer unproblematical in the way they were for Balzac when he said that the novel gave supreme access to the *sens caché* of reality. In brief, the novel is no longer a reliable guide to anything, except perhaps (if written in a certain way – what the French would nowadays call a 'self-deconstructing' way) as a guide to the absolute unreliability of everything. Sartre's novel is centrally situated within this general problematic. Part of its specific interest however is that its *precise* location in these terms is somewhat uncertain. Its position with regard to the sceptical paradigm, and the multiple paradoxes the paradigm generates, is ambiguous. How *La nausée* engages with this ambiguity, what kind of awareness it shows of its nature and implications, are what I chiefly want to talk about.

In this connection we might perhaps start by citing another Sartrian metaphor, or more accurately an analogy. Sartre once remarked that a great novel would be, *inter alia*, like a *stone*. That might not sound a terribly promising basis on which to found a new narrative programme; indeed, it might not seem to be anything we can make sense of at all. We might however recall here that stones (and their variants, pebbles, rocks, boulders) have enjoyed a rather vigorous symbolic life in a great deal of modern French thinking. It is, of course, central to *La nausée* itself, in that Roquentin's first experience of existential nausea comes when he picks up a pebble on the beach ('that pebble,' he later reminisces, 'the origin of this whole wretched business'). Elsewhere it provides the decisive element in Camus' allegory of the Absurd, his adaptation of the story of Sisyphus, whose perpetually defeated attempt to roll the boulders up to the top of the mountain illustrates the permanent contradiction between the human desire for meaning and the world's resistance to that desire (in the terms of *La nausée*, the contradiction between the desire for 'story' and the anguish of 'contingency'). In the context of specifically literary theory and practice, our stone or pebble turns up in at least two other important contexts. First, in the brilliant, though nowadays little read, imaginary Socratic dialogue by Valéry, *Eupalinos.* Valéry's Socrates picks up a pebble while walking along the sea-shore. Washed for centuries by the sea, the pebble, in terms of smoothness and roundness, is perfect. The question it prompts is whether a perfection produced by the random forces of nature can properly be compared to the perfection of a work of art. Socrates' answer is an emphatic 'No', on the grounds that its perfection is accidental, a result of the play of contingent forces, whereas a condition of the aesthetic artefact is the conscious, ordering activity of the human mind and the human hand. The other example I should like to note here is Francis Ponge's short, and deceptively simple, prose poem, 'Le Galet' (or 'Beach Pebble'). Ponge's pebble is also perfect, but its status is ambiguous. It is not clear whether the real object of Ponge's attention is the thing itself or the word *galet* which denotes it; his poem oscillates ambiguously and ironically between the referential and self-reflexive functions of language, apparently miming the material properties of the thing when in fact exploring, and playing with, the material properties of the word – not so much a naming of objects as an object-ifying of names. It is a deliberately cultivated, and in its implications wide-ranging, ambiguity, raising in its own low-key way the characteristic 'modernist' queries about the possibilities and constraints of the relation between language and reality.

Stones thus appear to get around quite a lot in the modern French literary consciousness. But Sartre's novelistic stone or stone-like novel is quite different from either Valéry's or Ponge's respective pebbles. What Sartre has in mind is neither Ponge's ambiguous interlacing of the referential and self-reflexive, nor Valéry's rigorously classical insistence on the ordering power of imagination and convention. What Sartre envisages – it is in fact an extraordinarily naive version of a very naive traditional theory of mimesis – is a novel that would resemble the stone in its pure contingency, a novel so unselfconscious, so freed from artifice and convention, as to give us an unmediated image of the raw chaos of things, the world in its pure, meaningless 'being-there'. It is, of course, fantasy. What such a novel might conceivably look like and, more pertinently, to what extent *La nausée* can be intelligibly analysed in terms of this programme, are very open questions indeed.

It is nevertheless around a fantasy of this sort that a good deal of *La nausée* is organised. In the first place, what underlies it is precisely what in principle is entailed by Roquentin's experience of nausea. The symptoms and consequences of Roquentin's moments of nausea – with the beach pebble, the beer glass, the tree root, etc. – have been much discussed, and I don't propose to rehearse them in any detail here. Nor do I propose to discuss either their philosophical context (the existentialist theory of contingency) or the view that they represent less a philosophical outlook than a psychiatric condition; the recuperative implication of the latter view is that all Roquentin's troubles could be adequately dealt with were he to see a good doctor – the riposte to which is given by *La nausée* itself, in the figure of Dr Rogé, voice of Experience and Wisdom, whose wisdom consists in 'always explaining the new by the old'. But, in the most general terms, Roquentin's nausea is the symptomatic expression of the falling away of all familiar frames of reference. It entails the abolition of difference, the break-down of classification, the erasure of distinctions, in a process whereby identities fuse and merge to form a soft, gelatinous mess within which no structure of differentiation and intelligibility can any longer hold. In Roquentin's words, nausea spells the disappearance of 'the world of human measures', the rubbing-out of the 'feeble landmarks which men have traced on the surface [of things]'. Nausea is akin to an experience of 'melting': 'The veneer had melted, leaving soft, monstrous masses, in disorder – naked, with a frightening, obscene nakedness.' Or, in Roquentin's aural metaphor, the world is not so much a store-house of information, a source of messages we can confidently decode, as the place of an 'inconsequential buzzing'.

Within this generalised dissolution of all human systems of ordering and representation, there is however one that comes in for particularly heavy treatment: the system of narrative. 'Stories' ('histoires') are at once a prop and a mask; they support us, make our world habitable, by blinding us to the pure superfluity of existence, the unmotivated or (in Sartre's slightly more moralistic way) 'unjustifiable' nature of our being-in-the-world. From this point of view the key passage in *La nausée* is the following; it is a long one, but worth quoting at length:

> This is what I have been thinking: for the most common-place event to become an adventure, you must – and this is all that is necessary – start *recounting* it. This is what fools people: a man is always a teller of tales, he lives surrounded by his stories and the stories of others, he sees everything that happens to him through them; and he tries to live his life as if he were recounting it. But you have to choose: to live or to recount. For example, when I was in Hamburg, with that Erna girl whom I didn't trust and who was afraid of me, I led a peculiar sort of life. But I was inside it, I didn't think about it. And then one evening, in a little café at St Pauli, she left me to go to the lavatory. I was left on my own, there was a gramophone playing *Blue Skies*. I started telling myself what had happened since I had landed. I said to myself: 'On the third evening, as I was coming into a dance-hall called the Blue Grotto, I noticed a tall woman who was half-seas-over. And that woman is the one I am waiting for at this moment, listening to *Blue Skies,* and who is going to come back and sit down on my right and put her arms around my neck.' Then I had a violent feeling that I was having an adventure. But Erna came back, she sat down beside me, she put her arms around my neck, and I hated her without knowing why. I understand now: it was because I had to begin living again that the impression of having an

adventure had just vanished. When you are living, nothing
happens. The settings change, people come in and go out,
that's all. There are never any beginnings. Days are tacked
on to days without rhyme or reason, it is an endless monotonous addition. . . . There isn't any end either: you never
leave a woman, a friend, a town in one go. . . . That's living.
But when you tell about life, everything changes; only it's a
change nobody notices: the proof of that is that people talk
about true stories; events take place one way and we recount
them the opposite way. . . . I wanted the moments of my life
to follow one another in orderly fashion, like those of a life
remembered. You might as well try to catch time by the tail.
[pp. 61–3]

The central emphasis of this way of looking at narrative lies in
the opposition of two terms: Event (*évènement*) and Adventure
(*aventure*). Much has been made of this distinction, partly because
of its relation to Sartre's philosophical writings, partly because of
its bearing on recurring problems of twentieth-century narrative
theory. In fact, the point at issue is, on the surface at least, a
relatively simple one. 'Events' are what occur in real life; 'adventures' are what occur in books (although they can also occur in
real life to the extent that we model our lives on books). Events
constitute free-floating, undetermined, discontinuous series of
'happenings'. Adventures, on the other hand, are happenings
converted into significant order, causal sequence, meaningful
pattern; in brief, adventure equals event plus intelligibility.

The intelligibility in question is basically of a temporal sort.
Time, in the aspect of event, is time in its 'everyday slackness',
where 'days are tacked on to days without rhyme or reason', as 'an
endless monotonous addition'. The time of adventure, on the
other hand, is time 'caught by the tail'. It not only, according to
the classic Aristotelian formula, has a beginning, a middle and an
end, portents and resolutions, anticipations and closures. Above
all, it is time organised in function of a significant end. Narrative
versions of experience occupy a teleological structure wherein
what comes before is determined by what comes after – in the
world of story 'the end is always there, transforming everything'.
In story, everything is, so to speak, back to front: life as narrative
is one that 'unrolls backwards: the minutes don't pile up

hahazardly one after another any more, they're snapped by the story's end which draws them toward it and makes each of them draw to it in its turn the moment that precedes it'.

In this conflation of remarks we can read the terms of Roquentin's (and Sartre's) critique of the presuppositions and procedures of narrative. Narrative (or adventure) imposes factitious order on the contingent disorder of experience; it makes artificial sense of what is inherently without sense; it attributes design and purpose to what is formless and superfluous. Stories, in brief, are an epistemological confidence trick. In itself, this set of propositions is hardly news – we will find a virtually identical set of ideas in, say, Gide's notion of narrative as 'forgery' or 'counterfeiting', not to mention a whole number of other sources (moreover by no means confined to what is often polemically, and wrongly, assigned to the preserve of 'modernism'). What gives Sartre's version of this particular theme its particular edge, or sense of urgency, is that it is not limited to query of a purely epistemological order. Or rather, the epistemological doubts over the credentials of narrative are closely linked to considerations of a social and ideological character. Stories, narrative orderings, are not just sources of epistemological error, they are also sources of dishonesty (or what Sartre calls 'bad faith'). The fictions consecrated by Fiction serve discredited utilitarian ends. For we do not simply recount or listen to 'stories': we perceive ourselves and others, we arrange our lives, construct our worlds according to its comfortable and comforting dispositions: 'a man is always a teller of tales, he lives surrounded by his stories and the stories of others, he sees everything that happens to him through them; and he tries to live his life as if he were recounting it'. What is emphasised in this remark – it is a stress that will be repeated over and over again in the ideological arguments about the novel that surround the later emergence of the *nouveau roman* – is what has come to be known as the 'sociality' of writing. The phrase is to be understood not just in the older sense of the social conditioning of literature, but in the more active sense of literature itself being an intervention in the social construction of reality; as directly complicit in forming the compacts and arrangements whereby we collectively fashion an arbitrary order as if it were the natural order of things. (The paradigm of this ideological and cultural conspiracy, as it were, in *La nausée* itself is the picture gallery devoted to the portrait of the notables of Bouville.)

The life of Roquentin represents a concerted and anguished attempt to cast off the blandishments of story in order to face reality in its non-narrative 'nakedness', that 'obscene nakedness' which appears before one's eyes when the 'veneer' of all human fictions has 'melted'. The difficulty with this otherwise courageous project (if we accept the assumptions that lie behind it) is that Roquentin's 'life' is for us precisely a life *recounted*, directly in the form of the diary he keeps, indirectly as a 'novel' written by Sartre. And the question, of course, is: how do we situate *this* story in relation to the devaluation of story proposed by Roquentin himself? What exactly is the status of this devaluation? Does the charge of bad faith refer only to a certain *class* of narratives (from which Sartre's narrative is exempt on the grounds that it gives us something radically different from the traditional fare); or does it refer to all forms of story-telling, as a disposition inherent to narrative as such, or indeed, more broadly, to any kind of articulated account of the world? Is *La nausée* a book that remains faithful to the implications of 'nausea'? Or are the terms of the argument such as to make that sort of claim a contradiction in terms? And, if the latter, to what extent does *La nausée* show an awareness of this paradox? One way of putting all these questions in a kind of shorthand would be to say: is *La nausée* 'stone' or 'story'?; or, more precisely, does this set of alternative scenarios represent a set of realistic choices?

If we follow the implication of the stone metaphor (i.e., the idea of a novel free of bad faith, which surrenders itself to the world's contingency) we will of course come up with something (though with *how* much is not very certain). For example, we might point to the device of what might be called the story-that-crumbles: for instance, in the passage I cited earlier, the story of the woman in Hamburg, Erna, reconstructed as Adventure and then deconstructed back into Event, the latter version cancelling out the presuppositions of the former. Again, we might point to certain ways of handling time made possible by manipulating the conventions of the diary form. There is the sense of narrative indeterminacy in the undated 'first' entry and the future tense on which Roquentin's manuscript closes ('Tomorrow it will rain over Bouville'). There are the frequent movements between tenses, in a manner that suggests a certain merging of narrated and narrating time, as in the Paris restaurant episode: 'When I felt tired I came into this café and fell asleep. The waiter has just woken me up, and I am writing this while I am half-asleep. Tomorrow I shall go back to Bouville.' This strategy of shifting temporal perspective is evidently designed to evoke a life as it is being lived; instead of that commanding narrative preterite of classic fiction whereby, in Roland Barthes' phrase, life is converted into 'destiny' ('aventure'), here we see an attempt to match the rhythms of writing to the texture of existential reality itself – in which past, present and future, memory, experience and project are not allowed to settle down into some pre-arranged design.

Finally, we could perhaps cite certain critical experiences with and in language: the famous incident, of course, with the tree root in the public garden, where that primary instrument of differentiation and classification, the principle of *naming*, breaks down; in Roquentin's words, 'things have broken away from their names . . . I am in the midst of Things that cannot be given names'. The implication is that, stripped of the human and humanising labels which language confers, things appear before Roquentin in their original ontological condition of pure contingency. A similar implication could be drawn from the various hallucinated sequences of *La nausée* (e.g., the episode where Roquentin roams the streets in a semi-demented state after having read the newspaper item about the raped and strangled girl); in the interpenetration of fact and fantasy, what comes under pressure is syntax itself: the sentences both proliferate and disintegrate at the same time, in a wild interchange of subjects and predicates, no longer capable of holding together that system of identity and difference from which alone the consolations of intelligible reality can be had.

These, then, would be so many marks of a narrative trying to escape from the bad faith of traditional story, in search of a new kind of narrative authenticity. But it is precisely here that we encounter all the critical paradoxes of which I have already spoken. The items I have referred to may be deemed figures in the effort to dramatise the senselessness of existence, but they are not themselves senseless. They make sense, if only of that senselessness, in the same way that to talk of the unnameability of objects is still to name them (if only as the 'Unnameable' – the paradox around which Beckett's *L'Innommable* endlessly circulates). That is, the linguistic and literary apparatus of *La nausée* is not like the pebble on the beach picked up by Roquentin or by Valéry's Socrates; its elements are not random and contingent, but the product of human choices made within a uniquely human medium. They are *devices* (in the strong sense given to the term by the Russian Formalists) designed to create certain impressions and effects. One intended impression is of course what it is like to experience the world as pure contingency; but they are not themselves contingent. On the contrary, they are items in a rhetorical and narrative repertoire, as indeed is everything else in *La nausée*. Perhaps one could make the nature of the paradox a little clearer, in an illustrative way, by returning to that aspect of the text with which I began: the use of metaphor.

For a text whose presuppositions would seem to demand the systematic elimination of metaphor, it is perhaps surprising that *La nausée* is absolutely saturated in it. What, for example, are we to make of bits of newspaper described as 'sedate as swans', or Adolphe's braces possessing a 'sheep-like stubbornness'? Is this simply Sartre, as Robbe-Grillet would have it, being unreflectingly guilty of the very anthropomorphism that his own argument would require him to refuse? One rather sophisticated account of Sartre's metaphors (Fredric Jameson's) advances the view that Sartrian metaphor is really 'false metaphor'.[2] By this is meant a process of exaggeration whereby the traditional claims and implications of metaphorical representation are undermined; through the use of hyperbole, wilfully exaggerated or excessive metaphorical development, Sartre *decomposes* metaphor; through its very excess, it announces itself as metaphor, a literary construct whose very literariness is the mark of its distance from reality. The classic example is the elaborate figurative structure built around the episode of the tree root:

> . . . that long dead snake at my feet, that wooden snake. Snake, claw or root, it doesn't matter . . . that big rugged paw . . . that hard, compact sea-lion skin . . . a small black pool at my feet . . . a greedy claw, tearing the earth, snatching its food from it. [pp. 185–91]

Metaphor, in this context, is 'false' in so far as our expectations of its expressive power are constantly defeated; the figures are dramatic yet impotent; a series of figures in which one displaces the others, yet where all, individually or collectively, circle around what they can never express. It is the dance of figurative language around an absence – the existential reality of the root (its 'superfluity') on which metaphorical discourse (or indeed any linguistic form at all) can never gain purchase. This is an interesting argument, and does help to make sense of some of Sartre's more baroque inventions. It does however have an unwarranted implication. On this view, metaphorical excess in *La nausée* not only leads us to posit a reality 'beyond' metaphor (beyond the humanising appropriations of language), it also creates the possibility of passing through that excess into direct contact with reality itself; metaphor, undone, gives the occasion for transforming absence into presence. Thus, in the example of the root, 'beyond' its diverse figurative representations, so baroque as to blow up in our faces, we 'somehow' (Jameson's word) sense the reality of the root as a pure physical substance. This however will not do (as the implied unease of the impressionistic 'somehow' itself indicates). Neither in Sartrian metaphor, nor in any other, is there a 'beyond' to which the text gives us access; the idea of a non-textual reality to which a text takes us is a contradiction in terms. If, as Jameson suggests, metaphor is posited in *La nausée* as a substitute for what *cannot otherwise be named*, then, from the point of view of the reader of Sartre's text, there is simply nothing more to be said or done on the matter. The metaphor is the ground of our activity as readers; we are held within the metaphorical play of the text because there is nowhere else for us to go, except perhaps towards silence. To take the central, most extended example of the text, as readers we can know what is entailed by the experience of 'nausea' only by being told what it is *like* – i.e., through a set of metaphorical representations of which the key term is, precisely, 'nausea' itself. 'I have no need to speak in flowery language,' remarks Roquentin, 'I am writing to understand certain circumstances. I must beware of literature.' But a paragraph later we find him writing, 'the next day I felt as disgusted as if I had awoken in a bed full of vomit'. This statement is hardly 'flowery', but it is certainly literary, as is the whole of the texture of *La nausée*.

For the reality of *La nausée* is that of literature and not of 'existence'. Individual stories may crumble, but a general story is told (the life of Roquentin) in ways that do not massively offend our standard expectations of intelligibility. Time, in our ordinary experience of it, is certainly questioned, but equally certainly does not disappear. (Indeed, there are various instances in *La nausée* of precisely that kind of narrative anticipation, such as the hints that finally culminate in the revelation of the Autodidact's homosexuality, which, according to the terms of the existential critique, should not be there.) Metaphor may be made to behave in peculiar, self-deconstructing ways, but it still behaves as metaphor. Syntax, both in the strict grammatical sense and the looser sense of the syntax of narrative, may at certain junctures be threatened, but it never completely falls apart. The main point in stating all this, however, is not to say that *La nausée* is a safe traditional novel after all (a silly claim), but that, given the rigidities we often find these days in the quarrel of the Ancient and the Moderns, the general categories in question, though they may be equivocated, strained and stretched in a variety of ways, cannot simply collapse. Without those properties, narrative would be what Roquentin describes the world as being: an 'inconsequential buzzing'. That might be good existentialist epistemology, but it is doubtful whether writing based on such a formula would retain our attention for very long. A text that was an 'inconsequential buzzing' might be many things (it might, for instance, be in some way like a stone), but it would not be a *text*. It should of course be clear where all this is leading us. If novels are written in bad faith, then, to some degree, they are necessarily so. As Kermode argues,[3] the truth of the world may be contingency, but it is not the truth or reality of narrative; for narrative to exist, it must possess, as constitutive conditions of its existence, properties which a contingency theory denies to the world.

One answer to such a dilemma would be to abolish narrative, or, more radically – since the extreme point of the argument touches language itself – to command silence. This indeed is one of the alternatives of the choice starkly presented by Roquentin: 'il faut vivre ou raconter' ('you have to choose: to live or to recount'). Sartre, however, has chosen to recount, and so too will Roquentin, his exit from the novel being an entry into the literary vocation. Quite what we are to make of Roquentin's decision to write is, I think, highly uncertain. There could be an intended irony here: Roquentin's turning to literature as a means of personal salvation is a cop-out, modelled on the apotheosis of the Proustian narrator, just as Anny's (derided) philosophy is modelled on the Proustian epiphany of the 'moment parfait'. It could, on the other hand, be taken straight, implying Sartre's belief in a form of literary consciousness and a literary practice situated beyond bad faith. One suspects that it is the latter implication that is the case; Sartre seems as committed to his hero's vocabulary of 'salvation' as Roquentin himself. The difficulty lies in squaring this decision with the logic that informs Roquentin's demand that we must choose between the irreconcilables of 'living' and 'telling'. Indeed, the exact terms in which Roquentin evokes his literary project chime oddly with what he has earlier been at pains to stress: 'Another kind of book. . . . The sort of story, for example, that could never happen, an adventure. . . . A book. A novel . . .'. 'Story'? 'Adventure'? 'Novel'? – these, of course, are the very terms, reserved in the earlier assault on human fable-making for his utmost contempt, now reappearing as the main emphases of an affirmed and affirmative literary programme, one that will 'make people ashamed of their exist-ence'. But in what ways will this be 'another kind of book', dif-ferent from the books he has previously denounced? A further difficulty here is that we are given very little detail as to what this programme will in practice involve. The chief clue is through the analogy with the haunting jazz song 'Some of These Days'. Yet, despite some metaphysical mutterings about transforming 'exis-tence' into 'being', the analogy is not particularly informative. What, then, makes it so special? In particular, why is the jazz melody attributed 'redeeming' and 'cleansing' powers, whereas the 'consolation' Roquentin's aunt derived from Chopin's *Preludes* after her husband's death merely fills him with disgust? What makes jazz authentic and Chopin fraudulent? Within the terms of the argument of *La nausée* does the distinction really stand up, or is there an element of special pleading at work here – Chopin rejected because he is part of the cultural baggage, the drawing-room mythology of the bourgeoisie; 'Some of These Days' celebrated because it belongs to the more marginal and informal ambience of the outsider-culture?

In fact, the hypostasising of the jazz melody simply displaces, rather than resolves, the problem that confronts both Roquentin and the reader of *La nausée*: what does it mean to *write*? Does

Roquentin's project represent a way of overcoming the problematic disjunction between 'recounting' and 'living' without being caught in the morass of *mauvaise foi*? If so, what grounds does *La nausée* itself offer for us to be able to believe in this as a convincing possibility? On the other hand, is Roquentin's book the object of Sartre's irony? If so, what then are the implications of the ironic stance for the fact that Sartre himself has written a book? The problem, it will be seen, is entirely circular, its logical structure akin to the conundrum of the Cretan Liar paradox. It is not, however, a question of shredding *La nausée* in the logic-chopping machine or of turning the circle into a noose with which to hang Sartre; that is ultimately a sterile game to play, and moreover can be played with very many modern writers indeed. The question bears less on the fact that *La nausée* is inescapably inscribed within paradox than on how much *awareness* it shows of its own paradoxicality. Does it generate a level of self-reflexive monitoring large enough to make the critique of fictions it contains a full-fledged auto-critique? Is it a fiction that, in questioning the value of fictions, remains alert to its own fictive character? Or does it tacitly seek to proclaim itself as 'another kind of book', one which closes the gap between fiction and existence, language and thing, 'story' and 'stone'? The latter, we have seen, is an impossible dream (it is also a very ancient one). It would be bizarre if Sartre, while seduced by the dream, were not also aware of its impossibility; indeed, the first section of *La nausée* itself virtually permits of no other conclusion. Yet it is not certain. *La nausée* hesitates over its relation to the paradoxes it inhabits. It is a novel that cannot quite make up its mind as to what it is, what it would like to be, what it could be. It is emphatic (even moralistically so) in its rejections (seeking to sweep away a whole tradition of narrative as the debris of a bankrupt bourgeois culture). But it is unclear in its prescriptions, explicit or tacit. For many the hesitation is fatally disabling, the sign of a fundamental incoherence. It is however perhaps equally arguable that its confusions are in some ways an exemplary illustration of the dilemmas of 'modernism'; that, through those very confusions, it meets head-on, if somewhat awkwardly, the difficulties which the more sophisticated cleverness of other novelists tends perhaps to elide in the complacent security of a transcendent, all-knowing Irony.

NOTES

1 Page references for passages in French are to Jean-Paul Sartre, *La Nausée*, Paris, Gallimard, 1938. Page references for passages in translation are to *Nausea*, trans. Robert Baldick, Harmondsworth, Penguin Books, 1965.
2 Fredric Jameson, *Sartre: The Origins of a Style*, New Haven, Conn., Yale University Press, 1961.
3 Frank Kermode, *The Sense of an Ending*, New York, Oxford and London, Oxford University Press, 1966.

5 Ralph Waldo Emerson: An introduction[1]

Anita Kermode

In 1832 Emerson abandoned his career as a Unitarian minister – a career in which he followed his father and grandfather before him – to pursue a more difficult and precarious calling. This was the first of many abandonments – abandonment became, indeed, a way of life for Emerson – but in none of them was he unfaithful to the spirit of his new vocation. He became a prophet. To be so titled would make him uneasy; 'prophet' was among the numerous words that troubled him because of their power to bestow a spurious identity. He did not like to be identified. And although he is so often called a Transcendentalist, the very chief of Transcendentalists, this too is a label he actively mistrusted. Nevertheless, he began to lecture and to write transcendentally and prophetically, as spokesman and interpreter not of God's will (in the old sense), but of the veiled and silent will of America.

In the eyes of his forebears, the early Puritan settlers, America *was* the realisation of God's will, and his most rooted convictions echo theirs. 'One thing is plain for all men of common sense and common conscience, that here, here in America, is the home of man' (NAL, p. 241).[2] But he is speaking less of the United States than of a spiritual state – one that we might possess, however, in the actual American landscape, if we could but open our eyes and see. The voice of the spiritual America might plainly be heard, if we could but stop our ears to the buzz of competing voices, to the intrusive noise made not by 'man', but by men caught up in getting and spending, in the pursuit of ends and results.

From his provincial study in Concord, Emerson appointed himself seer and guardian of that landscape, articulator of that

73

hidden voice. It was an audacious move (and accompanied always by much private anxiety). It also initiated Emerson's long and unresolvable struggle to define the characteristics that would distinguish an authentically *American* literature from writing that was merely a function of the literature industry in America. There was always enough 'literature', even in America. What Emerson looked for was something so different that it might not even be recognisable as 'literature'. He looked for an *American* literature that would demonstrate what he called 'an original relation to the universe'. Perhaps he is beginning to sound chauvinistic, but, like the Puritans before him, he was not in any narrow sense of the word a nationalist. The elusive difference I speak of – between an American literature and a literature that merely accumulates in a place known as America – involved for Emerson a more essential difference, one with which you will already be acquainted in the English Romantics, especially in Coleridge. This is a distinction between the *primary* language of what they (and he) called the Reason (or Soul) and the *secondary* language of what they (and he) called the Understanding. 'Reason in her most exalted mood' – Wordsworth's phrase: this would perhaps be the mood characteristic of a truly American literature.

Yet the difference I mention cannot be thought of, finally, as obtaining between one kind of literary object or enterprise and another kind, as dividing the sheep from the goats. Emerson knew it as a difference which was inherent in the mind itself and which generated that 'double consciousness' to which he imagined us as ordinarily condemned: on the one hand, the life in us of the Reason or Soul, privileged by a direct and immediate access to spiritual reality; on the other hand, the life of the Understanding, depending for its knowledge of reality on casual and oblique contacts with the world of experience, on the sensory data it can gather and classify. These two lives, he complained,

> never meet and measure each other; one prevails now, all buzz and din; and the other prevails then, all infinitude and paradise; and with the progress of life, the two discover no greater disposition to reconcile themselves.   [ML, p. 100]

As a prophet, Emerson proclaimed the way out of this impasse, into a visionary America where consciousness would at last be reconciled with itself. But as a peculiarly modern and self-conscious prophet, Emerson studied the impasse – he studied in himself the play of a double consciousness. He enquired of his thoughts, of his utterances, of his very metaphors: from whence did they come, at any given moment? Did they spring from the deep impersonal Soul intuitively in touch with the primary activities of Nature, of the Universe? Or were they borrowed – the literary cast-offs and exuviae of departed genius? Or were they inherited from the common stock of myths and metaphors at work in the culture at large? 'Life consists', said Emerson provocatively, 'in what a man is thinking of all day.' And how could you determine the sources, primary or secondary, of your mental life?

Emerson recorded the drama of a consciousness striving to realise itself, literally to *create* itself, out of its own momentary and divided impulses; and seeking then to free itself from the limitations of its own creations, its own representations. At the same time he was able to project this drama as the representation of a central American consciousness. 'My giant goes with me wherever I go.' Emerson's first person singular acquired nearly mythic dimensions in its effort to shed its own mythologies and to give voice to the hitherto mute and undescribed elements of its experience, to make 'the dumb abyss be vocal with speech'. He looked to discover modes of thought and of speech that had not yet been fixed into *thoughts*, into *sayings*, or that had just abandoned them, escaping out into free space. To say 'I think this', or 'I think that'; to identify oneself: 'I am so and so', 'I am such and such a one' – all this for Emerson was no more than an aspect of quotation. He imagined being able to say, simply, 'I think', 'I am'.

This Emersonian vocal drama proved to have great carrying power. Just at the time when America was entering its most active period of industrial and territorial expansion, Emerson proposed counter-images of an extravagant interior, or spiritual, expansion. America was reluctant to support its native arts, its native thinking; Emerson invested the figure of 'Man Thinking', of the American Scholar, with enormous glamour, indeed with heroic attributes. The encouragement he gave was indispensable; without it, what is now called the American Renaissance would doubtless never have happened. His subsequent influence too has been very great, and – this is just as important – very embarrassing.

I say 'embarrassing' because, if we remembered nothing else of Emerson, we'd remember the moments when he calls on us to forget. He begins his prophetic career, in 1836, in the book *Nature*, with this bold appeal to forgetfulness:

> Our age is retrospective. It builds the sepulchres of the fathers. It writes biographies, histories, and criticism. The foregoing generations beheld God and nature face to face; we, through their eyes. Why should not we also enjoy an original relation to the universe? Why should not we have a poetry and philosophy of insight and not of tradition, and a religion by revelation to us, and not the history of theirs?
>
> [ML, p. 3]

Repeatedly he declares that we can never sufficiently disinherit ourselves, rid ourselves of tradition, of history, of *propriety*: that is to say, of our property; but more than that, of our very claims to ownership, to proprietorship; and more even than that, of our most intimate sense of 'ownness', of owning ourselves, our own proper names, our own proper identities. 'Propriety' carries all these senses, as well as the sense of mere conformity and correct behaviour, when Emerson says:

> The one thing which we seek with insatiable desire is to forget ourselves, to be surprised out of our propriety, to lose our sempiternal memory and to do something without knowing how or why. . . . The way of life is wonderful; it is by abandonment. [ML, p. 290]

We can never sufficiently abandon ourselves, our sense of propriety. Man 'postpones or remembers'; like Hamlet, he looks before and after; he broods on the fathers. But

> when we have new perception, we shall gladly disburden the memory of its hoarded treasure as old rubbish. . . . When good is near you, when you have life in yourself, it is not by any known or accustomed way; you shall not see the face of man; you shall not hear any name; the way, the thought, the good, shall be wholly strange and new. It shall exclude example and experience. [ML, p. 158]

This is quite a radical exclusion. It is already going far to exclude 'example' from the sense of having 'life in yourself', and to reject any previous models for 'new perception'. But it is going very far to reject 'experience' as well. You might declare yourself a radical individualist; you might, sublimely, claim to break with the example of the fathers, to refuse your inheritance, to accept no authority over you. But in that case you would probably seek to justify such claims by appealing to the authority and integrity, the propriety, of your own experience. You might appeal, as Wordsworth does in *The Prelude*, to the history of your own mental development, to the principle of your essential self-sameness (that is to say, once again, your propriety). But Emerson speaks of breaking not only with the fathers, the precedents, but with oneself, one's own experience and sense of self-sameness. You must abandon yourself to the discontinuities of your own ego. Only then can you stop repeating, quoting, 'I think this', 'I think that', 'I am so and so', and discover how to say 'I think', 'I am'.

During one of these passages of radical exhortation, Emerson seizes upon an image, a metaphor of original being:

> These roses under my window make no reference to former roses or to better ones; they are for what they are; they exist with God to-day. There is no time to them. There is simply the rose; it is perfect in every moment of its existence.
>
> [ML, p. 157]

This may remind you of Gertrude Stein's famous words (and if we remembered *her* for nothing else, we'd remember her for this): 'A rose is a rose is a rose.' You would be right to hear in that sentence an echo of Emerson's roses. Gertrude Stein is a very Emersonian writer. But if you do hear a reference to those former roses of Emerson, those roses which themselves make no reference to former roses or to better ones, then you can also hear how Gertrude Stein tries to exclude the reference even as she makes it. If you were simply to say, 'A rose is a rose', that would be like Emerson saying, 'they are for what they are'. And you might mean by it any number of profound things. But what if you improve on that by saying, 'A rose is a rose is a rose'? You have permitted no room for reference or allusion, for what we might call the *literary* dimension of language. Gertrude Stein doesn't have to add, by way of explanation, 'there is no time to it, there is simply a rose'. The provocatively meaningless form of her statement makes explanation superfluous. She has, so to speak, gone

Emerson one better. One better rose. It's as if she had managed to forget, even at the moment of remembering them, Emerson's roses. As if, triumphantly, she were saying: *his* statement refers, even while denying them, to former and better roses; but mine does not. Mine is the better rose, the better expression of how to exclude example and experience, of how to make words, like roses, exist in a perfect present.

This is sneaky, but it doesn't exactly solve anything. If Gertrude Stein's famous words mean anything to us, they do so by virtue of belonging to a recognisable tradition, a tradition that defines what real, authentic American writing sounds like. And Emerson did more than anyone to shape this tradition in its modern form, to announce its typical themes, its typical metaphors or tropes, and also its typical problems. We have in the passage I've quoted one of these themes: there should be no time, no history to American words; they should exclude example and experience. And we have one of these metaphors: the roses of European poetic tradition being Americanised, made local and abrupt and even bare, stripped of their literary trappings and associations. They just happen to be there, they are like 'found objects'. In other words, we have metaphorical roses turned into a type of anti-metaphor.

And we have, implicitly, a problem. Even though the roses actually growing under Emerson's window do not refer to former roses or to better ones (nor do they refer even to themselves; they have no sense of propriety), Emerson's words about them do indeed refer, not only to roses both former and better, but also to themselves. Roses may well *be*; but words refer, they mean, they allude. Archibald MacLeish, a recent and sub-Emersonian poet, is remembered for his line: 'A poem should not mean, but be.' However, there are no short-cuts to being of the sort that Mac-Leish and, more cleverly, Gertrude Stein propose. Emerson himself knew this well. The habit words have of referring, of remembering, of postponing, is not in itself a problem; yet it becomes one if like Emerson you imagine that writing might, at certain moments, coincide with pure, original Being – that it might become, to use one of his most privileged metaphors, 'transparent'.

And as an extension of this difficulty concerning reference, we encounter the problem of influence. It is a problem, as we've seen with Gertrude Stein, of acknowledging influence and denying it at the same time. In so far as they *are* meaningful, her words tell us less about what it is like to be in touch with pure Being than they do about what it is like to be in touch with the roses of previous literature, including, specifically, Emersonian roses. It is a complex fate to be influenced by Emerson, who spoke out so strongly against influence and told us so memorably to forget. We must, he said, 'consider literature ephemeral and easily entertain the supposition of its entire disappearance'. 'In our ordinary states of mind' we are in danger of idealising literature; 'we deem not only letters in general but most famous books parts of a pre-established harmony, fatal, unalterable'. But it is precisely such memorable words, such imagined harmonies, that become, in the end, fictions which impose on our freedom and usurp the Soul's right to an original relation with the universe.

> Our exaggeration of all fine characters arises from the fact that we identify each in turn with the soul. But there are no such men as we fable; no Jesus, nor Pericles, nor Caesar, nor Angelo, nor Washington, such as we have made.
>
> [ML, p. 436]

And no Ralph Waldo Emerson either, we may presume.

And therefore Emerson remains an embarrassment to American writers. They are shy about alluding to him. Statesmen often do, and businessmen, astronauts, tennis champions. Tracy Austin has a quotation from 'Self-Reliance' on her bedroom wall. The writers are evasive. Ezra Pound's watch-word, 'Make it New', is pure Emerson; but although Pound discussed, alluded to and quoted all manner of predecessors, he did not mention Emerson. Wallace Stevens, the most Emersonian of poets, alluded frequently to Mallarmé, to Valéry, and so on; but he did not mention Emerson. Walt Whitman simply lied; he claimed never to have read Emerson until *after* publishing the first versions of *Leaves of Grass*. (Later on, though, he fessed up: 'I was simmering, simmering, simmering; Emerson brought me to the boil.').

So, if you are reading American literature for the first time, it might be wise to take Emerson's advice. Forget, for the moment at least, the biographies, the histories and the criticism. But not, for the moment at least, Emerson! Read him instead – not all in one lump, but intermittently, as you go along; let him circulate among the other writers. Yet there is no obvious place to begin, with Emerson, and no obvious direction to take. He himself had a deep aversion to directions, to linked sequences of thoughts or things. 'If you desire to arrest attention, to surprise, do not give me facts in the order of cause & effect, but drop one or two links in the chain.' Some advice to himself in his journal. Minutely linked sequences, facts arranged in the order of cause and effect – such are the mimetic tricks that conjure in books the illusion of 'a pre-established harmony, fatal, unalterable'. Such are the rhetorical arrangements that support our sense of personal identity and foster our belief in fine and fabulous 'characters'. Such are the chains of literature, that oppress and hamper the movements of the soul. Emerson, writing, drops links in the chain as he goes, and he likes to read as he writes, discontinuously, for the sake of freedom. The poets, he says,

> are liberating gods. . . . They are free, and they make free. An imaginative book renders us much more service at first, by stimulating us through its tropes, than afterward when we arrive at the precise sense of the author. I think nothing is of any value in books excepting the transcendental and extraordinary. [ML, p. 335]

Arrivals make Emerson uneasy; he writes as if every sentence might be a new departure. So if you try too hard to follow him and to fix his sense in mind, you lose touch with him. 'There are no fixtures in nature', he says, and there should be none in books. The poet 'unfixes the land and the sea'. Emerson's volatile way of 'making free' rather exasperated Henry James Senior: 'O you man without a handle!' Henry Junior called him 'a clue without a labyrinth'.

Let us, arbitrarily, pick up this clue in 1838, as Emerson addresses the students of Dartmouth College. He imagines these young men as beset by two chief anxieties, which his address aims at helping them to overcome. The first is not exclusively American in nature; it is the modern burden of feeling that one has come too late into the world. The world seems old, even finished; the language seems old, second-hand, worn-down; the human seems to have degenerated into the mere dwarfish shadow of some previous gigantic and powerful self. Men feel alienated from their own potentialities, and from the natural world as well, because they have forgotten that the natural world was never any more, or less, than the strong projection, outward, of their own mental structures and capacities. Since they fail to recognise the world as projection, as production, they do not understand how it might become introjection – how it might be taken inside, again, to nourish their dwindling energies.

But on top of this, Emerson imagines the young men as bearing a specifically American burden of anxiety and guilt. This springs from their awareness of

> the historical failure on which Europe and America have so freely commented. This country has not fulfilled what seemed the reasonable expectation of mankind. Men looked, when all feudal straps and bandages were snapped asunder, that nature, too long the mother of dwarfs, should reimburse itself by a brood of Titans, who should laugh and leap in the continent, and run up the mountains of the West with the errand of genius and of love. [NAL, p. 100]

But what have Americans actually got to show for themselves? Nothing but a culture still derivative and, in all essential respects, empty.

It's in this context that Emerson takes, figuratively speaking, to the woods (a trope that will become very familiar in American literature). Here, in the woods, we can experience the momentous possibility of a new *description* of the world. 'By Latin and English poetry,' he begins, 'we were born and bred in an oratorio of praises of nature, – flowers, birds, mountains, sun, and moon'; yet of all these fine things the chanting poets have known nothing that is real or essential; 'the merest surface and show' is all their song can offer. But, Emerson continues,

> go into the forest, you shall find all new and undescribed. The honking of the wild geese flying by night; the thin note of the companionable titmouse, in the winter day; the fall of swarms of flies, in autumn, from combats high in the air, pattering down on the leaves like rain; the angry hiss of the wood-birds; the pine throwing out its pollen for the benefit of the next century; the terpentine exuding from the tree . . .
> [NAL, p. 106]

This, he implies, is not the oratorio of 'poetry', woven of empty words – 'flowers, birds, mountains, sun, and moon' – but living

81

music of the forest, a savage composition already, for whoever has ears to hear. 'Indeed,' he goes on,

> any vegetation; any animation; any and all, are alike un-attempted. The man who stands on the seashore, or who rambles in the woods, seems to be the first man that ever stood on the shore, or entered a grove, his sensations and his world are so novel and strange. Whilst I read the poets, I think that nothing new can be said about morning and evening. But when I see the daybreak, I am not reminded of these Homeric, or Shakespearean, or Miltonic, or Chaucerian pictures. No; but I feel perhaps the pain of an alien world; a world not yet subdued by the thought; or, I am cheered by the moist, warm, glittering, budding, melodious hour, that takes down the narrow walls of my soul, and extends its life and pulsation to the very horizon. *That* is morning, to cease for a bright hour to be a prisoner of this sickly body, and to become as large as nature. [NAL, p. 106]

Overcharged with old descriptions of the world, with 'pictures', we have lost the capacity to *see*. But go into the forest, simply open your eyes and ears, and you'll discover that you've arrived not late, but early. It's daybreak, it's morning. Here, Emerson imagines an original relation to the universe in terms of the figure, or trope, of the 'first man' of all, a man literally without examples and without experience. He's got nothing but his own feet, to project himself physically into the world, and his own eyes and ears, to project himself mentally. The first man has an innocent eye. As Wallace Stevens put it, 'You must become an ignorant man again/And see the sun again with an ignorant eye.' But we know that the innocent eye sees nothing. Emerson knew this too; he says in the great essay 'Experience':

> We have learned that we do not see directly, but mediately, and that we have no means of correcting these colored and distorting lenses which we are, or of computing the amount of their errors. [ML, p. 359]

Nevertheless, figuratively speaking, experience might be 'corrected', the distortions of sight yielding to the recognitions of insight. The first man is a figure of speech. Through the stimulation of such figures, the mind might recover earliness, in 'a world not yet subdued by the thought'. Sensations of this kind are brief; they last only for 'a bright hour'. But they help the soul to recover its powers and to know itself 'as large as nature'. And '*that* is morning', that momentary expansion of consciousness. 'Morning', here, is not the sunrise mimed in poetry; nor is it even the actual daybreak observed by some solitary wanderer in the forest. It is the freeing of the 'I', here and now, from the constrictions of identity, of self-ness. Liberation gets expressed, in this passage, by the way Emerson moves from 'daybreak', as a natural event, to 'morning', as the metaphorical equivalent of an invisible, a non-empirical, a psychic event. It is not going out into the forest that counts. What counts is the rhetorical or descriptive activity of converting this naturalist's excursion into a figure, a metaphor, a trope. And tropes or metaphors, Emerson says, are what support and realise

> the centrifugal tendency of a man . . . his passage out into free space, and they help him to escape the custody of that body in which he is pent up, and of that jailyard of individual relations in which he is enclosed.   [ML, p. 333]

You will encounter in American literature many versions of this morning scenario, in which the self undergoes an exhilarating and also painful transformation. But let us go on to the next paragraph in the Dartmouth address. Emerson has just described a landscape momentarily freed from what Wallace Stevens calls the 'doctrine' of landscape, freed from Homeric and Miltonic and Shakespearean 'pictures'. He has described a corrective act of *re*-description. And at this point he moves away from a scene that appeals primarily to what we might call the outward eye, and begins to describe a landscape that has been interiorised, that is being reflected as it were in some inner eye. It is now that the forest becomes an *American* forest:

> The noonday darkness of the American forest, the deep, echoing, aboriginal woods, where the living columns of the oak and fir tower up from the ruins of the trees of the last millennium; where, from year to year, the eagle and the crow see no intruder; the pines, bearded with savage moss, yet touched with grace by the violets at their feet; the broad, cold lowland, which forms its coat of vapor with the stillness of subterranean crystallization. . . .   [NAL, pp. 106–7]

Notice how the forest is being invested with a sublimity that it
lacked in the previous paragraph, and how vastly extended it has
become, both in space and in time. It is as if Emerson were
suggesting that an act of radical re-description might in itself be
enough to redeem that sense of historical failure he spoke of
earlier. The American land is still ready to mother a brood of
Titans – but these Titans are perhaps to be America's poets,
rather than her men of action: that's the implication. Notice how
the forest is changing into a reflective, a symbolic landscape. The
lively discord, the innocent details of the last paragraph – geese
and flies and turpentine, honking and pattering and exuding:
things simply occurring as they occur – are here displaced by
things juxtaposed in significant pairs, suggesting their emblematic value. 'The noonday darkness'; this is the trope of contradiction which the rhetoricians call an 'oxymoron'. And the land is
now charged entirely with oxymoronical, with *rhetorical* forces.
'Living columns of the oak and fir' are set against 'the ruins of the
trees of the last millennium'. The eagle, traditional emblem of
nobility and sovereign solitude, is matched with the antithetical
crow, emblem of all that is vulgar, commonplace, gregarious. The
woods are 'deep' and they are 'echoing': they resound with patterns, with forms, with harmonies 'never recorded by art' and yet
already organised, already landscaped, as it were.

The aboriginal land is already a landscape. 'America is a poem in
our eyes', said Emerson. And here, in the Dartmouth address, he
communicates a sense of the mind discovering a correspondence
between its own newly awakened powers and powers which are
inherent in the American land itself. Throughout his writing, the
word he uses for this elated feeling of discovery, of correspondence, is 'transparent'. When the mind wakes up and recognises
itself in the world *out there*, that world becomes 'transparent'.

> The ruin or the blank that we see when we look at nature, is
> in our own eye. The axis of vision is not coincident with
> the axis of things, and so they appear not transparent but
> opaque. The reason why the world lacks unity, and lies
> broken and in heaps, is because man is disunited with him-
> self.   [ML, p. 41]

To be reunited with oneself is to recognise the world as one's own
double – as 'this shadow of the soul, or *other me*.' At such moments

it no longer seems a jumble of meaningless 'things'; it reappears as a figurative world, as a rhetorical and linguistic world, as an allegorical extension of the soul. But before this can happen, the old metaphors and descriptions must be cleared away, like 'hoarded treasure' now perceived as 'old rubbish'; one must expose oneself to the alien things of the world – geese, flies, all – as if one were the first man, unprotected. It is only after exposure that transparency is possible, when the world exists (as Emerson puts it in *Nature*) 'in the apocalypse of the mind'.

The word 'apocalypse', as I'm sure you know, comes from the Greek for 'unveiling' or 'revelation'. And the awakenings that Emerson describes are indeed apocalyptic; they derive their rhetorical force from their deep and multiple roots in the powerful Jewish–Christian tradition of Apocalypse. This new yet aboriginal American land, which demands new perception, evokes the novelty of the natural creation as it might have appeared at the mythical beginning of time. But even more, it evokes the novelty of the supernatural world that will appear at the end of all time – at the end not of 'the last millennium' but of the approaching Millennium; the world that was unveiled to St John in the *Book of Revelation*:

> And I saw a new heaven and a new earth: for the first heaven and the first earth were passed away; and there was no more sea. . . . And he that sat upon the throne said, Behold, I make all things new. And he said unto me, Write . . .
>
> [Rev. 21:5]

These are the prophetic words that come back to Emerson whenever he meditates the possibilities of an authentically American writing. Goethe is impressive, to be sure, but in him

> the Muse never assays those thunder-tones which cause to vibrate the sun & the moon, which dissipate by terrible melody all this iron network of circumstance, & abolish the old heavens & old earth before the freewill or Godhead of man. [J, VII, p. 366]

We live in an age of hobgoblins:

> Public Opinion is a hobgoblin, Christianity is a hobgoblin, the God of popular worship a hobgoblin. When shall we

>   attain to be real & be born into the new heaven & earth of
>   nature & truth?   [J, VII, p. 240]

Emerson's forest, his novel and alien American landscape, echo, deeply, with biblical metaphors of revelation, metaphors derived from what he called the most and indeed the only original book ever written. But in the passage we've been considering there are echoes of writing much less 'original', in Emerson's radical sense of the word. 'The noonday darkness' of the forest may well remind us, for instance, of Milton in *Samson Agonistes*: 'O dark, dark, dark, amid the blaze of noon.' But Emerson has explicitly claimed that the new world he sees before him reminds him of *no* Miltonic pictures. It does not refer to former or to better pictures.

This returns us to the difficulty I mentioned earlier, the difficulty posed for American writing by memory and by influence. The only writer, said Emerson, 'who can be entirely independent of this fountain of literature and equal to it, must be a prophet in his own proper person'. What a tricky word this turns out to be: 'proper'. 'A prophet in his own proper person' – what can this mean? A prophet is someone who, precisely, does *not* speak in his own proper person; he speaks rather in and for the voice of God, or what Emerson calls 'the Godhead of man'. The voice of prophecy can be recognised by its *lack* of propriety; it exemplifies just that abandonment of one's own proper person which Emerson so yearningly imagines: 'The one thing which we seek with insatiable desire is to forget ourselves, to be surprised out of our propriety, to lose our sempiternal memory and to do something without knowing how or why. . . .' To be a prophet in one's own proper person sounds like an odd, perhaps oxymoronical, state of affairs. So too is it contradictory to write in a way that sounds, even if remotely, like Milton, just at the moment when you assert your ability to forget Milton and to be entirely independent of this fountain of *other* literature.

But the power to displace the fountain of literature by a fountain of revelation – that is to say, by a radically 'new' description of reality – this power can only be felt to proceed from a strongly individual voice, one which does speak in its own proper person (even if this is an invented person). And such a voice must sound strong enough, individual enough, to persuade us that it is inde-

pendent of the 'fountain of literature' just when it is most pro-
foundly alluding to, referring itself to, that fountain (a 'fountain'
which has, nevertheless, no original source; for 'literature' never
begins, it just carries on). Emerson bequeathed this problem –
perhaps I should say, this opportunity – to all American writers,
and most obviously to Whitman, who speaks in his own invented
proper person (I, 'Walt Whitman, an American, one of the
roughs, a kosmos') exactly when he is claiming to speak, prophetically, for the Godhead in man.

The special poignancy of Emerson's desire to forget himself
and to begin anew springs from his curious faith that metaphor
might *literally* take the place of truth. His metaphors of apocalyptic endings and beginnings might be, themselves, the vehicles
of a renovatory force. These figures of a radical newness are
presented not merely as the harbingers and patrons of change,
but as the actual place of change, the place in which poetry,
eloquence, might for once embody what Emerson calls 'practical
power'. 'The true romance which the world exists to realize will
be the transformation of genius', of imagination, 'into practical
power'. A romance, a figurative construction, but really, but
literally, a true romance.

And this particular form of literal-mindedness also has its roots
in a tradition. Behind it lies a long and complex history of asser-
tions that America was in fact to be the scene of apocalyptic
transformation. Emerson's Puritan ancestors had believed that
God intended the American wilderness to provide the historical
setting for the literal fulfilment of the scriptural promises. Their
errand, as God's new Chosen People, was to build the city on a hill,
to plant the New Jerusalem in the western deserts, to prepare for
the great, the final Millennium. America *was* the Promised Land,
where the world awaited the realisation of a new heaven and a
new earth.

Emerson revised the rhetoric of these earlier prophets – he
spoke of a new description, a new perception, rather than of a
New Jerusalem – but it retained in him its old urgency and
conviction of privilege, as the voice of a place in which, if the ideal
had any meaning at all, it had meaning as an aspect, already, of
reality. And that kind of rhetoric, even in its most degraded
forms, still exercises something like practical power in America. I
was listening on the radio, just before the recent election, to a

Ronald Reagan propaganda recording. Ronald Reagan, hero of many a True Romance, said, 'God put this country here between two shining seas for a purpose.' He said that God made this country to be populated by a new kind of human being, called 'an American', who would give the world a new start. He ended by saying, 'America *can* be a shining city on a hill.'

Well, Emerson dreamed of a new kind of voice in literature – or rather, beyond literature; at the very end of 'literature' – but he doubted his own strength to invent it. He very often records his sense of failure, of betrayal by his own sense of propriety – for Mr Emerson of Concord was indeed an extremely proper person. He wrote in his journal, after one of his lectures:

> Alas! alas! I have not the recollection of one strong moment. A cold mechanical preparation for a delivery as decorous – fine things, pretty things, wise things, – but no arrows, no axes, no nectar, no growling, no transpiercing, no loving, no enchantment.   [J, VII, p. 339]

He committed his faith to the future. 'Our American literature and spiritual history are, we confess, in the optative mood.' And he admits to looking 'in vain for the poet I describe. . . . Time and nature yield us many gifts, but not yet the timely man, the new religion, the reconciler whom all things await.'

But his own strongest moments, his arrows and axes, come when he *is* writing in the optative mood, and postponing to an unrealised future the timely man, the timely poet. It is this mood that most vividly expresses his need for freedom, which surpasses always his desire for fulfilment. For Emerson cannot even imagine, wish-fulfillingly, the arrival of the central man, the liberator, the reconciler, without sensing immediately that this act of imagination has put his own liberty under threat. The figure of the timely poet, who is a prophet in his own proper person, establishes at once, by its very compellingness, a form of mental tyranny. For Emerson nothing is more important, more valuable, more desirable, than freedom of mind. It is important, valuable, desirable in proportion to the difficulty of achieving it and to the impossibility of sustaining it.

> On the brink of the waters of life and truth, we are miserably dying. The inaccessibleness of every thought but that we are

in, is wonderful. What if you come near to it; you are as
remote when you are nearest as when you are farthest.
Every thought is also a prison; every heaven is also a prison.
Therefore we love the poet, the inventor, who in any form,
whether in an ode or in an action or in looks and behavior,
has yielded us a new thought. He unlocks our chains and
admits us to a new scene.   [ML, p. 336]

A new scene. But for how long? *Every* thought is also a prison;
every heaven is also a prison. Emerson is stimulating partly
because of his nervously accelerated sense of time. He's always
leaving the scene before you've even got your hat and boots off.
He admires Swedenborg for the sheer rapidity of metamorphosis
in his writing, the speed at which his images displace each other.
'The figs become grapes whilst he eats them. . . .' Yet very soon
Emerson rejects Swedenborg, complaining that he is too systematic, that he tries to fix the play of his language into permanent
structures of thought. But there are no fixtures in nature. Emerson abandons Swedenborg for the same reason that he abandons
all the potentially central men who have briefly enchanted him:

> . . . he nails a symbol to one sense, which was a true sense for
> a moment, but soon becomes old and false. For all symbols
> are fluxional; all language is vehicular and transitive, and is
> good, as ferries and horses are, for conveyance, not as farms
> and houses are, for homestead.   [ML, p. 336]

No one has affirmed more hopefully and vibrantly than Emerson the possibility of new invention, new description. But no one
has been more acutely aware of the distorting seductiveness of the
new thing, the new voice, the new symbol. We turn it into a fetish
or fixation, which quickly acts to block and confine, instead of to
release, the mind's creative energies. We become narcissistically
attached to our strongest creations – we appropriate them, claim
them as our own property – and then, mistaking them for nature,
for reality, use them not for conveyance but for homestead. '*Build
therefore your own world*': that is the exalted message of his book
Nature. But Emerson feels the risk of inertia in that metaphor.
Later he turns it upside down: 'Every spirit makes its house, but
afterwards the house confines the spirit.' *Don't fence me in*, is
Emerson's perpetual song. But he knows how much more is at

stake than simply pulling up stakes and moving further out West. He is more than a cowboy of the imagination. 'We cannot let our angels go', he observes. 'We do not see that they only go out that archangels may come in.' But then he measures the dangerous power of archangels. Finally, devastatingly, he says, 'Nothing but God can root out God.'

So, although he is very strong as a prophet of the constructive, the creative imagination, he is even stronger as a voice speaking for de-construction, for de-creation, for dissolution. The greatest value of metaphor is that it can make things *dis*appear. It can make us feel 'that the solid seeming block of matter has been pervaded and dissolved by a thought'. I'd like to leave you now with an image of Emerson in his most characteristic mode of disappearance: Emerson departing, splitting. And I really do mean splitting, since to depart like this calls for a radical act of dissociation, a splitting of the ego that, when it is developed within the framework of narrative fiction, by Poe or Melville or Hawthorne, can look distinctly pathological. Try to imagine how strange, how uncanny or even quite mad such a perception of things might seem were it to be embodied in the hero of a novel, a novel set in Boston, or New York, or even on board a whaling ship.

> The things we now esteem fixed shall, one by one, detach themselves like ripe fruit from our experience, and fall. The wind shall blow them none knows whither. The landscape, the figures, Boston, London, are facts as fugitive as any institution past, or any whiff of mist or smoke, and so is society, and so is the world. The soul looketh steadily forwards, creating a world before her, leaving worlds behind her. She has no dates, nor rites, nor persons, nor specialities, nor men. The soul knows only the soul.   [ML, p. 265]

That, if you think about it, is a frightening vision. It is astonishing that Emerson remains so unfrightened by it.

NOTES

1 This was the first in a series of lectures on Emerson, Poe, Melville and Hawthorne.

2 All page references are to the following texts, cited with initials:
NAL: R.W. Emerson, *Nature, Addresses, and Lectures*, ed. R.E.
   Spiller and A.R. Ferguson, Cambridge, Mass., Harvard
   University Press, 1979.
ML: *The Selected Writings of Ralph Waldo Emerson*, ed. Brooks
   Atkinson, New York, The Modern Library, 1940.
J: *The Journals and Miscellaneous Notebooks of Ralph Waldo
   Emerson*, 16 vols, ed. W.H. Gilman, Cambridge, Mass.,
   Harvard University Press, 1960–.

6 Hawthorne's illegible Letter

Norman Bryson

There are few bodies of writing more intractable to the reader
who seeks the continuous production of meaning than the work
of Nathaniel Hawthorne, and the fate of that work in critical
hands is admirably suited to demonstrate the comedy of inter-
mixed confusion and adulation which writing elevated to 'classic'
status can expect to encounter. To call a particular work a 'classic'
may seem harmless enough, but it's a label with a number
of less-than-innocent implications. For once a work has been
declared to be a 'classic', strategies of obscurantism denied the
work of low survival-power can at once be mobilised. At its most
unarguable level, the designation 'classic' means simply that a
piece of writing has enjoyed interest over several generations;
and while the differing generations are given licence to stress
changing and even incompatible aspects of the text as it passes
through time, 'classic' status serves as a conservative force always
able to gather together multiple and divergent readings into a
higher unity. For the classic work is agreed to inhabit a realm of
inviolable endurance where even the most contradictory interpretation cannot diminish the work's standing. Indeed, for a
work to provoke vigorous reaction over a long span testifies to
some aloof grandeur whereby the generations may come and go,
but the work remains fundamentally unaltered. Two, or several,
or many descriptions of the work, however mutually exclusive,
none the less are felt to 'bring out' different facets of an ever
stronger unity. A critic who is deliberately attacking a prevailing
view of a classic work is never in opposition to the coherence of
the work itself, only to previous and one-sided readings: the

92

commentary produced will, in the course of time, be placed alongside those it attacked, and the vigour of both readings will serve as proof of literature's superiority to what is written about it. The warring critics will only have released different energies latent in the unified work: multiplicity of interpretation is seen as evidence of immutable grandeur. Moreover, it's often the case that individual critics will attempt, as part of their logistics, to present a self-sufficient reading, one that coheres and produces a seamless fabric of meaning independently of the interpretations already in existence. The task is to yield an interpretation which treats as difficulties to be surmounted, where they are not ignored, moments in the text where continuity appears deficient. And, later, the student encountering manifest discrepancies and discontinuities between critical readings is faced with the often more arduous task of attempting to hold together in the mind critical views which have actually been designed to be untenable together. Reading, now expanded to include criticism, must involve itself in ever more complicated epicycles and adjustments in order to accommodate into a cohesive overview text, critical opinion, and whatever fresh insights that may have been provoked by the work itself. The effort here is one of delicate negotiation which aims always at retrieving unity out of plurality. Classic status demands it: in the power structure of reading, it is the diplomatic incompetence of the reader which is first to be blamed if the desired holism of meaning is not forthcoming, and after that the pugnacity and dogmatism of critics, but only as a last recourse will the classic work itself be queried, to ascertain whether or not the effect of continuous structuration of meaning was intended or not.

With Hawthorne especially the classic designation has, I think, proved disastrous, in that it is often precisely the effect of breaking, tearing, destroying continuous meaning which is the writing's aim. Here I would like to distinguish between three kinds of non-continuous writing: texts which withhold meaning, texts which prevent meaning, texts which destroy meaning. Into the first, 'withholding', category would come all those fictions which tantalise the reader with a promise of disclosure always deferred. For example, Faulkner never reveals to us the 'true' events which took place in and around Sutpen's Hundred; Pynchon snatches away from us the secret of the contents of Lot

49; and Hawthorne's preacher in *The Minister's Black Veil* takes with him to the grave the meaning of the double fold of black crepe. Into the second, 'preventive' category would come Benjamin Constant's *Adolphe*, in which the text itself, Adolphe's confession, lies in a state of becalmed impassivity between the outbursts of interpretation which flank it, the various prefaces and appendices which take up, in relation to the confession, their divergent, impassioned, theatrical attitudes of apology and attack. All Constant's effort in writing the confession, one might say, has been to perfect its dispassion, its deadpan, offering a surface so smooth and resistant that the explanatory missiles aimed at it from both sides will fall back defeated into the outside. And into this category would no doubt also come the purged, ascetic, anti-explanatory writing of Robbe-Grillet; the enterprise of cleansing and erasing human meanings from the world. With both these categories, meaning is a dimension of the text which is absent, posited as occurring in some place where the writing is not, the always elsewhere, in a utopian and veridical history of Sutpen's Hundred, in the pages which would have to tell us about the contents of Lot 49 if the text had not chosen to end with the descent of the auctioneer's hammer, in the secret world the minister inhabits behind the impenetrable veil. Interpretation is what lies either side of, but never within, Adolphe's confession, just as it is the state of affairs prior to Robbe-Grillet's work of effacement or erasure.

The Scarlet Letter differs from these categories in that for the reader the experience of being inside a meaning, inside a guided interpretation, happens all the time. It is not the realm of the off-stage, the prior, or the occulted: the reader is in the thick of it. And by placing the reader in a position where he or she is called upon at all times to be interpreting, explaining, ordering, and from which there is no escape, Hawthorne is able to achieve what these other categories necessarily cannot – to make vivid to the reader the experience of having meanings torn, slashed, destroyed.

Ultimately I want to show this happening at the level of the individual sentence. But an early stage in this disturbing process begins when we ask the unavoidable question: is *The Scarlet Letter* attacking or is it reinforcing the Puritan ethos it describes? Critical argument on this point has produced notoriously conflicting results. If we turn first to the anti-Puritan side, there is of course much evidence suggesting that the novel is a celebration of Hester Prynne's independence, of individual courage against collective cruelty, of the promptings of the heart against social repression. The chapter 'The Market Place' shows us the Puritan community as a body of sadistic tormentors, torturing to the point of loss of consciousness a woman Hawthorne intervenes to describe, in a markedly non-Puritan image, as 'the image of Divine Maternity . . . the world was only the darker for this woman's beauty, and the more lost for the infant she had borne' (p. 83).[1] Publicly and privately interrogated, Hester heroically refuses to reveal the identity of her lover. Despite the pain of being ostracised, she has the endurance to believe that 'the torture of her daily shame would at length . . . work out another purity than that which she had lost; more saint-like, because the result of martyrdom' (p. 105). Over the years, continual acts of charity transform the emblem of her shame into a sign of respect: 'They said that it meant Able; so strong was Hester Prynne, with a woman's strength' (p. 180). And in the forest love-scene, Hawthorne states that nothing less than 'the sympathy of Nature' supports the lovers' 'mystery of joy' (p. 220). As Hester casts away her stigma and removes the cap confining her luxuriant hair, 'All at once, as with a smile of heaven, forth burst the sunshine, pouring a very flood into the obscure forest, gladdening each green leaf, transmitting the yellow fallen ones to gold, and gleaming adown the gray trunks of the solemn trees' (p. 220).

That Dimmesdale is unable to withstand the influx of repressed impulses as they emerge into consciousness is, for Hester, a further contingent misfortune. Hester, made strong and self-reliant by her suffering, can cope with the reawakening of her dormant sexuality: that Dimmesdale cannot, that he should move first into crazed submission before the newly released drives, and then into self-consuming sublimation, is only further proof of the dangers of Puritan restraint. Hester can withstand even the final betrayal of her plans by her lover; and in the years after Dimmesdale's death she continues to grow in stature until the scarlet letter 'became a type of something to be sorrowed over, and looked upon with awe, yet with reverence too' (p. 274). In her last years, she becomes the legendary comforter and counsellor of distressed womenfolk, the prophet of a time when 'the whole relation

95

between man and woman [would be established] on a surer ground' (p. 275).

Such might be the roughest sketch of the anti-Puritan, pro-Hester case. Yet interpenetrating it, almost piercing it, is what one might call, taking the phrase from musicology, its 'mirror inversion'. For in her solitary cottage by the sea 'thoughts visited Hester', Hawthorne tells us, 'such as dared to enter no other dwelling in New England; shadowy guests, that would have been as perilous as demons to their entertainer, could they have been seen so much as knocking at her door' (p. 183): thoughts of murdering Pearl among them. When at last asked by Pearl what the scarlet letter signifies, the supposed paragon of Emersonian self-reliance utters a plain lie – 'I wear it for the sake of its gold thread!' (p. 198); in the process also going back on her promise to Governor Bellingham that the letter would be used as a means of explaining to her daughter the nature of sin. Hester is involved in both social hypocrisy and private deceit, and when Hawthorne darkly states that 'The scarlet letter had not done its office' (p. 184), we are given authorial confirmation of a view of Hester strangely at odds with the idea of authentic and courageous rebellion. The Nature that sanctions the lovers' reunion, despite its brief and resplendent flash, is also 'that wild, heathen Nature of the forest, never subjugated by human law, nor illuminated by higher truth' (p. 220). And the sense of the lovers' irresponsibility cannot be overlooked when, at the end of the sunlit chapter, we catch sight of Pearl among the creatures of the forest – first the harmless partridges, pigeons and squirrels, but immediately followed by the sinister fox and wolf. Hawthorne is careful to disclaim responsibility for the image of a child abandoned by its parents to be reared by wolves – 'here the tale has surely lapsed into the improbable' (p. 222) – but once presented to us, the image remains, and with it, accusation that, in abandoning themselves to the flesh, Dimmesdale and Hester are perpetuating the state of social non-being and non-identity which is their legacy to Pearl. Dimmesdale is too deeply enmeshed in guilt to declare himself to be Pearl's father until the end, but throughout the forest scene we are made aware that not the least of the sins of which Hester and Dimmesdale might be accused is gross negligence of Pearl's emotional needs. The couple may rationalise Pearl's horror at Hester's removal of the scarlet letter by their whispered 'Children will not abide any, the slightest, change in the accustomed aspect of things that are daily before their eyes' (pp. 226–7), but it is clear that until Dimmesdale tells Pearl, in person, that he is her father, she will continue to be driven to such desperate conclusions as her claim that she was not 'made' but plucked off a rosebush, or that a scarlet letter will spontaneously appear on her gown when she grows to womanhood. The moment Dimmesdale makes his public confession, 'A spell was broken' (p. 268); Pearl is able to cry fully human tears, and before long she is married to her European nobleman. But Hester in the forest is either woefully ignorant or wilfully dismissive of her daughter's need for social recognition and integration. Whichever way we interpret Hester's attitude, Pearl's disturbed state is sufficient cause for us to doubt whether her mother's self-abandon in the forest is the mature assertion of individual right which the first, anti-Puritan view claimed.

The point to emphasise is that Hawthorne, in presenting us with contradictory views of Hester, is not writing 'ambiguously' in any easily recuperable sense. We cannot take the body of our selections which constitute the pro-Puritan text, and that other body of anti-Puritan citations, and superimpose them one upon the other to produce a stereoscopic richness or depth; we cannot just lay the image of Hester as hero over the image of Hester as villain, to yield the plenitude of the 'rounded' character. Contradiction between the meanings that gather at the textual place 'Hester' is carried, systematically, to the extreme point where a kind of textual fission begins to take place.

The work of reading may seem at first to lie in fusing the two texts and the two Hesters into a 'complex' unity. And if Hester could be isolated from the novel, seen and analysed independently, perhaps this might be achieved. But the same duplicity or breaking of the characterology extends itself like a chain reaction throughout the novel's cast. Let us take the case of Chillingworth. There is so much evidence against him that he might seem the least problematic character in the text: guilty of pressuring Hester into marriage before she was experienced enough to recognise the folly of such a match, guilty of desertion, and above all guilty of the cardinal Hawthornian sin of violating the sanctity of a human heart – we might, as readers, feel relieved that at least one figure in the book is as black as he is painted. Yet Hawthorne

renders even this much uncertain by relegating the task of condemnation to the group which the reader, from the first scaffold
scene, is least happy to be associated with: the prejudiced, super-
stitious and crudifying Boston mob.

> A large number – and many of these were persons of such
> sober sense and practical observation, that their opinions
> would have been valuable, in other matters – affirmed that
> . . . the fire in his laboratory had been brought from the
> lower regions . . . that the Reverend Arthur Dimmesdale . . .
> was haunted either by Satan himself, or Satan's emissary.
> [p. 149]

In so far as the reader of the first scaffold scene is opposed to the
kind of gothic cruelties which characterise the Bostonian imagination, he or she cannot identify with this form of attack: we want
Chillingworth condemned, but not by such a jury and not in this
way. And even this is challenged when, in the scene by the shore,
Hester forces Chillingworth to recognise the fiend he has
become. 'It was one of those moments – which sometimes occur
only at the interval of years – when a man's moral aspect is
faithfully revealed to his mind's eye' (pp. 189–90). Just as the
image of an heroic Hester is pierced by its opposite, so Chillingworth, the Puritan as sadist and tormentor, becomes the Puritan
as masochist and victim – the sinister presence becomes the path-
etic. And once broken, the villainous image of Chillingworth can
never wholly be restored. There is, after all, no reason to doubt
the claim that without Chillingworth's ministrations Dimmesdale
would have long since died. Chillingworth's motive for holding
Dimmesdale back from his recantation is arguably a further impulse of charity: all Chillingworth has wanted is that Dimmesdale
relieve himself of the private burden of silence, not that he
destroy his reputation. And in the Conclusion, Hawthorne intervenes to tell us that 'In the spiritual world, the old physician and
the minister – mutual victims as they may have been – may,
unawares, have found their earthly stock of hatred and antipathy
transmuted into golden love' (p. 272).

There is, of course, one dramatic moment in which Hawthorne
might have established how it is we are to view Chillingworth:
the moment when Chillingworth discovers whatever is or is not

'there' on Dimmesdale's breast. But at precisely that moment the writing plunges into gothic darkness:

> With what a ghastly rapture, as it were, too mighty to be expressed only by the eye and features, and therefore bursting forth through the whole ugliness of his figure, and making itself even riotously manifest by the extravagant gestures with which he threw up his arms towards the ceiling, and stamped his foot upon the floor. [p. 159]

In its excess, the writing partakes of precisely that kind of melodramatisation or diabolisation of reality which has led to the persecution of Hester and Pearl; or rather, the style in which Chillingworth is described seems now to emanate from *himself*, not from the author. At exactly the moment when Hawthorne is called upon to finalise the image of Chillingworth – sadistic inquisitor finally reaching the truth, or hallucinating victim of Puritan over-exegesis – he exchanges authorial identity for that of his character. And one can see why this must be. The narrative strategy demands that the two images of Chillingworth be kept distinct. From another part of the text, from what Barthes called the 'hermeneutic code', comes a force which makes an equally insistent demand that one or other of the images be confirmed. Meeting at the description of Chillingworth's reaction, the forces start to tear the text apart: to ensure that the policy of apartheid finally wins, Hawthorne sacrifices or relinquishes his own identity.

It might be possible to analyse the same narrative duplicity in the case of Dimmesdale, were it not for a further twist of the narrative screw. On the plane of psychology, Hester, Chillingworth and Dimmesdale hardly lead separate lives at all: feeding off each other's mutually reinforcing weakness and guilt, at times merging telepathically with each other's thoughts, they seem less like three individual cases than a single, symbiotic organism. This unification on the psychological plane has an immediate consequence on the plane of narrative – if it is not the case that psychology of interdependence is the derivate of the narrative aims. For within this enclosed system, difficulties the reader encounters with one character have their immediate repercussions in the ways the other two are to be assessed. Thus, for as long as

we view Hester as the hero of an anti-Puritan text, certain consequences follow. The courage with which Hester withstands the
pressure to name her lover makes Dimmesdale's failure to confess seem by contrast the basest of crimes, in which cowardice,
hypocrisy and betrayal are united. For as long as we feel it possible
that the repression of Hester's sexuality is both unjustified and
incomplete, and are waiting for a moment of outright rebellion,
Dimmesdale's reticence must arouse our impatience, if not our
contempt. The meeting between the lovers in the forest then
comes as the book's natural climax, and Dimmesdale's cry, 'Do I
feel joy again. . . . Methought the germ of it was dead in me' (p.
219), is the revitalisation we have been waiting for. Dimmesdale's
reversion, beginning with the infantile pranks of 'The Minister in
a Maze' chapter and continuing through to the volte-face whereby his ungovernable libido is rechannelled into recantation, must
then be seen as a falling away from natural grace, a second
betrayal of Hester, and worse in that he no longer has the excuse
of cowardice.

But if Hester is a villain, the consequences are otherwise. When
we recall that her mind has been taught 'much amiss' (p. 217) by
its phantom counsellors, that her treatment of Pearl is menda-
cious and negligent, that her plan to escape is – given her lover's
condition and temperament – at the least unrealistic, then
Dimmesdale's 'reversion' at the end is a less culpable affair than it
is if our sympathies are with sexual liberation at all costs. For
within this perspective, the central drive of the narrative is less the
expectation or hope that Dimmesdale will reach a stage of genital
maturity, than that he may find in himself the strength to realise
that neither a life under Chillingworth's accusing eye, nor a life of
flight with Hester can satisfactorily resolve the contradictions of
his predicament. Only public confession will suffice, and the
narrative may then be seen to culminate not in the 'Flood of
Sunshine' chapter but in 'The Revelation of the A'. Hence the
book's thrice-repeated scaffold scenes: in the first, Dimmesdale
commits his crime of concealment; in the second he tries, through
flagellating by moonlight, at the scene of the crime, to atone for
his misconduct; in the third he has realised that the root of his
conflict is secrecy, and, heroically rejecting the easy escape Hester
has arranged, he undoes the crime of silence at the heart of the
book.

Hawthorne, in other words, denies us an absolute Dimmesdale, and forces us to recognise his use of a relative fictional method whereby what Dimmesdale is depends on what Hester and Chillingworth are; and if they are broken, fragmented, torn, then so is he. But more is at stake than the coherence of an individual character. For the difficulties the reader encounters now concern the whole shape of the narrative. Are we dealing with a story centred on the drama of erotic liberation, consistently dark, and reaching an interrupted climax in the forest scene? Or is the centre of the novel elsewhere, in Dimmesdale's cowardice, moving in three developing stages from initial crime (concealment), to provisional amendment (quasi-public revelation), to final resolution (full confession)? Answers to such questions are hard to find: the text refuses to select a fixed position, and neither author nor reader can have the satisfaction of giving the text any certain termination, or closure.

But neither is the text simply 'open'. Perhaps the most exemplary kind of openness is the end of Pynchon's *The Crying of Lot 49*: 'Either Oedipa in the orbiting ecstasy of a true paranoia, or a real Tristero.'[2] Either conspiracy or insanity: and either way there will be destruction – Oedipa will lose one of these possibilities. But the destruction will occur outside the text. It is not part of reading: hence its painlessness. Again, if one had access to a veridical history of Sutpen's Hundred, all the impassioned interpretations of the people whose lives have been touched by the events there might be construed as waste; but even so the individual acts of interpretation would retain their validity and their power, however divergent they might be from a 'true' account. (I will not labour the point that such an account would only be another 'version'.) In other words, there can be openness without pain.

The effacement of meanings occurs *before* the writing of the Robbe-Grillet text; it is the precondition of its form. The interpretative missiles launched from both sides of Adolphe's confession cannot penetrate its resistant surface. But the reading of *The Scarlet Letter* is a destruction from within. In a retrospective description such as this the narrative strategies can be seen as orderly and completed design. But at the local reading level, at all those numberless moments out of which that retroactive design is built, one experiences not the gradual emergence of pattern, but an ongoing process of tearing or rending the fabric of meaning.

> Such was the sympathy of Nature – that wild, heathen
> Nature of the forest, never subjugated by human law, nor
> illumined by higher truth – with the bliss of these two spirits.
> [p. 220]

With almost each word the unfolding sentence switches direction, reverses its loyalties; the effect is one of internal war. One image of a character fights with another, one narrative shape fights with another for the possession of the sentence, and the only moments of truce come from sentences whose allegiance is at the same time to all sides and to none: 'Be true! Be true! Be true!' (p. 211).

Nor is there any evident rationale for this destruction of the text by itself; and in this respect the work must be placed in a different category from, in particular, the *nouveau roman*, where an ample theoretical justification for withholding a stable position from the reader is an essential accompaniment to, almost a condition of, the practice of writing. Hawthorne's refusal to create stabilised characters, and his denial to the text of evident climax or thematic centre, are crucial sources of interest in the narrative, and yet they remain mysterious. We can, if we choose – though the argument is hard to sustain – attempt to 'close' the 'openness' by claiming that 'closure' is the pandemic disease of the Puritan society the book is out to attack. Thus, the instances of premature or prejudiced judgment whereby the Hawthorne villain immutably places or fixes a fellow human being can be seen as the central negative act which the whole rhetoric of the fiction seeks to undermine. Hester and Bellingham trying to decide whether Pearl is an angelic or diabolic agent; the community withholding from Hester and Pearl any identity except that typified by the scarlet letter; Chillingworth relentlessly probing the recesses of Dimmesdale's consciousness with the single and exclusive purpose of ascertaining guilt or innocence – all are involved in Manichean ethical judgments which, whether the verdict be positive or negative, remain confined within the most rigid and reductive of frameworks. And it may be that Hawthorne's motivation in the writing of *The Scarlet Letter* was based on the intuition that the reading act is suspiciously, dangerously, similar to this kind of thinking. Denial of fixed characterology, thematic centrality or clear climaxing *may* thus be an ethical choice on Hawthorne's part: perhaps even a strategy whereby Hawthorne could expiate his sense of complicity in the cruelty of his inherited culture, by rendering impossible precisely that kind of judgmental activity which was its most conspicuous and rebarbative characteristic.

While the desire for such self-distancing from a dark inheritance may to some degree account for Hawthorne's calculated uncertainties, the writing will go to such extremes to achieve a state of inner nescience – the radical refusal of the text to supply certain knowledge – that other, and less directly biographical, factors must be looked for. It is reasonably safe to assume that at certain points in the text Hawthorne makes a vigorous claim in favour of the 'ontological certainty' of the world, and against those habits of mind which estrange the subject from direct perception of the world's 'otherness'. No discomfort perplexes Hawthorne's historical placing of the mass hallucinations of the early Puritan community:

> Nothing was more common, in those days, than to interpret all meteoric appearances, and other natural phenomena, that occurred with less regularity than the rise and set of sun and moon, as so many revelations from a supernatural source. Thus, a blazing spear, a sword of flame, a bow, or a sheaf of arrows, seen in the midnight sky, prefigures Indian warfare. Pestilence was known to have been foreboded by a shower of crimson light. [p. 174]

No hesitation here menaces a stable distinction between real and imaginary worlds. Yet far more characteristic of the text is Hawthorne's emphatic refusal of description to an innocent or given real. One is partly blinded to the extent of the refusal by the repeated device of alternative interpretation:

> *but whether* it had merely survived out of the stern old wilderness, . . . *or whether*, as there is fair authority for believing, it had sprung up under the footsteps of the sainted Anne Hutchinson, as she entered the prison-door, – *we shall not take upon us to determine.* [p. 76; my italics]

The device is beguiling: event, followed by one, two or three glosses, then the grandiose assertion of the authorial prerogative not to choose from among competing versions. Repeated until it

103

takes on the familiar guise of a stylistic tic, the device assures us of Hawthorne's continuing presence even while it purports to register, among other things, his aloofness and distance from the tale. One hardly notices the deftness of the transition from this fastidious refusal to quibble over details, to the large-scale subversion of the narrative at the level of plot. For, on a small scale, Hawthorne so inoculates us against the expectation of veridical accounts of the real that it is only afterwards, as we cast our mind over the completed shape of the book from the final page, that we feel the shock of realising the extent of the information, crucial to the intelligibility of the story, that has been withheld from us.

Above all, the 'A' on Dimmesdale's breast. Since we have already experienced a blurring of this item several times before – the word 'adultery' is conspicuously absent from the text, and the initial has been merged with 'Able', 'Angel' (p. 177) – we are partly anaesthetised against the discomfort of never being in a position to know whether Dimmesdale's 'A' exists or not. But so much hinges on this question that the text's silence expresses far more than a desire to exploit 'the Marvellous'. If we were told that Dimmesdale, in an excess of self-punishment, had branded himself with the letter of his shame; if, conversely, we could be certain that Chillingworth's ecstatic revellings before the unbuttoned chest of Dimmesdale had caused a private hallucination; if Hawthorne would side with or against the opposing camps of 'eye-witnesses' who both did and did not see an 'A' on the dying minister's breast – then maybe we could establish what it in fact is to be an 'eye-witness' in Hawthorne's world. The use of fictional uncertainty cannot at this point be rationalised ethically, as might perhaps be argued in the case of Hawthorne's destabilisation of character. Rather, it extends that destabilisation beyond the question of the judgment of individual persons to the larger question of the legibility of the world.

For at its deepest level, *The Scarlet Letter* questions the viability of any narrative within a world where to see is not necessarily to know; where to have the impression of knowing bears an uneasy relation to the evidence of the senses. All of Boston 'knows' Hester for an adulterer, even though no one in that community has the least knowledge of any of the circumstances surrounding her adultery; the community similarly 'knows' Dimmesdale to be a saint, despite his every protestation from the pulpit to the contrary. Hawthorne will go so far as to present this 'knowledge' as false, but hesitates his text on the brink of any alternative truth. That perfect Puritan correspondence between inner state – adultery, and by extension, spiritual preterition – and outward sign – the 'A' – can be questioned only by subverting assumptions considered so normal within narrative that quite innocuous passages become tainted with the idea of a duality between inwardness and exteriority:

> A writhing horror twisted itself across his [Chillingworth's] features, like a snake gliding swiftly over them, and making one little pause, with all its wreathed intervolutions in open sight. His face darkened with some powerful emotion, which, nevertheless, he so instantaneously controlled by an effort of his will, that, save at a single moment, its expression might have passed for calmness. [p. 88]

Nothing in this description is firm: Chillingworth's state is not presented from the inside, and all we learn of it is that it is 'some' emotion of powerful impact. Yet we cannot go on to examine his outward appearance, since this, too, is unspecified – what does a face that writhes like a snake look like, and how could such a grimace also pass in a trice, for calmness?

The difficulty of understanding the inner state from the outward signs, and the further difficulties resulting from denial of inner/outer correspondence, are typical of what we find in the novel. Hester's strange demonic musings produce no outward trace on her saintly person; Dimmesdale suffers from an inner malaise which is never fully externalised; Chillingworth, demonstrating the obverse of this process, becomes externally the very type of caricature of revenge, yet his motivation may be pure. The darkest, the most disturbing, insight in the book, both for the reader and for the text, is that there may be *no* law of connection between outer and inner worlds. What manifests as intense psychological torture may be the guise of love. A flood of sunshine in a sylvan glade may betoken the depravity of the natural world. Believing that one is far from sanctity may mean that sainthood is burgeoning. The condition Hawthorne presents is one of a deep ignorance of the connections between physical and mental phenomena: we cannot see the world clearly, since we project so intensely on its face; yet even if we do see the world clearly, there is no guarantee that the external appearances before us are stable signs of fixed internal states.

Though this may be an acceptable world-view, one which might, for example, yield a rich poetic literature, it is hard to see how fiction can survive at all under such conditions. For the law of inner/outer correspondence is one of fiction's enabling conventions: the man rubbing his hands and counting piles of coin is a miser; the woman painted an inch thick is a whore; the man who wears yellow gloves and sports an opera hat is a dandy. It is from conventions such as these that fiction grows, qualifying caricature into character, expanding and refining stereotype into psychological and social 'truth'. Hawthorne retains the outwardness of typology, and even resorts to its crudification. (One problem in the scene of the interview between Hester and Chillingworth on the beach is that Chillingworth has become so exclusively the type of diabolic revenge that he lacks probability, so that the two actors in the scene seem to inhabit the differing and not easily compatible realms of character and caricature.) But simplification of behaviour and appearance is no guarantee that the caricature is, within, as it manifests without.

The peculiarly anti-realist – in the sense of the novel as a record of the real – nature of Hawthorne's art can be emphasised by contrasting his declared fictional intention with that of the European realist programme. 'La société française allait être l'historien, je ne devais être que le secrétaire.'[3] For Balzac, the act of writing is conceived as an act of transcription of a society whose intelligibility is not in doubt. The world is legible *already* – Balzac even speaks of 'Le monde écrit'.[4] As each character is introduced, a body of knowledge shared by both author and reader (but it is the author who knows more, whose superior knowledge of the given world the reader desires to possess) will, by reference to physical appearance, to dress, accent, gesture and the various agreed psychologies of money, love, ambition, age and so forth, successfully place, with a kind of immutable and self-confident certainty, the exact position in society that a given character occupies. Sollers has described this kind of classic realist fiction as 'la manière dont cette société se parle'[5] – the way society speaks itself, as though there were no problematic within the transference of knowledge from society to print, except possible limits to the percipience of the writer. Certainly there is room for ideological commentary – Balzac claimed to be guided by 'deux vérités éternelles: la Religion, la Monarchie'[6] – but it is always comment on that which already stands, appendix, to be taken up by the reader as a detachable point of view, a discardable deviation or digression from the overriding task of re-duplication. For George Eliot, the same obliteration of self-hood before an unassailably given reality dominates the process of fiction-making: the texts are presented as the attempt to 'give a faithful account of men and things as they have mirrored themselves in my mind.'[7]

But with Hawthorne, it is precisely the contract for the transmission of information to a reader who knows much, from a writer who knows more, which is under attack. First, in the opening of 'The Custom-House' section, Hawthorne claims that he is not responsible for the text which follows: it is a 'mysterious package' (p. 61), wrapped in the scarlet letter itself, with all that entails of fluidity of significance. The 'inmost Me', that organising and controlling consciousness which, in the Balzac or George Eliot text, acts to arrange into patterns of intelligibility the data of the world, is kept, Hawthorne rightly warns, behind a 'veil' (p. 36). The whole communication of the text, so far from following a model of transmission from A to B, resembles the utterance of the Sybil: the author 'casts his leaves upon the wind' (p. 35), sure only that once his production is circulated, its fate will be beyond his control. 'Some authors', from whose company Hawthorne excepts himself, imagine that the production of a novel resembles such 'confidential depths of revelation as could be fittingly addressed, only and exclusively, to the one heart and mind of perfect sympathy' (p. 35). Intent from the beginning to stress that his text will remain outside the constraints imposed by such intimacy, Hawthorne mocks this approach to fiction: such hopes of a perfect relay of data from author to reader make the mistake of supposing that between the two parties there is a stable contract, a prior relationship, a shared world.

Hawthorne seeks to stimulate or coax the reader into the expectation of such a relationship, but stage by stage its viability recedes. His work operates to render conscious to the reader, and then to subvert and dislocate, the expectation that in a novel, hitherto unknown or misunderstood facts about a real world will be conveyed from one terminus, replete with information, to another, hungry for information; and that the message will form a constant, unified structure of meaning. The fiction acts to dislodge the assumptions and assurances of the realist text: that characters are fixed enough in essence for us to pass ethical judgments; that external appearance is the unerring reflection of inward state; that the novel exists to re-duplicate the pre-established text of the world. If that world-text is illegible, then so must be the fiction to which it gives rise.

NOTES

1 All references are to *'The Scarlet Letter' and Selected Tales*, Harmondsworth, Penguin English Library, 1970.
2 Thomas Pynchon, *The Crying of Lot 49*, New York, Bantam Books, 1967, p. 137.
3 Honoré de Balzac, *La Comédie humaine*, Paris, Pléiade edition, 1951–5, vol. I, p. 7.
4 Ibid., vol. XI, p. 213.
5 Philippe Sollers, *Logiques*, Paris, Editions du Seuil, 1968, p. 228.
6 Balzac, *La Comédie humaine*, vol. I, p. 169.
7 George Eliot, *Adam Bede*, London and Edinburgh, Blackwood, 1876, p. 149.

7 Passion, narrative and identity in *Wuthering Heights* and *Jane Eyre*

Tony Tanner

We learn from Elizabeth Gaskell's incomparable biography of Charlotte Brontë that one day the father of the Brontës wanted his children to reveal their true feelings to him. So he put masks on their faces and, thus concealed, invited them to give absolutely truthful answers to his questions. To be honest, his questions were not such as to bring out the secret inner life of his children, but we may take the occasion as in one way being a prophetic paradigm of what the children, and most importantly Emily and Charlotte, would subsequently do. They put on narrative masks and revealed feelings and problems and inner contestations which could never surface in Haworth Priory. We are exceedingly familiar with the idea of 'masks' by now. But I want to start by suggesting that the different choices of narrative devices made by Emily and Charlotte are not only intimately related to what the books are about: these decisions, I think, already latently contain the ultimate meaning of the novels. In this sense the chosen form really is in large part the content. Let us consider the adopted narrative techniques in the two novels in question. Neither uses an omniscient third-person authorial voice. Emily chooses as a narrator a figure who is in all crucial respects her opposite – male, emotionally etiolated, and a product of the modern city. He in turn gets most of his evidence from Nelly Dean. That is to say that between us and the experience of Catherine and Heathcliff there is Lockwood's journal and Nelly Dean's voice – a text and a tongue, thus effecting a double translation, or refraction of the original story. Catherine and Heathcliff are as far as possible away from the narrative, and they recede into terminal

109

dissolution when nothing can be narrated because nothing can be differentiated. They become rumour and legend as they cease to be corporeal identities. Charlotte chose a precisely opposite technique. Jane Eyre – a potentially passionate woman with some experiences not unlike her creator's – tells her own story not only in but on her own terms. Her narrative act is not so much one of retrieval as of establishing and maintaining an identity. She survives. She is her book. Catherine and Heathcliff escape – from houses, from identity, from consciousness, and indeed from the book. This gives some indication of the different ways in which the two imaginations worked.

Wuthering Heights has often been regarded as pure romance, a timeless drama which has no particular reference to nineteenth-century England. Yet we notice that the book does not start 'Once upon a time . . .' but with a date – 1801. And, in addition, it is Lockwood we encounter first. Why? I think there are a number of reasons which make the book immeasurably richer than it would otherwise have been, but two comments by other authors might help us here. They are both addressing themselves to the problem of how to write about the supernatural or the demonic, the timeless, the utterly non-civilised. Thomas Mann (referring to his narrative method in *Dr Faustus*) succinctly says that for ironic purposes it was better 'to make the demonic strain pass through an undemonic medium'. Henry James, writing about ghost stories, asserts that '[supernatural] prodigies, when they come straight, come with an effect imperilled; they keep all their character, on the other hand, by looming through some other history . . .'. So the demonic intensity of Heathcliff is refracted through the very undemonic, emotionally timid, Lockwood. By showing us Lockwood and Heathcliff as inhabitants of the same universe, Emily Brontë, it seems to me, increases the impact of her story. Because part of the force of the book comes from the fact that a passionate yearning for timelessness and placelessness is forced to inhabit time and place, 1801. By making us see Lockwood and Heathcliff existing in the same space, Emily Brontë can show how space can become uneasy, problematical, holding incompatibles.

Let us look a little at the way the novel opens, for a good deal of the novel is contained, in embryo, in the first three chapters, in which Lockwood describes his first meeting with Heathcliff and his first entrance into Wuthering Heights. As Lockwood records his penetration into the house, considerable ironies are generated. For instance, he thinks of Heathcliff as a gentleman like himself, who prefers not to manifest his good feelings; or again, his domesticated eye can only see the wild dogs as tame pets (an error he will pay for when they set on him!). He even tells about a recent amorous incident in his own life which is comically the reverse of the story we are to hear. He reveals that he once found himself attracted to a girl, but when he managed to draw her glance, 'I shrank icily into myself, like a snail . . .' (p. 48).[1] This is a good example of the attenuation and deadening of feeling which can be a result of 'civilised' existence, where individuals live more and more separately and their passions diminish into egotistic self-withdrawal. On Lockwood's second visit to the house he sees Cathy (the daughter) and makes two embarrassingly wrong guesses as to her relationship with the other men. This only serves to show what an utterly alien world he has moved into: he can have no notion of what goes on in this house. He gets it all wrong. His urban/urbane discourse cannot comprehend the wild exiled depths he has stumbled into. He thinks in terms of a bland and tempered sociability, but in the house all is hatred, violence and anarchy. There is an additional point. He thinks in terms of conventional relationships. But Heathcliff is disruptive of genealogy and the whole web of familial relationships which make for social clarification and continuity.

Again Lockwood is set upon by the dogs and has to stay the night. This effectively takes him deeper into the secret of the house, for he is shown into a bedroom which, in turn, contains a small sort of closet (rooms within rooms) which makes a panelled bed. In this Lockwood seeks security. 'I slid back the panelled sides, got in with my light, pulled them together again, and felt secure against the vigilance of Heathcliff, and every one else' (p. 61). It is a revealing gesture. Lockwood, as a civilised man, likes to secure himself, to shut out possibilities of darkness and violence. In every sense he locks the wood. However, inside his refuge he notes various things. Some writing for a start – 'a name repeated in all kinds of characters, large and small' (p. 61), or rather three names, Catherine Earnshaw, Catherine Linton, Catherine Heathcliff. Here indeed is Catherine's problem – she cannot reconcile the three identities, and in which of them shall she find her self? The varying experimental inscriptions point to the insoluble dilemma of her life. Then Lockwood finds some diary entries by Catherine. They describe Catherine and Heathcliff's revolt against institutionalised religion and even civilisation itself. The fanatical Calvinist Joseph apparently forced two books on them – *The Helmet of Salvation* and *The Broad Way to Destruction*. In a gesture of revulsion they fling their books into the dog kennel (p. 63). It is a crucial repudiation of the Word. And to fling the books into the dog kennel suggests an inversion with larger implications. If they put the books in the dog kennel, where would they put the dogs? From an early age it would seem that Heathcliff and Catherine were associated with an inclination to reject the controls of orthodoxy and to 'unkennel' things more usually boxed up and confined.

Lockwood then goes to sleep and dreams and in his second dream he comes into contact with the drama of the book. Catherine, gripping his hand through a broken window, cries to be let into the house from the moors. Lockwood, in his dream, is hideously cruel: 'I pulled its wrist on to the broken pane, and rubbed it to and fro till the blood ran down and soaked the bed-clothes' (p. 67). When he gets his hand free he tries to bar the window and cries out: 'I'll never let you in, not if you beg for twenty years' (p. 67). It is notable that he tries to keep her out by piling up *books* to block up the gap in the window, trying to use print to stem the penetration of passion. He dreads any possibility of emotional leakage, any threat to his snail's shell. It is striking that Emily Brontë should use a dream to involve Lockwood in the violence and cruelty of Wuthering Heights, and I don't think it is just a matter of his somehow tapping the atmosphere of the place while unconscious. It is surely significant that the apparently 'civilised' Lockwood dreams of doing just about the cruellest and most sadistic act in a book full of cruelty. It suggests that Emily Brontë knew very well that in the most civilised effete mind there may well lurk a distorted and perverse proclivity to violence. The kind of extreme passional impulses embodied in Catherine are usually 'kept out' by society, disavowed and repressed by the individual. But in dreams – 'the return of the repressed' in a frighteningly grotesque form – Catherine represents a passion which society has excluded, cannot accommodate – just as Lockwood tries to keep her *out*. But in the world of this book the window which separates the house from the moor, the civilised from the uncivi-

112

lised, consciousness from unconsciousness, ultimately life from death, this window has been broken. Much of the power of the book stems exactly from this 'breaking of the window': things that are normally 'kept out' clamour for admission or come flowing in.

Let me turn now to the end. Again, we have three chapters from Lockwood and another date, 1802 (p. 336). The book started in storms and mists and snow, the very dead of Winter. It ends in 'sweet warm weather': wildness has given way to peace, storm to calm, and all kinds of savage disruptions and molestations to an image of a reconstituted society. To remind you of the picture Lockwood brings us, we have a new relationship between the young Cathy and Hareton, the legal inheritor whose *name* stands over the door of the house (remember Catherine's trouble with names). For a period Heathcliff has come between the house and the name, causing an anti-social rupture. This is now being healed. The new couple present a purely domestic scene of pleasant harmless peace. Hareton's 'ignorance and degradation' have dropped away from him under the civilising care of Cathy. Significantly, they come together over books – 'I perceived two such radiant countenances bent over the page of *the accepted book*, that I did not doubt the treaty had been ratified, on both sides, and the enemies were, thenceforth, sworn allies' (p. 345; my italics). The 'accepted' book is to be set against the *rejected* book – as in the gesture of Heathcliff and Catherine. Books, the written word, are the very essence of civilisation. To put it very simply, they accept human separation and recognise that we can communicate only indirectly – via sign systems. Accepting the book (in this novel) amounts to accepting the conditions of socialisation. Heathcliff and Catherine had no time for books – because they were not interested in any form of mediated communication. They desired actually to become one another – indeed, insisted on that identity. Such an impulse for total identification and assimilation is necessarily inimical to anything we can call society.

A word, now, about Heathcliff. He is a figure who in some way seems to transcend history – he is certainly not at home in it. He is the dark stranger from outside the home, the eternal alien of no known origin. He is found wandering in the streets of the great anonymous modern city (Liverpool), a gypsy child, an outlaw. Note that when Mr Earnshaw carries him home – i.e., to the *inside*

113

of the domestic circle – he is utterly exhausted by the effort. More, in the process of carrying Heathcliff, Mr Earnshaw finds that all the toys he had bought for his own legitimate children have been broken. We may sense that, from the beginning, Heathcliff, if contained, is more prone to cause destruction than further creation. (It is, for instance, unthinkable that he should have Catherine's child; he has no connection with social and familial continuity. He is himself alone: no parents, no successors. The son he has inherits none of his power – he is really the negative of a child, and dies before coming to life.) While Heathcliff and Catherine are children they are utterly happy. They live as one person inside what Emerson called 'the magic circle' of unselfconscious nature, sleeping together as they run together. But the essence of growing up is that individuals grow aware of their own separateness, their otherness and apartness from all other men and women. And it is exactly this severance – this emergence into separateness – which proves such a torment for Heathcliff and Catherine. Inevitably, one way or another, their energies will be devoted to breaking all the boundaries which make for this separation, to recapture some of that wild delight when, as one person, they ran over the moors all night.

Cathy is in some ways more complex than Heathcliff. She wants to be a 'double character', and indeed she suffers from something like schizophrenia as she tries to reconcile marriage (Edgar) and passion (Heathcliff). The division of energies is fatal and she dies between them (with Edgar, significantly, at his books). In her famous speech to Nelly just before her marriage she asserts that she and Heathcliff are inseparable and concludes: 'Nelly, I *am* Heathcliff!' (p. 122). For his part Heathcliff asserts that 'I cannot live without my life! I *cannot* live without my soul!' (p. 204). In effect they are both saying, I exist only because the other exists. Catherine feels her real self to be Heathcliff: Heathcliff feels that his life and soul are Catherine. This is the extreme form of that romantic passion which attempts to merge completely with another person – to end the inevitable, intolerable separation between two people. To be deprived of this kind of union, in Emily Brontë's world, is to suffer an utter hell of isolation and destitution (her poems return constantly to this sort of suffering). Clearly, there is in this sort of passion a drive towards death. As Catherine says, if she cannot have Heathcliff she will choose to die. On the other hand, if she could merge totally with Heathcliff that too would mean death – the annihilation of the boundaries which contain and separate the living individual. This is hinted at in the one passionate embrace of Catherine and Heathcliff, which is at the same time an embrace of love and an embrace of death. Heathcliff seems to be crushing Catherine into himself, to be merging himself into her. After she dies his one real desire is to share her grave – an event he prepares for by having one side of her coffin removed. Death is the final release from separateness, the individual merging back into the endless continuum of sheer matter and Being. There Heathcliff and Catherine can merge into each other and become one, because there everything is merged with everything else. Unconscious nature is a pure unity and, even from the beginning of their lives, Heathcliff and Catherine are really seeking to rejoin it. Their energies are ultimately aimed at destroying the 'shell' of the separate self.

At the end Heathcliff and Catherine are once more sleeping peacefully in the same bed, as they did as children; though now they have entered the second stage of unselfconsciousness: death. The second Cathy and Hareton 'accept' separateness and survive as restorers of a calm society. They will find their identities in marriage: Heathcliff and Catherine lose their identities in an unsocialised and unsocialisable passion. In their way they finally elude Lockwood's narrative 'framework' – he works with traces and indirect evidence for much of the time – just as, in a different way, Cathy and Hareton conclude it.

Matthew Arnold saw in *Jane Eyre* only 'hunger, rebellion and rage', while a contemporary reviewer considered the book 'pre-eminently an anti-Christian composition' and associated the novel with Chartism and the threat of social rebellion. Yet we can now see that the novel is most importantly about the creation of a self out of nothing except consciousness and sensation – and language. That is to say, Jane Eyre has none of the things that most people have to help them establish their first sense of reality – no family, no friends, no ties, no house (she is made to feel utterly unwanted and alien in the Reed household – aptly named Gateshead Hall, for they do indeed lock Jane up and try to imprison her mind). She has no connections, no context. She is alive but has no place in which to live. Let me remind you that the book starts in winter in extremes of cold, and this mood continues well into the book; while when Rochester 'proposes' it is mid-summer. The important point about this is that all of Jane's early experiences are of cold, literal cold, shivering freezing fingers, no bodily comfort, but also icy looks, harsh hands, cold treatment, the chilling deprivation of warm contacts and real mutuality. I stress this because when she comes to write her life she in effect arranges her experience according to a range of metaphors drawn from these early physical and mental experiences. Experience is usually cold, too cold. This of course leads to a yearning for some kind of warmth, melting, and fire, and I shall say more about this later on. But in her experience she also notes that if things thaw too suddenly they overflow, and that if fire gets out of hand – literal fire but also mental and emotional fire – it consumes and destroys. Experience can be too cold, but it can also be too hot – the geographic realms of the West Indies and India are equivalents of emotional and psychic areas of excessive heat leading either to madness and derangement or a loss of self through scorching aridity.

Now let me bring in language and narrative. Jane Eyre has to write her life, literally create herself in writing: the narrative act is an act of self-definition. Given her social position, the only control she has over her life is narrative control. She is literally as in control of herself as she is of her narrative. Early in the book when she tells her life story to new friends – like Helen Burns – she is liable to lose control, become incoherent with resentment and rage and suppressed emotions – just as she is driven 'out of herself' by being locked up in the red room. Helen tells her that she must learn to tell her story with more control, and this is a crucial lesson. For what Jane's narrative can contain, and order, and control, she herself can. A loss of narrative control is analogous to a loss of self-arrangement. From this point of view her identity is her text. This is particularly important in her dealings with the two key men in her life: they each in different ways try to take her to extremes, in effect to take her into non-lingual areas where the elemental annihilates the societal. Jane Eyre instinctively knows that if she allows herself to be taken into these extreme areas she will not be able to maintain her identity – though she has that in her which is drawn to such non-lingual extremes, to passional dissolutions of the self. What she has to do is to assimilate aspects of these extremes into her narrative. You can regard narrative – particularly 'autobiographical' narrative – as an exercise in assimilation and exclusion. The narrator decides what enters his/her narrative world, and in what form it enters; hence Jane's metaphoric and symbolic treatment of her experience. In *Wuthering Heights* Heathcliff and Catherine try to get beyond language – they throw away their books – and by the same token try to get beyond identity – they finally throw away their social roles. And they die. But Jane, aware of what lies outside language and identity, struggles to assimilate and contain the non-lingual and trans-lingual aspects of experience in her narrative – and she lives. Lives not as some false self or distorted role that other people try to impose on her, but lives with her own self-created, self-defined identity.

One other point here about Jane's narrative. Jane is nourished on nursery tales by Bessie (with the usual fantastic figures to be found in such stories): one of her favourite books is *Gulliver's Travels* which, let me just remind you, proposes the creation of extreme fictive realms in which people are impossibly small or impossibly large (or are animals – horses and apes). In addition, Jane Eyre admits that she needs a kind of compensatory fantasy world to make up for the boring routines of her actual one (as we know Charlotte Brontë needed, for a time, her 'Angria' fantasies). Thus, when Jane hears something strange on the 'third story' at Thornfield, she is drawn to it as a realm which nourishes her imagination, starved by the stagnation of the lower two storeys. 'Then my sole relief was to walk along the corridor of the third story . . . and, best of all, to open my inward ear to a tale that was never ended – a tale my imagination created, and narrated continuously; quickened with all of incident, life, fire, feeling, that I desired and had not in my actual existence' (p. 141).[2] The general point I am making is that Jane has a gift for narrative – imaginative, given to 'enlargement' and symbolic extremes – which is larger than the very constricted compass of her actual social existence, or indeed almost non-existence (she is 'nobody'). In her life she is subjected to pressure which would take her beyond the boundaries of her imaginary narrative altogether – into another kind of non-being, not inside society but outside it.

What she needs is somehow to make her life both as ample and controlled as her narrative. The domestic must be intensified; at the same time, the elemental must be socialised. The medium for this is language and imagination – that 'third story' which brings meaning and significance to the two below it. But there is also madness on the third storey (Mrs Rochester): this indispensable dimension of consciousness is necessarily ambiguous, and Jane has to tread – and fantasise – carefully.

So while there is much in the book that is drawn to wildness, abandon, the unhindered release of accumulating emotion, there is also much that contests the imperatives of passion and asserts the need for control and containment. Domestic and civilised realities are honoured and acknowledged at the same time as internal and external storms are raging. We often see Jane Eyre in different houses and rooms standing close to the window, more involved with the unstructured space and the climatic extremes outside the glass than with the often painful routines and orderings within the house. Yet the one time she leaves all houses and abandons herself to the elements – in her flight from Rochester – she is brought close to death, and at the nadir of her exhaustion she stands outside a house looking enviously *in* at the comfortable domestic routine. Jane Eyre has to learn how to control the dialectic of inside and outside, containment and release, structure and space, just as she has to establish for herself a sort of middle psychological geography, avoiding the extremes of the West Indies and India, and even the wicked south of France where Rochester would take her as a mistress but not as a wife. From one point of view her narrative is an act of psychological cartography. And at the end Jane is safe, inside a house having negotiated the outside; in England, a psychological England, not in the West Indies or France or India; and honoured by a legal marriage, not enslaved as a mistress or an object to be used.

When we first see Jane she is standing apart, prevented from 'joining the group'; she retires into the window seat behind the red curtains and studies, first, the cold winter landscape outside and then Bewick's *History of British Birds* (pp. 39–40). Inevitably 'birds' communicate a sense of liberty, a free circling in the immense spaces of the air. (And of course, Jane's surname contains a pun on that freest of elements – and more than once she is described as a bird – e.g., by Rochester: 'I see at intervals the glance of a curious sort of bird through the close-set bars of a cage' (p. 170).) But Bewick's book has another significance. Musing on the illustrations, Jane's imagination is drawn to the notions of the Terrible Arctic Zone – 'those forlorn regions of dreary space': she thinks about 'death-white realms'; she is drawn to the picture of 'the rock standing up alone in a sea of billow and spray; to the broken boat stranded on a desolate coast; to the cold and ghastly moon glancing through bars of cloud at a wreck just sinking' (p. 40). The lonely rock, the broken boat, the sinking ship – these images of the threatened promontory and boat with no firm land at hand adumbrate various stages of her life and the continuous threat to Jane's precariously emerging sense of her own identity. If 'air' is the element which attracts her, water is the one which warns of possible dissolution. On one occasion before Helen Burns dies, and just after a moment in the woods feeling how pleasant it is to be alive, she suddenly has a moment of what we may call metaphysical dread, or in Laing's term 'ontological insecurity'. Her mind tries to understand the idea of life after death – 'and for the first time it recoiled baffled; and for the first time glancing behind, on each side, and before it, it saw all around an unfathomed gulf: it felt the one point where it stood – the present; all the rest was formless cloud and vacant depth; and it shuddered at the thought of tottering, and plunging amid that chaos' (pp. 110–11). This feeling of being 'at sea', of not having any certain ports behind or ahead in life (which equals a loss of a sense of origin and destination), of their being only the palpable 'now' that one can be sure of – this is a basic and recurrent predicament for Jane. At another time she experiences temporal dislocation, a sort of existential amorphousness: 'I hardly knew where I was; Gateshead and my past life seemed floated away to an immeasurable distance; the present was vague and strange, and of the future I could form no conjecture' (p. 81). That is, she cannot bring definition to the tenses of her life – was, is, will be. Awash in time, her life is in danger of losing all grammar and syntax. She also experiences a comparable spatial dislocation: 'It is a very strange sensation to inexperienced youth to feel itself quite alone in the world, cut adrift from every connexion, uncertain whether the port to which it is bound can be reached, and prevented by many impediments from returning to that it has quited' (p. 125). At the end she is not only in possession of

Rochester's house, Ferndean, she also has his watch in her keeping; i.e., she is finally in control of time and space. (Her own paintings reveal something of her fears: one 'represented clouds low and vivid, rolling over a swollen sea: all the distance was in eclipse; so, too, was the foreground, or, rather, the nearest billows, for *there was no land*' (p. 157; my italics). There is only a wreck, a cormorant holding a bracelet, and a sinking corpse. This is the very image of that 'formless cloud and vacant depth' into which she fears she might plunge. Other paintings, of a wild woman's face in the sky, of a face 'blank of meaning but for the glassiness of despair' resting on an iceberg, likewise reveal her dreads and dreams (p. 157). They portray wild or miserable lone human faces being reabsorbed into the elements – sinking into the sea, rising into cloud. They hinge on the notion of the evaporation or dilution and vanishing of the distinct human form.)

Given that she has no assured place, no fixed location, Jane Eyre's sense of identity is necessarily very vulnerable. When Rochester tries to deceive her into a false marriage he effectively tries to appropriate her by an illicit act of renomination, calling her 'Jane Rochester'. But it only makes her feel 'strange' – as though she cannot find herself in the name. When the potentially bigamous marriage is revealed she is even more lost. 'Where was the Jane Eyre of yesterday? – where was her life? – where were her prospects?' (p. 323). This loss of a sense of her own self goes even further when she is in flight from Rochester and wandering in the 'outside' world of nature. The birds she sees are no longer an attractive image for her but a reproach: 'birds were faithful to their mates; birds were emblems of love. What was I?' (p. 348). Not 'who' – but 'what'? Her sense of her own distinct being and human actuality is close to annihilation. The 'outside', then, offers her no sphere for self-realisation. But when she is 'inside' for the most part people try to 'imprison' her in different ways. When she is locked up in the red room – a traumatic experience – it is felt to be a 'jail'. There are other dungeons in the book – Lowood School, Thornfield as described by Rochester, even her little school in Yorkshire, while St John Rivers turns her mind into a 'rayless dungeon'. In a crucial scene a game of charades is played at Thornfield, and the word chosen to be enacted is 'Bridewell'. Bridewell was in turn a royal palace, an hospital, and a house of correction or prison. The name focuses Jane's problem.

She must 'bride well' (i.e., make the right marriage), otherwise she will find herself in one kind of prison or another – her sense of self negated by the volition of a more powerful other. It is worth noting that only twice in the novel does she make the clear and confident assertion, 'I am Jane Eyre', and these are both moments when a character who has at one time been a dominant and powerful menace to her unhelped independence appears before her weak, helpless, crippled or dying. I will return to these moments.

To summarise a little, the book is organised around five sep-arate establishments, the names of which suggest a progression through a changing landscape – Gates(head), (Lo)wood, Thorn-field, Moor(house) also known as Marsh(End); and Fern(dean Manor). In each of these establishments except the last, various pressures, influences and threats are brought to bear on her sense of her own identity. Initially she is regarded as – or 'transformed' into – an 'interloper and alien'. But the main threats come from the two men who try to impose 'bad' marriages on her. Rochester tries to impose a false identity and role upon her, turning her into a make-pretend wife whom he really wants for his mistress (his references to harems and 'seraglio' indicate his 'eastern' pro-clivities). That is the point of his efforts to heap all sorts of clothes and jewels on her before the 'wedding': he is literally trying to deceive her by dressing her up as a 'bride', i.e., to make her play a role in his fantasy. But she resists: 'I can never bear being dressed like a doll.' He calls her his 'angel' but she refuses this: 'I am not an angel . . . I will be myself' (p. 288); and later: 'I had rather be a *thing* than an angel' (p. 291), intimating she would prefer petri-faction to idolisation. Rochester thinks he has the 'power' to change the rules of society – indeed, to change reality itself. Two of his comments are pertinent here: 'unheard-of combinations of circumstances demand unheard-of rules'. Jane resists this line of argument, sensing that 'unheard-of rules' would be no rules at all. Concerning his mad wife, Rochester says: 'Let her identity . . . be buried in oblivion' (p. 336). Jane recognises that if he thinks he can do this to one woman he can do it to any woman – hence her flight, a flight from identity-oblivion. Passionally, she is all but lost, but 'mentally, I still possessed my soul, and with it the cer-tainty of ultimate safety' (p. 344). In her flight she discovers that 'I have no relation but the universal mother, Nature' (p. 349). It is not enough. We have come too far. We must find our identities in some kind of society, not simply in nature. Because of thought and reflection. We may decay with and in nature and mingle with its processes – but at the cost of a living identity. 'Life, however, was yet in my possession; with all its requirements, and pains, and responsibilities. The burden must be carried; the want provided for; the suffering endured; the responsibility fulfilled. I set out' (p. 351). There it is. 'I set out.' The human obligation.

Refusing Rochester and the 'stage-trappings' he tries to impose on her, Jane asserts: 'I shall not be your Jane Eyre any longer, but an ape in a harlequin's jacket – a jay in borrowed plumes', and insists instead: 'I will be myself' (p. 288). She would rather be a real Jane Eyre – no matter what the privations – than a false 'Mrs Rochester'. With St John Rivers the problem and threat take another form. Whereas Rochester offered – or threatened – too much fire, St John Rivers is at various times likened to a glacier, marble, stone, glass. His eyes are like 'instruments'; he speaks at key moments 'like an automaton'. He is a man of iron who forges his own chains: he locks too much up. His beauty is that of a dead classic statue; his religion is bitter and deathly. As he significantly says: 'I am cold: no fervour infects me', while Jane replies 'Whereas I am hot, and fire dissolves ice' (p. 409). Rivers gradually subdues her and she feels an 'iron shroud' (p. 429) gather round her. His ice and iron seem to be winning over her innate fire. She gets to the point where she agrees to go with him to India – but not as his wife. 'I abandon half myself', she meditates – but only half (p. 430). She will not marry him, and in her answer to his pressing proposal she makes a distinction which is central to the issues I have been discussing. 'And I will give the missionary my energies – it is all he wants – but not myself . . . my body would be under rather a stringent yoke, but my heart would be free. I should still have my unblighted self to turn to: my natural unenslaved feelings with which to communicate in moments of loneliness' (pp. 432–3). This is the crucial act of resistance and assertion of her own identity. Her inner life is to be her own; whatever else she gives she will hold on to her 'unblighted self'. Her response to the telepathic call from Rochester indicates a sure intuition of where life lies for her. In leaving Rivers she is fleeing from ice, stone, iron, and an inflexible religious will which is corrupted by detectable sado-masochistic impulses: she is fleeing, that is, from everything that threatens the death of her self and the cold, relentless extinction and obliteration of her inner life, her passional integrity.

Her journey to Rochester is marked by a symbolic suggestiveness. The way gets darker and more constricted with trees until she feels she has lost her way. There are no longer any roads – indeed, there is 'no opening anywhere'. It is as though she is returning to some pre-social space where all the conventional definitions are erased and where she can begin again. In the 'formlessness' of Ferndean she at last can re-form relationships and roles on her own terms. When she finds Rochester he is of course the helpless one now, in a semi-impotent state (blindness being a recognised symbol for some degree of castration) – his imperious desire and antinomian energies now tamed. And this is the second moment when Jane asserts her full free-standing independent identity as she announces to him, 'I am Jane Eyre' (p. 459). Rochester has of course throughout been associated with fire by Jane, where she sees Rivers in terms of ice. The latent fire – and need for warmth – in Jane is roused by the perceptible flames in his own temperament. Her worry is that she must not be consumed and annihilated in one sudden conflagration (such as partially blinded and crippled Rochester). Fire of course has always been the most ambiguous metaphor drawn from the elements. It has meant so many contradictory things: it is the very stuff of life and the most deadly agent of destruction; it is the gift of the gods and the eternal punishment of hell; it is Promethean illumination and the source of civilisation; and it is apocalypse, holocaust, judgment day. This radical ambivalence is suggested by the large number of references to fire in the book – indeed, David Lodge in an admirable essay has counted them: eighty-five references to domestic fires, forty-three references to figurative fires, ten literal conflagrations, and four references to hell fire. I simply want to refer to two key uses of fire. The 'fire' of uncontrolled passion (such as destroys Thornfield) is of course something which Jane must avoid, but that does not mean that Jane is to be seen as opposing the fire-element. Certainly she knows that she will die in extreme heat, or utterly lose her identity; but that does not mean she would be more at home in arctic wastes, geographically or psychologically. Indeed, we would perhaps do best to see her as a spirit of *controlled* fire. Let me point to a notable

123

coincidence. I mentioned that it is when two of the once-dominant opposing or coercive forces in her life appear before her humbled and incapacitated that Jane asserts her full identity: 'I am Jane Eyre'. Well, it is precisely at those two moments that we see her kindling a fading fire. In Mrs Reed's house the action seems merely an unconsidered reflex – 'the fire was dying in the grate. I renewed the fuel' (p. 265). But note that this is exactly when she is thinking of Mrs Reed dying upstairs. Jane is in charge of the fire in the house which once imposed on her a cold and miserable isolation. Again, when she returns to Rochester (who earlier had tried to draw her too close to the fire until she complained that 'the fire scorches me' – see chapter XIX), it is now her turn to be guardian of the fire while he sits by, helpless and passively grateful. 'Now let me leave you an instant, to make a better fire, and have the hearth swept up' (p. 461). And soon, through his dimmed eyes, he sees 'a ruddy haze'. It is in just such a nourishing but non-annihilating warm glow that Jane will now lead her life with Rochester. Not suffering extinction in either the extremes of cold (a dead marriage) or heat (an adulterous liaison), but completely and fully her own self, sustained by a controlled warmth of passion which is essential to the well-being of her inmost life. The excluded orphan has finally become that crucial domestic figure: the mistress of the hearth.

It is worth noting that one of the first lessons that Jane Eyre masters is 'the first two tenses of the verb *être'* – I am, I will be, or I was. This is indeed exactly what she has to learn to say with full confidence and authority, to know what the self is in time, to stabilise the self in its relation to what is around it. If you can say 'I am' then you can also say 'You are' – self-apprehension leads to proper recognition of the other. Learning to articulate and define and hold on to her own identity, Jane Eyre is also able accurately to identify others. In this way she is able to resist being absorbed into, or transformed into, false selves which other people wish to make of her for their own selfish means. She can resist the kind of manipulation, reification, and falsification which threaten her at every key stage of her life (her narrative devices are an inscription of this resistance). Catherine and Heathcliff want to say 'I am you', which may be good passion but is bad grammar: they want to destroy pronouns, tenses, genders, prepositional distances and differentiations – indeed, they want to get out of grammar altogether. On the other hand, Jane Eyre's achievement, and not only the subject of the book but the reason she wrote it, is the proper mastery of the verb *être*, or the attainment of the unchallenged ability to say 'I am Jane Eyre'.

NOTES

1 All page references in the first part of the essay are to Emily Brontë, *Wuthering Heights*, ed. David Daiches, Harmondsworth, Penguin English Library, 1965.
2 All page references in the second part are to Charlotte Brontë, *Jane Eyre*, ed. Q.D. Leavis, Harmondsworth, Penguin English Library, 1966.

8 Writing for silence: Dorothy Richardson and the novel

Stephen Heath

Writing in 1923 with his usual forcefulness, D.H. Lawrence stig-matised the contemporary serious novel: 'dying in a very long-drawn-out fourteen-volume death agony, and absorbedly, child-ishly interested in the phenomenon. "Did I feel a twinge in my little toe, or didn't I?" asks every character of Mr Joyce or of Miss Richardson or M. Proust.' The novel is sick with introspection, moribund with an interminable subjectivity: 'It is self-conscious-ness picked into such fine bits that the bits are most of them invisible, and you have to go by smell. Through thousands and thousands of pages Mr Joyce and Miss Richardson tear them-selves to pieces, strip their smallest emotions to the finest threads. . . .'[1]

Dorothy Richardson, Proust, Joyce. The three names, the three works, were often brought together and in many ways inevitably and rightly so. The first chapter of the first of the *Pilgrimage* novels, *Pointed Roofs*, was drafted by Richardson in 1913, the same year that the initial volume of *A la recherche du temps perdu* was published in Paris and that Joyce in Trieste was making progress on *A Portrait of the Artist as a Young Man*. Like theirs, Richardson's work was to last a lifetime, life taken up in a permanent act of writing; and while there is no record that they had any knowledge of hers, Richardson read their work and gave thought to it (reviewing *Finnegans Wake,* for example, as soon as it appeared[2]). In her 'Foreword' to the 1938 collected edition of *Pilgrimage*, Richardson is careful to make reference to both Proust and Joyce but then also, it should be noted, to try to suggest something of her own individuality.[3] For the bringing together of the three names could serve too easily to obliterate, leaving Richardson's work as a kind of subsidiary instance in a general discussion of Proust, Joyce and the modern novel. *Pilgrimage* should be part of such a general discussion but has also its specific concerns and problems and qualities which can serve to raise certain critical questions about that modern novel; Richardson can be linked to Proust and Joyce but is not simply a cipher of the imagination of the writer we might derive from them, their myth. Her life and her work, after all, involve many contexts: she was a governess and an intimate friend of H.G. Wells; she wrote regularly in the same film magazine, *Close Up*, to which H.D. contributed her 'Projector' poems; she reviewed on psychoanalysis and many other things for *Dental Record*, which she was asked to edit, and was approached by Brecht as to the possibility of becoming his translator; she was close at times to left-wing political groups and was in many senses and with many nuances a feminist, 'strong, un-doctrinaire, feminine socialism', in the words of the novelist John Cowper Powys, friend and admirer;[4] she was. . . .

But that exactly is the matter of her work: identity, one's self, its definition or not, life and book together as pilgrimage. And, of course, this is to come back to Proust and Joyce, with whose writing Richardson's intersects in its own specificity. I want briefly in the space of this lecture to sketch out something of that specificity and so to provide an introduction to *Pilgrimage* as significant modern novel.

Freud in 1908 spoke of 'the inclination of the modern writer to split up his ego by self-observation into many part egos'.[5] *Pilgrimage* is full of that inclination, informed by the necessity for self-observation. Its project is given in the title: a journey through a life in writing, a moving over questions and *the* question of identity. 'Which self?' (IV, 318) says Miriam, the central figure of the book, suddenly returning from other worlds to the conversational world around her and to its particular expectation of herself. What does it mean to say 'I am'? 'I suppose I'm a new woman' (I, 436); 'I'm a Tory–Anarchist' (IV, 179); 'I'm a free-lover' (IV, 254); I am. . . . Carried along in conversation, held in the gaze of others, caught up in the public realms of work and friendship and life, taken over by her own desires for attachment, Richardson's heroine can reflect and assume identities, a myriad of part egos, 'I am's'. Hence the name: *Miriam*.

Yet there is everywhere, too, a deeper aspect of the 'miriamness', the feeling of the misfit, the place not me. Miriam knows and continually learns this, has it confirmed by any occasion: a dinner party 'had, in bringing together three of her worlds, shown her more clearly than she had known it before, that there was no place for her in any one of them' (III, 474). Concomitant with which is then the experience, falling into silence, of something different, persistent and elsewhere, another reality: during the interval at a concert 'her consciousness fell silent and empty. To be filled, as the moments flowed through this motionless centre, only by an awareness of the interval between the two parts of the concert as a loop in time, one of those occasions that bring with peculiar vividness the sense of identity, persistent, unchanging, personal identity, and return, in memory, inexhaustible' (IV, 304). She too returns 'inexhaustible', a difference of self which is increasingly the point of her desire, what she wants: 'she *would* reach that central peace; go farther and farther into the heart of her being and be there, as if alone, tranquilly, until fully possessed by that something within her that was more than herself' (IV, 219).

Thus the pilgrimage, the writing, 'the strange journey down and down to the centre of being' (IV, 609). Thus *Pilgrimage*, written in 'scattered chapters', as Richardson put it in her subsequent 'Foreword' (I, 12), a continuous publication from *Pointed Roofs* in 1915 to *Dimple Hill* in 1938 and then begun again with sections of *March Moonlight* appearing in 1946 in *Life and Letters* – thirteen book–chapters of an inevitably interminable project, a perpetual work on oneself. Which is Lawrence's objection, the long-drawn-out self-consciousness; what a more recent critic, Miriam Allott, calls 'an alarming diffuseness and an uncritical subjectivity'.[6] Richardson herself took up such complaints in a question she formulated in one of her film pieces: 'But must we not, today, emerge from our small individual existences and from narcissistic contemplation thereof?'; and answered with a stress on the importance of 'mirroring the customary and restoring its essential quality'.[7] Film and writing have different possibilities, but restoring the essential, finding that in life, is the overall aim and ambition. What is 'narcissism' for the critics is necessary journey for writer and reader, oneself coming into being.

A sure way of missing the essential is the novel with its smooth version of reality and all its illusions of identity. Take Wells. In 1909 he deals precisely with the 'new woman' in the person of Ann Veronica, eponymous heroine of the resultant novel. From the initial crisis of resistance against her father's authority through to the final reunion with him after she has taken her full independence, Wells takes Ann Veronica out into the world and into a stand for freedom that leaves the constraints of the novel intact. Ann Veronica's career could shock in respect of the social conventions of the novel – Macmillan, Wells' habitual publisher, thought it 'would be exceedingly distasteful to the public which buys books published by our firm'[8] and refused it – but the conventional perspectives of the novel were still firmly there: 'the best love story I have ever done'[9] was just that, a story with all the fictions of character, description and so on, with all the usual orders of meaning. Ann Veronica is put in her novelistic place, rounded off into the required image, seen, supported and summed up, identified as the new woman and tied back into the love story, the old vision repeated and updated in the terms of the novel with its usual ending: ' "Oh, my dear!" she cried, and suddenly flung herself kneeling into her husband's arms. . . . "Blood of my heart!" whispered Capes, holding her close to him. "I know. I understand." ' For woman today, as Ann Veronica has to demonstrate, 'wants to be legally and economically free, so as not to be subject to the wrong man; but only God, who made the world, can alter things to prevent her being slave to the right one'.[10]

Wells is written into *Pilgrimage* as Hypo G. Wilson, introduced in *The Tunnel* in 1919 and a crucial presence in the novel thereafter. Ironically, and indicatively enough, the attempted seduction of Ann Veronica in Wells's novel by Ramage, a businessman neighbour of her father, is rewritten by Richardson in *Dawn's Left Hand* as Hypo's attempted seduction of Miriam. The same scenes recur – the evening at a performance of Wagner, the restaurant dinner in a private room – but now with the woman no longer an object of exchange, held for the reader in a novelistic adventure.

Ramifying through the multiple drifts of Miriam's mind, the writing glimpses the seduction, its scenes, almost as a quotation from a novel, from *Ann Veronica* and all the others, part of the material of the book and the life but curiously strange and distant, falling short of any truth. Much of this gap between the idea of the novel and the reality of Richardson's writing is epitomised in her title: *Pilgrimage* as opposed to *Ann Veronica*. Wells believes in the novel, cut and dried, can finish it off with the name of his character, described, narrated, fixed; Richardson can only say the writing, the pilgrimage-journey that is this unending book in which Miriam is dispersed in a flow of thoughts and memories and bits and pieces of incident and impression and atmosphere and that can never be cast up into a 'character'. There are indeed parallels to be remembered here with the work of Proust and Joyce, equally at odds in their own ways with the idea of the novel: the 'I' of *A la recherche* is not brought down to the usual novelistic fictions of a name, is only twice – and doubtfully – picked out as 'Marcel'; while in *Finnegans Wake* 'Joyce' is continually present through a series of transformations, a kind of running signature, but never settled into any final appearance.[11]

As might be expected, it is Hypo Wilson who suggests to Miriam that the novel is important, meeting with her fascinated resistance: 'The torment of *all* novels is what is left out. The moment you are aware of it, there is torment in them. Bang, bang, bang, on they go, these men's books, like an L.C.C. tram. . . .' (IV, 239). Novels are everywhere in life, spreading their fictions, giving us a role: ' "But perhaps he doesn't want to," said Miriam, suddenly feeling that she was playing a familiar part in a novel and wanting to feel quite sure she was reading her role aright' (I, 439); 'A haunting familiar sense of unreality possessed her. Once more she was part of a novel; it was right, true like a book. . . .' (II, 389); ' "Pray don't worry about the pace of my millinery, Mr Leyton." That was quite good, like a society novel' (III, 52); 'Alma's social tone, deliberately clear and level. It made a little scene, the beginning of a novel. . . .' (III, 337) The novel is important and irrelevant, turning you into its terms, and then again, after all, 'Perhaps novels are important' (IV, 614).

Thus Miriam, envisaging the possibility of writing, its necessity. But Hypo, with his 'hideous, irritating, meaningless word *novvle*' (IV, 239), offers available places, recognised slots, 'setting out the contents of the cruet as if they were pieces in a game': ' "Women ought to be good novelists. But they write best about their own experiences. Love-affairs and so forth. . . . Try a novel of ideas. . . . Be a feminine George Eliot. Try your hand" ' (IV, 240). Much earlier in Miriam's life in the book, another male acquaintance had told her to write: ' "Have you ever thought of committing your ideas to paper? There's a book called *The Confessions of a Woman*. It had a great sale and its composition occupied the authoress for only six weeks. You could write it in your holidays" ' (I, 268). Now Hypo has it all sorted out, the professional writer offering a professional career in the novel: ' "*Middles. Criticism*, which you'd do as other women do fancy-work. *Infant.* NOVEL." ' (IV, 240). Miriam, however, is elsewhere: 'But her interest had disappeared so completely that she went off in search of it' (IV, 240).

Writing is a necessity and a problem, the pilgrimage and the difficulty of its novel. When Miriam finally begins to write, she produces a mass of hurriedly written pages that lose everything she is writing for: 'These tracts of narrative were somehow false, a sort of throwing of dust that still would be dust even if its grains could be transformed to gold; question-begging, skating along surfaces to a superficial finality, gratuitously, in no matter what tone of voice, offered as a conclusion' (IV, 524). What is needed is 'to be rid of realism', as Virginia Woolf put it in a review of *The Tunnel*;[12] or, as Richardson herself suggests in her 'Foreword', to achieve the presence of a new 'independently assertive reality':

> . . . the present writer, proposing at this moment to write a novel and looking round for a contemporary pattern, was faced with the choice between following one of her regiments and attempting to produce a feminine equivalent of the current masculine realism. Choosing the latter alternative, she presently set aside, at the bidding of a dissatisfaction that revealed its nature without supplying any suggestion as to the removal of its cause, a considerable mass of manuscript. Aware, as she wrote, of the gradual falling away of the preoccupations that for a while had dictated the briskly moving script, and of the substitution,

131

for these inspiring preoccupations, of a stranger in the form of contemplated reality having for the first time in her experience its own say, and apparently justifying those who acclaim writing as the surest means of discovering the truth about one's own thoughts and beliefs, she had been at the same time increasingly tormented, not only by the failure, of this now so independently assertive reality, adequately to appear within the text, but by its revelation, whencesoever focused, of a hundred faces, any one of which, the moment it was entrapped within the close mesh of direct statement, summoned its fellows to disqualify it.   [I, 9–10]

The passage, typically complex, is an exact version of Miriam's situation with her tracts of narrative. Richardson in the 1938 'Foreword' looks back to initial attempts at writing in 1911 or before and is echoed by Miriam in *Dimple Hill*, also published in 1938, in about 1908 in the chronology of *Pilgrimage*; Miriam coming back at this point towards the close of *Pilgrimage* to the *Confessions of a Woman* advice she received at its beginning:

It was Bob, driving so long ago a little nail into her mind when he said, 'Write the confessions of a modern woman,' meaning a sensational chronicle with an eye, several eyes, upon the interest of sympathetic readers like himself – 'Woman, life's heroine, the dear, exasperating creature' – who really likes to see how life looks from the other side, the women's side, who put me on the wrong track and created all those lifeless pages. Following them up, everything would be left out that is always there, preceding and accompanying and surviving the drama of human relationships; the reality from which people move away as soon as they closely approach and expect each other to be all in all.
                    [IV, 525]

What is at stake is writing. The book records the necessity for the book that this book is; Miriam's pilgrimage to be undertaken is this *Pilgrimage* written through the recreation of a life which is indeed already the pilgrimage for Miriam and which she must now learn in writing, 'discovering the truth about one's own thoughts and beliefs'. Miriam and Dorothy run into each other, 'the form of contemplated reality having for the first time . . . its own say'; and the point is not that Miriam Henderson and Dorothy

Richardson with their rhyming, chiming names are one and the same; it is that there is no *one*, only the myriad, the flow that only by a fiction – the old idea of the novel – can be stopped in some simple unity, some given identity. Writing is the knowledge of this: 'to write is to forsake life' (IV, 609), perhaps, but to write is also to know life, to *realise*, to say 'I am' with the difference of the essential. The result is neither novel nor autobiography but an original record, a kind of 'writing life' in which Richardson creates herself simultaneously with Miriam, becomes like Proust in *A la recherche* a text to be read in its single multiplicity – 'cette lecture . . . un acte de création où nul ne peut nous suppléer', 'notre seul livre', 'la vie enfin découverte et éclaircie, la seule vie par conséquent réellement vécue'.[13]

May Sinclair, writing in 1918, found an expression for Richardson's new realism, one that was to know considerable success: 'stream of consciousness'.[14] The feel of a streaming reality is certainly strong in *Pilgrimage*. For Miriam walking through the streets of London over 'flags of pavement flowing', 'Life streamed up from the close dense stone. With every footstep she felt she could fly' (I, 416). Everything interlocks in movement: the 'sense of the sufficiency of life at first hand' (IV, 364) – the shape of paving-stones, the clarity of light after rain, the set of a room – permeates the writing and is also that 'quality of the atmosphere' (III, 287) into which Miriam is always dropping away from her public presence, and atmosphere and life at first hand are in turn the fact of response, of the flow of thoughts and memories and speculations, endless *reflections* in and out of mind, revolving lights (to take up the title of one of the book-chapters): 'she found herself gliding into communion with surrounding things, shapes gleaming in the twilight, the intense thrilling beauty of the deep, lessening colours. . . .' (III, 360). What one wants is then not so much to recapture time lost, though the past is always present in the here and now of self-experience, 'a bright moving patch-work' (III, 323), but rather to create the silence of oneself, to be, separate, constant in movement: 'There was no thought in the silence, no past or future, nothing but the strange thing for which there were no words, something that was always there as if by appointment waiting for one to get through to it away from everything in life' (II, 322). Dropping into 'a trance of oblivion'

(III, 287), Miriam can be herself, outside the life around her – the identities, the parts, all the novel; yet the trance is also the flow, the streaming of consciousness in and out of things and people and places, all the moments and intensities of life in which, from which alone oneself can be read.

One can say, one wants so much to say, 'I am myself' (I, 286): divine instants of the 'I' single, unique, mine; ' "It's me, *me*; this is *me* being alive," she murmured with a feeling under her like the sudden drop of a lift' (I, 245). The strong baritone voice of a woman sings 'Ai-me-moi!' and Miriam later remembers 'that it had brought her a moment when the flower-filled drawing-room had seemed to be lit, from within herself, a sudden light that had kept her very still and made the bowls of roses blaze with deepening colours. In her mind she had seen garden beyond garden of roses, sunlit, brighter and brighter, and had made a rapturous prayer' (I, 405). Beyond the prayer, the pilgrimage. How is one ultimately to say 'I am myself' if not in writing, the record-realisation of the unique, of 'the original contents of [a] mind' (III, 285)?

Hence the project of the book, stream of consciousness as self-creation, not the novel but writing, not the surface but the underlying movement, a kind of elliptical concatenation of pauses in what for the novel would be reality, a story in elsewheres and silences.

'Only of course there are so many kinds of silence. But the test of absolutely everything in life is the quality of the in-between silences' (III, 389). Thus Miriam to Hypo, deciding no longer to be beguiled into surface and conformity: 'Somehow make him aware of the reality that fell, all the time, in the surrounding silence, outside his shapes and classifications' (III, 360). For him that silence is merely a void, an emptiness from which to be rescued, to come back into the security of talking, conversation. For Miriam and the book, constant theme and demonstration, all conversation is 'a lie' (I, 308); talk goes on, smoothly renewing the surface, filling up the troubling silences: 'Their talk had gone on. It was certain that always they would talk. Archipelagos of talk, avoiding anything that could endanger continuous urbanity' (IV,

39). Under this conversational reality is another reality, forgotten and disquieting and essential:

> There are two layers of truth. The truths laid bare by common sense in swift decisive conversations, founded on apparent facts, are incomplete. They shape the surface, and make things go kaleidoscoping on, recognizable, in a sort of general busy prosperous agreement; but at every turn, with every application of the common-sense civilized decisions, enormous things are left behind, unsuspected, forced underground, but never dying, slow things with slow, slow fruit. . . . The surface shape is powerful, every one is in it, that is where free will breaks down, in the moving on and being spirited away for another spell from the underlying things, but in every one, alone, often unconsciously, is something, a real inside personality that is turned away from the surface. In front of every one, away from the bridges and catchwords, is an invisible plank, that will bear. Always. Forgotten. Nearly all smiles are smiled from the bridges . . . Nearly all deaths are murders or suicides. . . . [III, 181–2]

The surface is made up of bridges and catchwords, speech which 'does nothing but destroy' (III, 182), sets things 'in a mould' (III, 129) – a whole world of inevitable misrepresentation: 'nothing can ever be communicated' (II, 306); 'even in the most favourable circumstances, people could hardly communicate with each other at all' (III, 218). And this is more than criticism of some particular social use of language, it is language itself which is the object of a radical distrust. Language classifies, fixes, defines, producing a common ground of meaning that misses individuality, uniqueness, real meaning: 'language is the only way of expressing anything and it dims everything' (II, 99). What language does is to make statements, but statements have nothing to do with the movement of my thoughts and experiences, all the impressions of life: 'Anything that can be put into propositions is suspect. The only thing that isn't suspect is individuality' (IV, 328). To put it another way, language is technical, a kind of dull jargon which because of its necessary generality is always wrong, never fits the particular case: 'Every word. In telling things, technical terms must be used; which never quite apply' (III, 285). So that one is writing in the end for silence: caught in language, 'the only way of expressing anything', aware of its hopelessness, 'it dims everything', and then committed nevertheless to seize out of it some essential expression, to make space for the individual, to give 'the original contents of [a] mind': writing then as the project of that, falling into the silences.

At one point during the seduction, Hypo calls Miriam 'pretty':

> 'You *are* a pretty creature, Miriam. I wish you could see yourself.'
>
> With the eyes of Amabel, and with her own eyes opened by Amabel, she saw the long honey-coloured ropes of hair framing the face that Amabel found beautiful in its 'Flemish Madonna' type, falling across her shoulders and along her body where the last foot of their length, red-gold, gleamed marvellously against the rose-tinted velvety gleaming of her flesh. Saw the lines and curves of her limbs, their balance and harmony. Impersonally beautiful and inspiring. To him each detail was 'pretty', and the whole an object of desire. [IV, 231]

'Pretty' is his *observation*; he can only see, has only a linguistic vision of things. Thus the relationship between Miriam and the Amabel mentioned in the passage is picked up at once by his 'intelligent eye, blinkered in advance with unsound generalizations about "these intense, over-personal feminine friendships" ' (IV, 315). But for Miriam and the reader the relationship with Amabel is never exactly defined; or rather, it is exactly defined precisely in as much as it is not dropped into any generalisation, is removed from any summary definition. Seeing through the experience of Amabel, 'her own eyes opened by Amabel', Miriam – and the reader with her – sees differently, away from 'the clumsy masculine machinery of observation' (IV, 315).

The distrust of language goes along then with an opposition between women and men, and that opposition finds indeed political and social articulation in the book. The writing often engages through Miriam militant positions and offers a violent reaction to men and their world, to their impossible repression: 'They despise women and they want to go on living – to reproduce – themselves. None of their achievements, no "civilization", no art, no science can redeem that. There is no pardon possible for man. The only answer to them is suicide; all women ought to agree to commit suicide' (II, 221). Elsewhere it marks through her a distance from militancy: the experience of the suffragette demonstrations is recorded through Amabel's participation as mediated by Miriam's removed and doubtful consciousness. Hers is an 'intermittent feminism' (IV, 504), intermittent because the commitment is to individuality, the unique complex of oneself, and because of an extreme version of the essential untouchability of women, their radical separation, something that feminists – 'an insult to womanhood' – fail to grasp: 'Those women's rights people are the worst of all. Because they think women have been "subject" in the past. Women never have been subject. Never can be. . . . Disabilities, imposed by law, are a stupid insult to women, but have never touched them as individuals' (III, 218).

The opposition between women and men, their difference, is thus crucial, and crucial with regard to language and meaning. Everywhere one has 'this muddle of men and women with nothing in common' (I, 376); throughout Miriam is confirmed in 'her certainty that between men and women there can be no direct communication' (IV, 223). Indeed, they speak different languages: 'She may understand his. Hers he will never speak nor understand. In pity, or from other motives, she must therefore, stammeringly, speak his. He listens and is flattered and thinks he has her mental measure when he has not touched even the fringe of her consciousness' (II, 210). Miriam moves her friend Michael to uneasy anger by her insistence that women 'can't be repre- sented by men. Because by every word they use men and women mean different things' (IV, 93).

Women must speak in their own language, but the opposition between women and men is accompanied by the distrust anyway of language: there is no communication between the sexes, but there is no communication in language either, 'nothing can ever be communicated'. Is language then irredeemably male? Men and language deal in statements; men and their books, sums of language, close things up, finish off: 'Clever phrases that make you see things by a deliberate arrangement, leave an impression that is false to life. But men do see life in this way, disposing of things and rushing on with their talk; they think like that, all their thoughts false to life; everything neatly described in single phrases that are not true. Starting with a false statement, they go on piling up their books' (III, 14). To learn this language – but is there any other? – is to fit with men, quoting the surface as ' "clever" women' do: 'To write books, knowing all about style, would be to become like a man' (II, 131).

In a famous passage of her review of *Revolving Lights*, Virginia Woolf spoke of Richardson's invention of a woman's sentence:

> She has invented, or, if she has not invented, developed and applied to her own uses, a sentence which we might call the psychological sentence of the feminine gender. It is of a more elastic fibre than the old, capable of stretching to the extreme, of suspending the frailest particles, of enveloping the vaguest shapes. Other writers of the opposite sex have used sentences of this description and stretched them to the extreme. But there is a difference. Miss Richardson has fashioned her sentence consciously, in order that it may descend to the depths and investigate the crannies of Miriam Henderson's consciousness. It is a woman's sentence, but only in the sense that it is used to describe a woman's mind by a writer who is neither proud nor afraid of anything that she may discover in the psychology of her sex.[15]

It is a passage that is worth holding on to in all its nuances and turns: a woman's sentence, but not because it is in its very form some essential expression of the woman writer, since men can write such sentences too; a woman's sentence because it is used to explore a woman's mind; but then again too because it is rooted in 'the psychology of her sex', because there *is* the difference, some feel of an essence that allows its identification nevertheless as 'the psychological sentence of the feminine gender'. On the one hand for Richardson, 'Everybody is a special category' (IV, 327); on the other, but at the same time, as it were, women share a common silence, a common elsewhereness to assertion and position, what Richardson calls in an article on 'Leadership in Marriage' their ' "shapeless" shapeliness'.[16]

Men's writing is a refusal of this, and a relief from it: 'It is because these men *write* so well that it is a relief, from looking and enduring the clamour of the way things state themselves from several points of view simultaneously, to read their large superficial statements. Light seems to come. . . . But the after reflection is gloom, a poisoning gloom over everything' (III, 275). Reality is multifarious, a mesh of diffuse and diverging intensities beyond statement or position. What is needed is a sentence, a writing, that can suspend the frailest particles, stretch to the extreme, envelop the vaguest shapes. And this is a sentence of the feminine gender, for women are multifarious, essentially beyond statements, positions ('women can hold all opinions at once, or any, or none': III, 259). What Sinclair calls 'stream of consciousness' in Richardson is thus a critique of the idea of the novel, a perception of reality, and a psychology of women.

The 'female psyche' is one of the great concerns of the early decades of the twentieth century when Richardson is living and writing, a concern contemporary with the powerful development of women's struggles to change their condition and definition: on the one hand, it is part of those struggles, raising questions of the reality of women's experience and of new representations; on the other, it is a reaction to them, attempting to make up the old fictions of identity, confirm the place of 'the woman'. It is in this context that the issue of *The Adelphi* to which Richardson contributes an article 'About Punctuation' will also contain a piece on 'The Ugliness of Women' ('I believe that in every woman born there is a seed of terrible, unmentionable evil'),[17] or that D.H. Lawrence in the 1920s will be writing popular newspaper features with titles such as 'The Real Trouble About Women' and 'Women Don't Change' ('women are women').[18] Psychoanalysis is important here too, serving largely to set out the terms of debate with its new conception of sexuality and its particular methods for exploring and understanding the psychical apparatus. Richardson herself was fully aware of this: one of her good friends, Barbara Low, was a psychoanalyst and the author of *Psycho-Analysis: A Brief Account of the Freudian Theory*, which she reviewed in 1920 for *Dental Record*; another close friend, Winifred Bryher, was analysed by Hanns Sachs and the latter wrote on psychoanalysis and film for *Close Up*. Barbara Low, moreover, enthused over Lawrence's *The Rainbow*, read in manuscript, when she first met Richardson in 1915; Richardson then sent *Pointed Roofs* to Lawrence's publisher, Duckworth, where the reader, Edward Garnett, judged it 'feminine impressionism' and recommended its acceptance.[19] These intellectual and literary interconnections thus bring us back to the novel, itself massively caught up in the concern with woman and her representation: Wells' *Ann Veronica* is one kind of example, Joyce's *Ulysses* another, with its final 'female monologue' as Molly–Penelope lies musing in bed praised by Jung, no less, as 'a string of veritable psychological peaches'.[20]

Richardson's work is near to all this (we should note, just to continue the interconnections, that sections from *Interim* were published alongside episodes from *Ulysses* in *The Little Review* in 1919–20 which also ran articles comparing Richardson and Joyce[21]). When John Cowper Powys talks of Richardson bringing to light 'a complete continent, a submerged Lost Atlantis of feminine susceptibility', there is no great distance from Jung's praise of Molly's monologue, Arnold Bennett's for Joyce's supreme understanding of 'feminine psychology'.[22] And this is not simply a male image, not simply a determined misreading. Richardson herself uses phrases of this kind and can refer to Jung's work to do so, defining 'the unique gift of the feminine psyche' and discussing 'the essential characteristic of the womanly woman'.[23] The ' "shapeless" shapeliness' mentioned earlier is another such identification of woman, and *Pilgrimage* anyway, as was seen, is everywhere involved in questions of the nature of women and men, their difference and separation. *Pilgrimage* is not the *Confessions of a Woman* Miriam is advised to write, but at the same time it has something nevertheless of a reality of that title; 'a lifetime might be well spent in annotating the male novelists, filling out the vast oblivions in them' (IV, 240) and that is at once part of the dissatisfaction with the novel and Hypo's contents-of-the-cruet slots but also a part of the project of Richardson's novel, part of how it reads. Resistance is the risk of essence, the opposition turns on an alternative representation that is always potentially another definition, another given place.

The same Virginia Woolf who commended Richardson's invention of 'the psychological sentence of the feminine gender' also believed that 'It is fatal for anyone who writes to think of their sex' and that the act of writing is androgynous, the writer male and female together.[24] Powys said something the same about

Richardson specifically: 'All authentic human genius is, in some degree, bi-sexual. . . . she is the first *consciously to turn the two elements upon each other* in a reciprocal fury of psychological interpretation'.[25] These notions of androgyny and bisexuality, however, are still bound up with thinking of sex, male plus female, female plus male; are still locked into assumptions – ideas, positions, representations – of the one and the other. An aspect of the fatality is then precisely the difficulty of distinguishing the alternative from the accepted representation and of avoiding the mere repetition, but now as value, of the place already assigned as limitation: men are on the side of language and classification and statement; women are elsewhere, but this is an old story of the illogical, emotional woman; women have a shapeless shapeliness, and this too has been heard before, men make shapes, stand out erect, women flow, like ALP in the closing pages of *Finnegans Wake*. Joyce famously leaves the Molly chapter of *Ulysses* unpunctuated, eight long unstopped sentences until the final 'Yes.': 'Do you notice how women when they write disregard stops and capital letters?';[26] Richardson agrees: 'Feminine prose, as Charles Dickens and James Joyce have delightfully shown themselves to be aware, should properly be unpunctuated, moving from point to point without formal obstructions' (I, 12). But why should this be if not by reference to the representation of women as 'the woman', 'the feminine', as unformed, fluid, inconsistent?

In her essay 'About Punctuation', also referred to in the 1938 'Foreword', just after the remark on feminine prose quoted above, Richardson makes a different emphasis: 'in the slow, attentive reading demanded by unpunctuated texts, the faculty of hearing has its chance, is enhanced until the text *speaks* itself'.[27] Punctuation as we know it is developed concomitantly with print, with the *book*, moving from a foundation in the encounter of voice and language to a logic of truth and its subject (punctuating for 'the better understanding of the sense' as opposed to 'for the ease of breath' is not a common conception in English, for example, until the beginning of the eighteenth century, when it goes along with the general desire to 'fix' the language as a stable instrument for a free exchange between speaking subjects grounded in universal reason, common sense).[28] Without punctuation there is no single point of view; without punctuation the text speaks itself: multiple possibilities all at once, no one subject, no standard communication (early in *Pilgrimage* Miriam is offended by the word 'standard', as in 'standard book': 'It suggested fixed agreement about the things people ought to know and that she felt sure must be wrong, and not only wrong but "common" . . . standard readers. . . .' I, 235). What Richardson is emphasising is again the question of identity and the fictions of its stability, its representation, in which the novel, books, talk, language itself all participate, with which they are complicit. So *Pilgrimage* is non-standard (compare *Ann Veronica*): no endings (the last of the book–chapters stops on a question, none of them comes to any conclusion), no go-ahead narrative timing (the chapters are more and more unparaphrasable, resistant to any summary), ellipses and fragments, long intricately claused and variformly punctuated sentences, 'an astonishing variety of patterns'.[29]

This it is that is simultaneously referred, and by Richardson herself, to 'the feminine', and we can perhaps grasp why it should be that modern writing in the novel runs into such a reference. Language itself is neither male nor female, but nor is it simply neutral: it exists only in use, which is to say in specific orders of discourse, and these bring with them, among other things, specific representations of their speaking subject. The stabilisation of language in respect of 'communication', 'free exchange', 'instrument' for the transmission of a general knowledge, a unity of 'thoughts', is the institution of a subject position that eradicates all contradictions of class and sexual differences: indifferent, a function of the general knowledge, the subject is male; women are relegated to any excess of language, any disturbance of the norm – female illogicality, diffuseness and so on. The novel, on the basis of this stable language and increasingly invested in as a crucial social mechanism, makes sense in the area of subjectivity, deals with the problems of the relations between the social and the individual, *represents*. Part of that representation importantly is the maintenance of the identity of the woman, stories, explorations, definitions that repeat and renew her place as a condition of the smooth operation of the whole system. 'Bang, bang, bang', Miriam's words to Hypo, novels issue statements, set out the terms of the available reality.

To challenge that is then quickly to write 'feminine', in contradiction, differently, to the established forms and fictions; Molly and ALP are inevitably the end of Joyce's two great texts as modern writing. Yet here, in this, the challenge works and jams; the given identities are called into question and are ever-present; opposition takes its stand on the old position. 'Male' and 'female', their identification, 'the man' and 'the woman', are after all the guarantee of stability, the very standard: the one and the other, different, unknown, the submerged continent, the formless, and so on and on. The moment the writing goes 'feminine', uses that as its point of displacement, it turns from the Wells novel but can also say the same thing. The chorus of over-eager male praise for Joyce's achievement at the end of *Ulysses* is indicative and right – Joyce has (re-)produced 'the woman' (and so the identity of 'the man' with her).

The interest and power of Richardson's work is that it intersects with this modern writing in the novel – is itself a major example – and provides a radical edge to what effectively becomes the stock reference to 'the feminine', 'the woman', breaks that *image*. *Pilgrimage* is full of a psyche and a psychology, common terms, to which at the same time in its writing it never gives a final hold. Reviewing *Clear Horizon* for *Scrutiny* in 1935, Q.D. Leavis wrote of Richardson that 'her pre-occupations date already as being those of a period when woman – as distinct from individual women – was a matter for defiant assertion'.[30] But this is quite wrong: woman was a concern and Richardson was concerned in the debates, and without condescension or dismissiveness, aware of their political importance; yet her essential value was always the individual, the intensity of a particular life, a unique reality ('independently assertive'). 'We all have different sets of realities', says Miriam to Hypo, who replies inevitably 'That, believe me, is impossible' (IV, 309). Writing her life, Miriam's life, Richardson is involved in and against that impossibility, a process of self-discovery. Individuality, the fact of *my* experience, is not outside but through language, existing forms, social modes; essence is a production in and with all the matter of reality, has a history in history: Richardson makes out a complex historical consciousness – personal, social and political necessarily all interwoven and traced into one another. What is important, the resistance, is to break the fixity of representations, their given identities, where one is 'called upon' (III, 239) to be; and the crux of that fixity, the

143

hold of the system, is the very proposition of 'one' – as though *I* were some figure from a novel, like Ann Veronica, and not a Miriam, a myriad of moments and intensities and inflections – and with it 'the man'/'the woman', the basic assumption of oneness, one and other, the difference on which identity can turn – so that to resist fixity, where I am called upon as *one*, is also and immediately to call into question the representation of sexual difference, fighting strongly through life and book against the oppression it sustains and writing for the individual.

What Lawrence dismissed as childish absorption is here, in fact, a kind of utopia of individuality, offered to the reader as such, as that experience. To write is to forsake life and to project the terms of its reality. 'Contemplation is adventure into discovery; reality' (IV, 657): writing is the form of contemplation, the fundamental silence. 'Fully to recognize, one must be alone' (IV, 657): writer and reader together, caught up in a movement, in the dispersion of writing, out of place, as on 'neutral territory, where one can forget one is there, and be everywhere' (IV, 657). *Pilgrimage* – writing for silence.

NOTES

1 D.H. Lawrence, 'Surgery for the Novel – or a Bomb' (1923), in Edward D. McDonald (ed.), *Pheonix*, London, Heinemann, 1961, pp. 517–18.

2 Dorothy M. Richardson, 'Adventure for Readers', *Life and Letters*, July 1939, no. 22, pp. 45–52.

3 Dorothy M. Richardson, 'Foreword' (1938), *Pilgrimage*, London, Virago, 1979, vol. I, pp. 10–12. All further references to *Pilgrimage* are to this Virago edition in four volumes and are incorporated in the text, specifying first volume and then page number. *Pilgrimage* was first published as a series of separate novels as follows: *Pointed Roofs* (1915); *Backwater* (1916); *Honeycomb* (1917); *The Tunnel* (1919); *Interim* (1919); *Deadlock* (1921); *Revolving Lights* (1923); *The Trap* (1925); *Oberland* (1927); *Dawn's Left Hand* (1931); *Clear Horizon* (1935); *Dimple Hill* was included in the first collected edition (1938); *March Moonlight* with the second collected edition (1967).

4 J.C. Powys, *Dorothy M. Richardson*, London, Joiner & Steele, 1931, p. 46.

5 S. Freud, 'Creative Writers and Day-Dreaming' (1908), *The Standard Edition of the Complete Psychological Works of Sigmund Freud*, London, Hogarth Press, 1959, vol. IX, p. 150.

6 M. Allott, *Novelists on the Novel*, London, Routledge & Kegan Paul, 1965, p. 196.

7 Dorothy M. Richardson, 'Continuous Performance: Narcissus', *Close Up*, September 1931, p. 183.

8 Letter to Wells from Frederick Macmillan (October 1908), cit. Norman Mackenzie and Jeanne Mackenzie, *The Time Traveller: The Life of H.G. Wells*, London, Weidenfeld & Nicolson, 1973, p. 248.

9 Letter from Wells to Macmillan (September 1908), cit. Mackenzie and Mackenzie, op cit., p. 235.

10 H.G. Wells, *Ann Veronica* (1909), London, Virago, 1980, pp. 295, 206.

11 In the shifting movement of *Finnegans Wake*, A comedy of letters!' (James Joyce, *Finnegans Wake* (1939), London, Faber & Faber, 1968, p. 425), 'Joyce' as a name never appears; only a series of transformations – 'joyicity' (p. 414), for example – that are never brought down to the 'proper name': 'since in this scherzarade of one's thousand one nightinesses that sword of certainty which would indentifide the body never falls' (p. 51). As for *A la recherche du temps perdu*, the name 'Marcel' in relation to the hero is used only twice in a text of some 3,500 pages, both times obliquely in the description of phrases employed by Albertine (Marcel Proust, *A la recherche du temps perdu* (1913–27), Paris, Gallimard 'Pléiade', 1966, vol. III, pp. 75, 157). Manuscript corrections to various sets of proofs for *A la recherche* suggest that Proust might have come to remove even these mentions; cf. Michihiko Suzuki, 'Le "je" proustien', *Bulletin de la Société des Amis de Marcel Proust*, 1959, no. 9, p. 74. The name 'Miriam' occurs more frequently in *Pilgrimage*, in conversational remarks addressed to her but also in the narration itself ('Getting close to the radiator, Miriam moved into a fathomless gentleness', IV, 43); Richardson's strategy is to drift the name across a peculiar created voice of record and analysis, as though somewhere between the first and third person, which leaves 'Miriam'

loose in the writing, a function of its movement.

12 V. Woolf, review of *The Tunnel* (1919), *Contemporary Writers*, London, Hogarth Press, 1965, p. 122.

13 M. Proust, *A la recherche du temps perdu*, vol. III, pp. 879, 880, 895.

14 'Nothing happens. It is just life going on and on. It is Miriam Henderson's stream of consciousness going on and on. . . . In identifying herself with this life, which is Miriam's stream of consciousness, Miss Richardson produces her effect of being the first, of getting closer to reality than any of our novelists who are trying so desperately to get close.' M. Sinclair, 'The Novels of Dorothy Richardson', *The Egoist*, April 1918, vol. 5, no. 4, p. 58, and *The Little Review*, April 1918, vol. V, no. 12, p. 6.

15 V. Woolf, 'Romance and the Heart' (1923), *Contemporary Writers*, pp. 124–5.

16 Dorothy Richardson, 'Leadership in Marriage', *The New Adelphi*, June–August 1929, vol. II, no. 4, p. 347 ('her state of being "all over the place" ', p. 345).

17 J.H.R., 'The Ugliness of Women', *The Adelphi*, April 1924, vol. I, no. 11, p. 1025.

18 D.H. Lawrence, 'The Real Trouble About Women', *Daily Express*, 19 June 1929; subsequently titled 'Give Her a Pattern', in Warren Roberts and Harry T. Moore (eds), *Phoenix II*, London, Heinemann, 1968, pp. 533–8; 'Women Don't Change', *Sunday Dispatch*, 28 April 1929; subsequently titled 'Do Women Change?', in *Pheonix II*, pp. 539–42 (quotation p. 539).

19 Cf. Gloria G. Fromm, *Dorothy Richardson: A Biography*, Urbana, Ill., University of Illinois Press, 1977, p. 77.

20 C.G. Jung, letter to Joyce (27 September 1932), cit. R. Ellmann, *James Joyce*, New York, Oxford University Press, 1959, p. 642.

21 Cf. e.g. William Carlos Williams, 'Four Foreigners', *The Little Review*, September 1919, vol. VI, no. 5, pp. 36–9.

22 Powys, op. cit., p. 29; Arnold Bennett, review of *Ulysses* in *The Outlook* (29 April 1922), in Robert H. Deming (ed.), *James Joyce: The Critical Heritage*, London, Routledge & Kegan Paul, 1970, vol. I, p. 221.

23 Richardson, 'Leadership in Marriage', p. 347; reference to Jung, p. 346.

24 V. Woolf, *A Room of One's Own* (1929), St Albans & London, Granada, 1977, p. 99.

25 Powys, op. cit., pp. 8–9.

26 James Joyce, letter to Stanislas Joyce (9 October 1906), in R. Ellmann (ed.), *Letters of James Joyce, Volume II*, New York, Viking Press, 1966, p. 173.

27 Dorothy Richardson, 'About Punctuation', *The Adelphi*, April 1924, vol. I, no. 11, p. 990.

28 The quoted phrases are from Michael Maittaire, *The English Grammar* (1712), cit. Murray Cohen, *Sensible Words: Linguistic Practice in England 1640–1785*, Baltimore, Johns Hopkins University Press, 1977, p. 51; Cohen discusses this development in punctuation, pp. 50–3.

29 This phrase is borrowed from Dorothy Richardson's 'Leadership in Marriage' (p. 346), where it comes at the end of a sentence that is itself an example of the characteristic shifting intricacy, turning any position into a complex process of qualifications. As Miriam reflects, 'If only one could speak as quickly as one's thoughts flashed, and several thoughts together, all with a separate life of their own and yet belonging. . . .' (III, 218).

30 Q.D. Leavis, review of *Clear Horizon*, *Scrutiny*, December 1935, vol. IV, no. 3, p. 329.

9 Voices of patriarchy: Gabriel García Márquez' *One Hundred Years of Solitude*

Susanne Kappeler

Praise of Márquez' novel is almost unanimous. Its sales records and multiple translation attest to the worldwide gratitude for a modern masterpiece, one that satisfies not just the refined tastes of academic *jouisseurs*, but equally the broader desire for the pleasure of reading. It may be *lisible* in comparison to the *nouveau roman*, but it does not for that reason fall within the category below the very best. On the contrary, its 'readability' is employed in the service of its keener pleasure, bursting the binary opposition between readable pleasure and the ecstasy of writing–reading.

The novel's delightful readability is its ploy of seduction; not the wily seduction of the innocent, but the conscious seduction between consenting partners who know where it is leading. In literary historical terms the seductive factor is epic. Yet the twentieth-century reader knows that this is not the era of epics; and Márquez knows it too.

Epic features are unmistakably present in *One Hundred Years of Solitude*, and most uncontestably, I would argue, in the first part of the book. There, the word is absolutely the Word, in a brazen assertiveness that allows no self-consciousness of a subject: it is the bona fide word of storytelling. The question, 'Who is speaking?' is beside the point in the presence of such authority of representation. We can hardly even speak of a voice in the singular, just as there is no 'viewpoint'. 'Representation' bespeaks post-epic awareness of a gap, a possible tension between *histoire* and *récit*. The truly epic word, however, does not represent: it speaks what *is*, and only that is which is spoken. Presenting, the epic is its own and only present, albeit in the narrative past tense; and even when it shifts into the past, we find ourselves once more in the present of that past, as in the cinematic cut to a flashback. Auerbach has made such a flashback in the *Odyssey* famous, sharply distinguishing the interpolated account of how Odysseus came by his scar from the psychological perspective of a memory.[1] No one actively recalls this story, neither Odysseus himself, nor the nurse Euryclea who recognises him by the scar: it is the epic voice itself which shifts into the present of that past event, with no linking through perspective, no view other than to what is in the focus of its present.

Characteristically, the epic mode strikes the modern reader as in a certain measure naive; though the term need not be pejorative. Rather, that *naïveté* is charming and endearing in its simplicity – the very voice of the childhood of literature. As with the child, time and space exist only within its own presence. But the epic word takes the utmost liberty in choosing its focus, taking the large grand view of the world at its beginning, or zooming in on to the minutiae of a specific afternoon in Macondo, Casa Buendía. 'The world was so recent that many things lacked names, and in order to indicate them it was necessary to point' (p. 9).[2] From the childhood of the world to the routine of years: 'Every year during the month of March a family of ragged gypsies would set up their tents, and with a great uproar of pipes and kettledrums they would display new inventions' (p. 9). Zooming in still further to the very afternoon in March of the year when 'they brought the magnet'. And on it goes on an even plane in the full present and presence of the entire scene of dialogue between Melchíades and José Arcadio Buendía, and the transaction which makes the magnet José Arcadio's. An occasional 'flash-forward' defines the present from the other side: 'Many years later, as he faced the firing squad, Colonel Aureliano Buendía was to remember that distant afternoon . . .' (p. 9). The narrative voice dwells on the lives and deaths of its favourite characters, or sums up the lives of less favoured ones in a single sentence, with the goal orientation characteristic of early narrative.[3] Its voice is life, and it bestows it only on those of whom it speaks, and who come to life only at its wilful call.

Amaranta, that shadow figure in the Buendía household and almost step-great-great-grandmother of Gabriel García

Márquez, is an obvious victim of epic arbitration. She exists only sparingly, in glimpses: we see her fleetingly 'lying in a wicker basket', abandoned by her mother who left her in search of her runaway son (p. 36). Then the care of her and of her coeval nephew is 'relegated to a secondary level', and having been left in the charge of the Guajiro Indian woman Visitacion, the two are raised on lizard broth and spider eggs and the Guajiro language (p. 38). Amaranta is briefly brought to the fore on the arrival of her companion-to-be Rebeca, with whom, now as a twosome, she sinks back again into narrative oblivion. Until one day when Úrsula looks up from her busy manufacture of candy animals: 'she looked distractedly towards the courtyard ... and she saw two unknown and beautiful adolescent girls doing frame embroidery in the light of the sunset' (p. 51). Úrsula's vision turns into her recognition of the girls' approaching nubility, which in turn leads first of all to her feverish enlargement of the house to accommodate future children's children. This in turn leads to the discovery of the residence in Macondo of a magistrate sent by the government. These events at once take over the narrative, or the narrative takes over these events and abandons again the lives of the two glimpsed girls.

Yet this arbitrary omnipotence of the epic is distinct from the omniscience of the nineteenth-century realist author. *His* or *her* view is the large and all-encompassing wisdom of the Creator of a universe, a gaze full of responsibility, control and order. The epic voice by contrast has the exaltation of youth, and if it is not exactly irresponsible (a characteristic perhaps more of post-realism), it is capricious and unashamed of its own ignorance and omissions. 'Epic is life, immanence, and the empirical', says Lukács in *Die Theorie des Romans*: it need not strive for the transcendence to God's view of the universe. Epic is life chronicled, rather than historicised, if we understand chronicle as 'a conjunction of non-causal singular statements which expressly mention [the] subject',[4] and history as explanatory interpretation of events. Such definitions are difficult, since even the chronicle, and certainly the epic, contain a rudimentary causality, though one that would not satisfy the 'objective' criteria of history. The epic chronicler in fact enjoys the privilege of assertion without having to supply his sources.

Thus the chronicling voice of *One Hundred Years of Solitude* may assert that 'Actually, Remedios the Beauty was not a creature of this world' (p. 164), and that 'Actually, [the muttering Aureliano Segundo] was talking to Melchíades' (p. 288). Actually Melchíades is dead; he has already died twice, and was buried as the first deceased in Macondo. Again, the epic voice may introduce its report with the boldness of 'That was what happened' (p. 160), and yet fail to give an account of who 'actually' sent that spurious letter announcing the death of Pietro Crespi's mother on the eve of his wedding to Rebeca. This voice may carry the aplomb of the General Truth, as in 'Then [Aureliano Segundo] married, as all sons marry sooner or later' (p. 169). On the other hand, the chronicle may side with the opinion of its protagonist of the moment, drifting temporarily in the third-person form of his or her consciousness. Frequently, the chronicler leans on Úrsula's opinion, without always having to judge or correct it with what was 'actually' the case. It is Úrsula's suspicion that the twins (Aureliano Segundo and José Arcadio Segundo) 'had been shuffled like a deck of cards since childhood' (p. 153) and, when they finally settled into their respective identities, had got it exactly wrong. At least, Úrsula in her blind and visionary old age 're-examined her old memories and confirmed the belief that at some moment in childhood [José Arcadio] had changed places with his twin brother, because it was he and not the other one who should have been called Aureliano' (p. 214). No need for the chronicler to settle the question.

Similarly, comment and judgment can be withheld at convenience, and events be listed with the characteristic indifference of chronicle:

> When calm was restored [after the bloody carnival], not one of the false bedouins remained in town and there were many dead and wounded lying on the square: nine clowns, four Columbines, seventeen playing-card kings, one devil, three minstrels, two peers of France, and three Japanese empresses. [pp. 167–8]

No stance, just an inventory. Describing the merry goings-on in the Street of the Turks, 'gambling tables, shooting galleries', sooth-saying and 'tables of fried food and drinks' are effortlessly followed by the 'Sunday mornings [when] there were scattered on

151

the ground bodies that were sometimes those of happy drunk-
ards and more often those of onlookers felled by shots, fists,
knives and bottles during the brawls' (p. 188). But from these
dead the narrative voice returns quickly and unperturbedly to the
living, for its business is life. Life includes, moreover, the categories of magic or the supernatural, which the chronicler exercises his right of asserting. The faithful ghost of Prudencio
Aguilar *is there*, in the Beundías' courtyard or bathroom, 'with his
sad expression' (p. 25), just as towards the end of José Arcadio
Buendía's life he is, 'actually, the only person with whom [José
Arcadio] was able to have contact' (p. 119). José Arcadio Buendía
has long become susceptible to the '*status quartus materiae*', the
fourth dimension, which he enters as easily as the Latin language
he has never learnt. José Arcadio Buendía himself will remain, in
stato quarto, under the chestnut tree after his death, perceived by
everyone except his obstinate and solitary son, the old Colonel
Aureliano, who urinates in primal fashion exactly under that
chestnut tree (p. 211). Aureliano was born with a sense of premonition, but premonitions and omens 'abandoned him' (p. 109)
after that last inspiration to demand that his death sentence be
carried out in Macondo, where indeed he survives it. But the
supernatural does not exclusively concern death and the lonely
dead who seek the company of the living, but is also pre-
eminently a part of life. It manifests itself most ebulliently in Petra
Cotes' 'supernatural proliferation' (p. 158), in her fecundity so
powerful as to generate progeny in her lover's cattle and multitude in his money chest, yet not, surprisingly, in herself.

Premonitions, omens and superstitions are often mentioned,
yet without the clarity of distinction from the 'real' or 'true' that
the modern reader would expect. Of Úrsula it is said: 'It was a
supposition that was so neat, so convincing that she identified it as
a premonition' (p. 145). A sentence spoken by a fluctuating subject, one that first identifies her idea as a supposition and then, as
if convinced, as a premonition proper. The reservation of the
first part is not sustained to the end of the sentence, where, for
consistency, it would have to read 'that she took it, or mistook it,
for a premonition'. To identify is a cognitive performative, fea-
sible only if, by definition, the identification is correct.

Consistency and non-contradiction are not, however, among
the goals or standards of the epic voice, whose only truth is that of

'life', of 'what happened', and whose order is the empirical rather than the structuration imposed on the empirical by a unitary subject. Indeed, the pattern of the sentence just quoted repeats itself on a larger scale, most crucially, for instance, in the episode of the three thousand workers and unionists at the station. Among them a Buendía, José Arcadio Segundo, is present, who thus provides a suitable locus for the epic narrative voice. Leaning imperceptibly on his consciousness, we learn of the gradual build-up of the strike, of the tensions and confrontations, and of the intervention by the army. And we share in the depiction of those soldiers who 'were all identical, sons of the same bitch', and who 'with the same stolidity . . . all bore the weight of their packs and canteens, the shame of their rifles with fixed bayonets, and the chancre of blind obedience and a sense of honour' (p. 246). And we live through the horror of the massacre at the station from within, always close to José Arcadio Segundo, who is 'the only survivor' (p. 253). But then the chronicle returns to its impartial business and voices as conscientiously 'the official version' (p. 252): 'there was no dead [sic], the satisfied workers had gone back to their families, and the banana company was suspending all activity until the rains stopped'. ' "You must have been dreaming," the officers insisted. "Nothing has happened in Macondo, nothing has ever happened, and nothing will ever happen. This is a happy town" ' (p. 252). Such is the power of the official word, as it was dispensed from the higher courts already earlier, when 'it was established and set down in solemn decrees that the workers [who were the plaintiffs] did not exist' (p. 246). We recognise this voice of political dictatorship and terrorism, as we recognise the silence of fear and acquiescence in its citizens and victims. The epic voice, however, is devoid of such recognition. It turns against its own earlier account, gainsaying it with 'the official version' and refusing to arbitrate with its elsewhere available 'actually, that was what happened'. José Arcadio Segundo is transposed into the hiding place of the fourth dimension, where the 'supernatural light' of Melchíades' room protects him from the sight of the searching military, although he is plainly seen by his trembling mother Santa Sofía de la Piedad and his twin brother Aureliano Segundo (pp. 253–4). The only narrative remnant of the massacre is José Arcadio Segundo's persistent memory, the subjective knowledge of the sole survivor. For the narrative voice is that of

153

chronicle, and not that of an investigative journalist or an omni-scient Author, who would have questioned the workers' families or counted the inhabitants of Macondo. The banana company is said to have suspended all activity 'until the rains stopped', and not, one notes, because there might not have been any workers left to take up such activity. As it happens, the rains go on for 'four years, eleven months and two days' (p. 256), after which the banana company packs up and disappears for ever.

In terms of a proper epic we should not, of course, ask after what is omitted, since all there is, and all that matters, is the narrative itself. Yet the open conflict of these self-contradictory voices pressingly raises the question of 'epic *naïveté*'. Adorno traces the roots of epic *naïeté* and follows its transformation in the later descendant of the epic, the bourgeois novel.[5] *Mythos* and narrative are in fundamental opposition, the former the embodi-ment of the ever-same, the latter, the *telos*, the dimension of difference and of the abstraction of rational discourse. Epic nar-rative, in Adorno's view, is the irresolvable attempt to capture the singular and concrete in the conceptual medium of generalis-ation. The reflection of this conflict in style makes it appear as silly, naive, unaware, and as clinging to the particular where it is already dissolving into the general – summed up by Adorno as *Urdummheit*. What traditionally is regarded as a bonus, the *naïveté* of the epic, becomes in his analysis the price. With the accuracy of description the epic tries to compensate for the falseness and untruth of discourse: the tricks of verisimilitude, 'history-likeness' (Kermode), 'reality effects' (Barthes).

Failure is thus immanent in the epic intention itself. The modern reader, moreover, no longer believes in the possibility of the project 'chronicle', the neutral and transparent presentation of 'things as they are'. Even the chronicle itself is necessarily historical, structuring, ordering, explaining its material in re-presentation, although one might call this an involuntary histori-ography. Above all, the epic chronicle contains the implicit assumption that the world makes sense, sense that is shared by its inhabitants and especially by its readers. The particular sense that the world of Macondo makes is the order of its unchallenged patriarchy. We have seen it innocently manifest in the general truth that 'all sons marry sooner or later', building the lines of children's children that are known 'by the house of their fathers'

(Numbers 1:18). It is the sons, too, who forge history, or at least events; who, in other words, together with their genealogies, make for epic narrative material. The women, in Macondo society as in the narrative, live in the kitchen, servicing and providing for their men of action. Amaranta, not even a bearer of children, appears only periodically to confirm an event, or to received into her care the child of one of the Buendía sons. The widowed Santa Sofía de la Piedad, 'the silent one, the condescending one, the one who never contradicted anyone, not even her own children' (p. 146), 'had that rare virtue of never existing completely except at the opportune moment' (p. 98). It is Úrsula, the matriarch, who holds a unique female position in that patriarchal texture. Her function in the narrative is primary, and not just the simple complement to that of her husband, the founding father José Arcadio Buendía. They may together stand at the apex of the family tree, yet while José Arcadio finds proliferating succession in his sons and grandsons, Úrsula is more like the stem which runs down that entire tree, supporting all its branches. Not until the advent of her great-great-granddaughter Amaranta Úrsula does she find even a partial heir to her name. The patriarchal line is defined by succession, by the chain of the houses of fathers, while the matriarchal function, it seems, is not so easily handed on, is possibly even unique. Hence, perhaps, Úrsula stays alive for well over a hundred years and for the greater part of the book, until the moment when her faith in the function and necessity of the matriarch begins to fade, and when her principal interest, to keep the family line going, begins to appear to her as dubious.

Curiously enough, it is Fernanda among the daughters-in-law who turns into the partial matriarchal successor as she takes over the rule of the house. Yet Fernanda's interpretation of that role introduces also a regime which is incompatible with, and indeed a travesty of, Úrsula's matriarchal values. Fernanda brings into the house the chilly breath of her bourgeois upbringing in the city, the funeral air of her rigorous etiquette and the prohibitive codex of her Saints' calendar. As domestic bursar and moral superintendent of the house she fulfils a fraction only of Úrsula's previous prodigious role.

It would lead too far to explore the full scope of Úrsula's matriarchal power and support, but we should consider the circumstances and implications of her abdication. Úrsula started out with the unquestioned values of patriarchy, focusing all her energy and attention on that prime patriarchal emblem, the House. She runs and maintains it, periodically rejuvenates and enlarges it, and effectively also provides the money, be it with her lucrative candy business or by burying assorted treasures in the garden for future necessities. Yet despite her own crucial function, her sense of rightness makes her fixate her hope on the men in her family. 'Head of the House' is a patriarchal title, to be filled, even if only nominally, by a male. Her own husband was early lost to the mundanities of domestic husbandry, squandering his time and the (first) family fortune in alchemical experiments. Her first son runs away with the gypsies, her second goes out to fight thirty-two futile civil wars. José Arcadio gets himself shot by a firing squad; Aureliano José, as well as the seventeen Aurelianos engendered during the thirty-two wars, incur the vengeance due to their father. Aureliano Segundo leaves the House to live with his mistress and spends his life feasting and drinking; José Arcadio Segundo becomes a worker at the banana company and a union leader soon bereft of workers and union. Those of the male Buendías who survive their abortive history-making end up retiring into the silver workshop or Melchíades' four-dimensional room, both shacks at the back of the House. It is about this time in the family history that something happens to Úrsula's unfailing good faith.

Intermittently she had been troubled by her repeated bad luck with her sons and their sons, as for instance when José Arcadio Segundo set out to build canals to cross the region by navigation which José Arcadio Buendía had tried to cross on foot.' "I know all this by heart," Úrsula would shout. "It's as if time had turned around and we were back at the beginning"' (p. 162). In her 'staggering old age' (p. 201), when she applies herself to turning her great-great-grandson José Arcadio into a future pope, her previous suspicion of the cyclical nature of time turns into the conviction of 'a progressive breakdown of time' (p. 201). The epic voice, however, adds a corrective to Úrsula's view: 'something that she herself could not really define and that she conceived confusedly as a progressive breakdown of time' (p. 201); and further on: 'The truth was that Úrsula resisted growing old even when she had already lost count of her age' (p. 201).

The original kind of time, the time of happy patriarchy and of happy epic narrative, was like a kind of space, the space of the eternal present. The passage of time would only flow through it evenly and calmly, as the ever-changing water through the river which remains the same. To Fernanda, 'one day seemed so much like another that one could not feel them pass' (p. 293). Characteristically, José Arcadio Buendía eventually falls into a trap of perpetual Mondays. 'He spent six hours examining things, trying to find a difference from their appearance on the previous day in the hope of discovering in them some change that would reveal the passage of time' (p. 71). But the space of time is left intact, untouched by any passage of time-flow. Many years later, his children's children gazing at Melchíades in the fourth dimension realise that it is

> always March there and always Monday, and then they understood that José Arcadio Buendía was not as crazy as the family said, but that he was the only one who had enough lucidity to sense the truth of the fact that time also stumbled and had accidents and could therefore splinter and leave an eternalized fragment in a room. [p. 283]

The time-flow may be dammed, or solidified and splintered like ice, that magic substance of José Arcadio Buendía's obsession and dreams. The young Aureliano, abandoned to his silversmith work, 'seemed to be taking refuge in some other time' (p. 48) as if it were another room.

The floods of rain bring a deluge of time – 'unbroken time . . ., relentless time, because it was useless to divide it into months and years, and the days into hours, when one could do nothing but contemplate the rain' (p. 261). Macondo is swamped by a pool of stagnant time, in which action, which is in need of moving time, becomes impossible. Waiting, the verb of duration, is the only one available to the subjects in this non-temporal discourse of activity. Aureliano Segundo and Petra Cotes cease to make love, and Úrsula is 'only waiting for the rain to stop in order to die' (p. 260). Even the transition to death is too active to be accomplished in this viscous medium of time.

The spatial, patriarchal time, like the present of the epic, is symmetrically abutted by the past and the future on either side. Memories and premonitions are the looking-glasses through

157

which they may both be glimpsed from the position of the present. When Macondo is stricken with the plague of insomnia, followed by the collective loss of memory, Pilar Ternera adapts her gift of cartomancy and reads 'the past in cards as she had read the future before' (p. 46).

Úrsula's first suspicion of something amiss with the common order of time is less a fundamental questioning of the spatial or patriarchal conception of time than a shifting of her attention towards the flowing element traversing the space of the present. Somewhere behind their backs, someone is redirecting the same old flow and letting it pass through their space again. Once, she had feared that that flow might dry up: ' "What's happening", she sighed, "is that the world is slowly coming to an end and those things [the annual visits of the gypsies] don't come here any more" ' (p. 154). Hence Úrsula, now in charge of the 'apprentice Supreme Pontiff' and suspecting a progressive breakdown of time, expresses her annoyance with 'this bad kind of time' (p. 201) in terms of her ingrained spatial conception of time, though complemented by her new awareness of the trick of the recycled flow. Time wears off, it seems, in this process of recycling, and the 'progressive breakdown' indicates a deterioration in the quality. Or even in the quantity, which, in a flow, is the same thing: 'When God did not make the same traps out of the months and years that the Turks used when they measured a yard of percale, things were different' (p. 205). ' "The years nowadays don't pass the way the old ones used to," she would say, feeling that everyday reality was slipping through her hands' (p. 201). What is wrong with this 'bad kind of time' is that it has lost its spaciousness, for you cannot fit as much into it as before. In the old days, 'after spending the whole day making candy animals, she had more than enough time for the children'; now, with nothing much to do and walking about all day with the little pope on her arm, she is compelled 'to leave things half done' (p. 201). Or remember the 'dying Colonel Aureliano Buendía, who after so much war and so much suffering from it [and after so many pages and chapters] was still not fifty years of age' (p. 201).

The subjects living in the expansive space of the continuous present relate in a curious manner to the flow of time that passes through it. Above all, growing old is something they do within that space, and has nothing or little to do with the passage of flowing time. Or it is something they don't do, as Úrsula, who resists growing old despite her hundred-odd years. Or Pilar Ternera, that deputy matriarch who is annexed to the House of Buendía like the stables or the granary in which she reads the cards of the first-generation sons, and who is 'also almost a hundred years old, but fit and agile in spite of her inconceivable fatness' (p. 205). Coping effortlessly with her blindness, Úrsula is merely annoyed and indignant at her clumsiness, deciding that it is 'not the first victory of decrepitude and darkness but a sentence passed by time' (p. 205) – another trick of the 'bad' time.

Úrsula is the only one to view the space time with the suspicion of the recycled flow. The other members of her family lose themselves in different corners of static time, in the 'attic of bad memories' (p. 158), in 'times reserved for oblivion, in labyrinths of disappointment' (p. 173), 'a trap of nostalgia' (p. 218), or in Melchíades' room of Mondays. With this new shift from the space of the present to the flow of passing time, however, Úrsula has taken the first step towards the discovery of history. The patriarchal order knows no history. It conceives itself as timeless, unchanging, ever-present. Its duration is filled with the anecdotes of events, with the episodes it celebrates in epics. We have seen the epic voice itself politely dissociate itself from Úrsula's subversive vision of time. The order of patriarchy has no history, it has a past represented in the present in ghosts and memories. For José Arcadio Buendía, the repetition of days or seasons or gypsies' visits only leads eventually to the solidification of his static conception of patriarchal time, a time that gets frozen into a perpetual Monday in March. For Úrsula, on the other hand, repetition becomes the trigger of suspicion:

> the insistent repetition of names had made her draw some conclusions that seemed to be certain. While the Aurelianos were withdrawn, but with lucid minds, the José Arcadios were impulsive and enterprising, but they were marked with a tragic sign. The only cases that were impossible to classify were those of José Arcadio Segundo and Aureliano Segundo [p. 152]

– the ones she thought must have been shuffled like a deck of cards. Drawing a lesson from history, 'she decided that no one again would be called Aureliano or José Arcadio' (p. 158). Yet she is overruled and the next child, son of Aureliano Segundo (who should have been José Arcadio Segundo), is named José Arcadio. Úrsula then draws the second lesson from history and decrees that he shall become 'a man who would never have heard talk of war, fighting cocks, bad women, or wild undertakings, four calamities that, according to what Úrsula thought, had determined the downfall of her line' (p. 158).

It was finally with her blindness that Úrsula acquired 'such clairvoyance as she examined the most insignificant happenings in the family that for the first time she saw clearly the truths that her busy life in former times had prevented her from seeing' (p. 203). She 'made a detailed recapitulation of life in the house since the founding of Macondo and . . . completely changed the opinion that she had always held of her descendants' (p. 203). There follows a whole page of Úrsula's revaluations (a page well worth quoting if space permitted) which shows these revaluations as *interpretations*. It is motivation for action, rather than deeds and effects, that now makes the new history of the Buendías. Thus it is pride rather than idealism that made Colonel Aureliano fight thirty-two wars, as it was pride rather than fatigue that made him lose them. Nor was it the suffering of the wars that made him withdraw from the family, but rather his fundamental 'incapacity for love' (p. 204). 'Amaranta, however, whose hardness of heart frightened her, whose concentrated bitterness made her bitter, suddenly became clear to her in the final analysis as the most tender woman who had ever existed', in whom the 'fear . . . of her own tormented heart had triumphed [in the] mortal struggle between a measureless love and an invincible cowardice' (p. 204). Comparison of repetition and a rebellious courage of interpretation turn Úrsula into the first historian in this book, an historian who overtakes even the epic chronicler who notes her findings down. It is not too surprising that the epic chronicler lags behind, chronicles her views without committing himself or approving them. For her history is also the history of patriarchy, and as such necessarily the critique of patriarchal order and the epic which it engenders. As the successive failures of the bearers of patriarchy are recorded, the values of their motivations are exposed. All that propelled them into action and out into the world, in turn rendered them incapable of love towards the family which is their very pride. Amaranta, the shadow figure of the House and of the narrative, is partially redeemed through the assessment of the vice of impossibility into which the patriarchal order condemned her. 'Rebeca, the one who had never fed on her milk . . ., the one who did not carry the blood of her veins in hers . . . Rebeca, the one with an impatient heart, the one with a fierce womb, was the only one who had the unbridled courage that Úrsula had wanted for her line' (p. 204). Rebeca, the unknown stranger dragging a bag with the bones of her parents, embodies the final verdict on patriarchy. And with it, for Úrsula, the judgment on her complementary matriarchal role and her ambition to nurture that line.

With history, the old past of patriarchy acquires a new dimension, as the desire to derive laws from the past to predict the future is the archetypal motivation of history. Memories are like the eidectic skills of Freud's *Deckerinnerungen*, static images that cover up what historical interpretation reveals, and they are 'devoid of lessons' (p. 214). On the other side of the present, history is complemented by prophecy, as the patriarchal memories are matched by glimpses of premonition. Prophecy is not the future, but the history of the future, the future perfect. Melchíades' parchments are the counterpart for the future to Úrsula's history of the past. 'No one must know their meaning until he has reached one hundred years of age' (p. 154), just as Úrsula had to become a centenarian before she began to know the meaning of history. And as her visionary sight came with blindness, so it is said of the parchments that 'the last man who read these books must have been Isaac the Blindman' (p. 297).

It is Aureliano, the 'Moses' who had been delivered in a basket from the nunnery, and who with his aunt Amaranta Úrsula engendered the last of the line, Aureliano with the tail of a pig, who will be the first and the last to read Melchíades' documents. When his pig-tailed son and cousin is devoured by the ants Úrsula had fought for over a hundred years, 'Melchíades' final keys were revealed to him and he saw the epigraph of the parchments perfectly placed in the order of man's time and space: *The first of the line is tied to a tree and the last is being eaten by the ants*' (p. 334). So he takes up his ordained task of deciphering the documents, which he can read without any difficulty although they are written in Melchíades' mother-tongue Sanskrit, and complicatedly encoded.

However, his desire to read 'his fate' (p. 334) and future is inseparable from his curiosity for his 'origin' (p. 335). His 'final protection', in the face of the imminent revelation of his fate, lies in 'the fact that Melchíades had not put events in the order of man's conventional time, but had concentrated a century of daily episodes, in such a way that they coexisted in one instant' (p. 335). He is protected, in other words, from the teleological linearity of ordinary narrative which could precipitate him prematurely into the abyss of his disclosed end. Thus he proceeds to read 'the chanted encyclicals' (p. 335) of Melchíades', not noticing the 'cyclonic' storm which uproots the House. 'He began to decipher the instant that he was living, deciphering it as he lived it, prophesying himself in the act of deciphering the last page' (p. 336). Before reaching the last line, however, he has understood that he will never leave this room, since it was foreseen that Macondo would be 'wiped out by the wind and exiled from the memory of men at the precise moment when Aureliano Babilonia would finish deciphering the parchments' (p. 336). The interpretation of the past and the history of the future conflate in that instance of the present where living and reading, historical being and its interpretation, merge together in an insoluble hermeneutical circle. Prophecy has joined history, squeezing out any tenable present for the subject Aureliano, shrinking the moment to the degree zero of total comprehension which can have no extension. For 'everything written ... was unrepeatable since time immemorial and forever more, because races condemned to one hundred years of solitude did not have a second opportunity on earth' (p. 336).

Aureliano Babilonia, with the gift of tongues and of deciphering, the first to be linked to the House of Buendía not through the house of his father but through his mother, is not one hundred years of age at the moment of this apocalypse. But with him as its last scion the Buendía patriarchy has come of age.

NOTES

1 Erich Auerbach, 'Odysseus' Scar', in *Mimesis*, Princeton University Press, 1953.
2 All references are to *One Hundred Years of Solitude*, trans. Gregory Rabassa, London, Pan Books, Picador edn, 1978.

3 Clemens Lugowski, *Die Form der Individualität im Roman* (1932), Frankfurt am Main, Suhrkamp Verlag, 1976, pp. 27–30. One of Lugowski's examples is on p. 27: '. . . gieng alssbaldt und ward ein Eremit . . .'; for an example in Márquez, see p. 238: 'A bullet lodged in his spinal column reduced him to his bed for the rest of his life'; or p. 242.

4 Morton White, *Foundations of Historical Knowledge*, New York, Harper & Row, 1965; quoted in Frank Kermode, *The Genesis of Secrecy*, Cambridge, Mass. and London, Harvard University Press, 1979, p. 103.

5 Theodor Adorno, 'Über epische Naivetät', in *Noten zur Literatur I*, Frankfurt am Main, Suhrkamp Verlag, 1958.

The editors, the author of 'Voices of Patriarchy: Gabriel García Márquez' *One Hundred Years of Solitude*' and the publishers wish to thank the following, who have kindly given permission for the use of copyright material: Harper & Row, Publishers, Inc., for extracts from *One Hundred Years of Solitude* by Gabriel García Márquez, translated by Gregory Rabassa. English translation copyright © 1970 by Harper & Row, Publishers, Inc.; Jonathan Cape Ltd, for extracts from *One Hundred Years of Solitude* by Gabriel García Márquez, translated by Gregory Rabassa. First published in Argentina 1967 by Editorial Sudamericana, S.A., Buenos Aires, under the title *Cien Años de Soledad*. First published in Great Britain 1970 by Jonathan Cape Ltd.

10 'Opinion' in *Troilus and Cressida*

Frank Kermode

'Opinion' is a complex word with a difficult history. When you consider the extent of its usage and the fluctuations of its meaning in varying contexts, you quickly discover that you must venture into areas of study more philosophical than literary, and into languages other than English. For the semantic spread of 'opinion' and of related words is not the effect of random linguistic change. It derives from deeply established ways of thinking about the truth of the world, and especially about statements concerning it, which may only seem to be true.

Troilus and Cressida is remarkable (among other things) for the intensity with which it dwells on the words 'opinion' and 'truth'.[1] It explores the conditions of knowledge and feeling which are suggested by the character of the relations between the two words, and between them and others. There are other plays by Shakespeare which seem in a measure obsessed by the semantics of a particular word: *Othello* by 'honest', *Hamlet* by 'act', *Macbeth* by 'time', *Coriolanus* by 'voice'. But *Troilus and Cressida*, so distinctive in other ways, is unique also in the degree to which its language is saturated by 'opinion' and by the various but interconnected ideas of which it is the centre. I shall try later to justify that word 'saturated'. But first I want to illustrate, of course much too simply and with inadequate documentation, the history and semantic range of the word 'opinion'.

Translators of St John's Gospel face, or ought to face, an interesting little problem when they come to 5:41. The Greek of that verse (*doxan para anthrōpōn ou lambanō*) can mean what the Authorised Version (AV) says it means: 'I receive not honour

164

from men'; but it can equally well mean 'I do not accept the
opinion of men', or 'I do not derive my opinion from men'. A
modern translator gives: 'Not that I accept human praise', which
is also correct.[2] The variety of sense to be legitimately discovered
in this simple Greek sentence may warn us that the word *doxa*,
'opinion', is very slippery. It would be fair to say that there is a
general preference for the first sense, as given by the AV and,
with small variation, by Brown and the New English Bible (NEB):
'I do not look to men for honour'. But the argument for 'I do not
accept the opinion of men', or something like it, is not negligible.
The context may even indicate a deliberate ambiguity. Three
verses later Jesus says – in the AV – 'How can ye believe, which
receive honour one of another, and seek not the honour that
cometh from God only?' The original is more accurately represented by NEB: 'How can you have faith so long as you receive
honour from one another, and care nothing for the honour that
comes from him who alone is God?' But both versions stick to the
word 'honour' to translate *doxa*, here distinguished by the context
into earthly and heavenly honour (*tēn doxan tōn anthrōpōn, ten
doxan tou theou*). This sharp distinction, here sharply expressed,
establishes a contrast which became traditional. Think, for
example, of these familiar lines from Milton's 'Lycidas'.

> Fame is no plant that grows on mortal soil,
> Nor in the glistering foil
> Set off to the world, nor in broad rumour lies,
> But lives and spreads aloft by those pure eyes
> And perfect witness of all-judging Jove;
> As he pronounces lastly on each deed,
> Of so much fame in heaven expect thy meed.

Here 'fame' in the opening line of the passage, and 'fame' in the
closing line, are both *doxa*, and have the same relation to one
another as *doxa* in John 5:44. The 'broad rumour' of the third line
could also be perfectly glossed as 'opinion' or translated into
Greek as *doxa*. Milton returned to the contrast between earthly
and heavenly *doxa* in *Paradise Regain'd*; when Satan offers Jesus
'fame and glory' (III, 25) he is always offering an earthly reward
which Jesus rejects in favour of a heavenly one.

> ... what is glory but the blaze of fame,
> The people's praise ...?   [III, 47–8]

This argument about fame was a favourite Renaissance topic, and Milton alludes to it in his *Defensio Secunda*: 'what itself conquers the most excellent of mortals . . . glory'. Glory may be, as Satan argued, 'the reward/That sole excites to high attempts the flame/Of most erected spirits'; or it may be what Cicero called it, *insipientium opinio*, the opinion of the foolish, the people's praise, the blaze of fame. There is no difference there. But the glory of God is also *doxa*; we still call the Gloria the doxology.

We may also note that in describing earthly *doxa* Milton emphasises its dependence on sight, and to a lesser extent on hearing: earthly glory is 'set off to the world' and a matter of 'rumour', but heavenly glory is perceived by the pure sight of God. One is controlled by earthly perceptions, by the treacherous senses; the other, by the truth those senses may not perceive. Opinion is not necessarily false or wicked; Milton also remarks that 'opinion in good men is but knowledge in the making' (*Doctrine and Discipline of Divorce*). It is certainly not truth, though it may not be ignorance. It is a third thing, though more likely to be bad than good.

Plato thought of opinion (*doxa*) as somewhere between knowledge and ignorance; it has to do with the world of sensory experience, not with the ideas, and so it cannot ever be identified with *epistēmē*, knowledge. It is concerned with appearances. Etymologically, the word *doxa* already contains this suggestion, for it is related to the verb *dokeo*, which means, transitively, 'to suppose, to imagine', and intransitively, 'to seem, to appear'. In fact John uses this verb in the very passage I used to demonstrate the ambiguity of *doxa*: 'Search the scriptures; for in them ye *think* ye have eternal life . . .' (4:39). According to Plato, rhetoricians are concerned with *doxa*, not truth; so are juries, which have to rely on the witness of others. *Doxa* stands somewhere between knowledge and ignorance. In the *Timaeus* it is specifically associated with the lower parts of the soul, with *sensation* (27e–28a). If you ask whether sensation can yield knowledge, Plato's answer is, of course, no: it yields *doxa*, opinion.

So we have a spread of senses for *doxa* that includes the following:

1   heavenly glory or honour;
2   the opinion others have of one – glory, honour, fame;

3   the same as 2 but with the strong implication that these are false qualities; that they are the product of what other people say, of ignorant popular acclaim;

4   the product of mere seeming or supposition or fantasy (*dokeo*), dependent on the vagaries of human perception, sensation and appetite.

We can now proceed from *doxa* to *opinion*, in which we shall discover the same range of senses, except the first, which is present only by implication and contrast. The word has now lost most of its pejorative connotations, but they were strong, perhaps predominant, in the English of Shakespeare's time. 'Public opinion', now regarded as a sort of ultimate tribunal ('the bar of public opinion'), would have connoted for Shakespeare the dangerous fickleness of his mobs. The first remark of Coriolanus to the Roman populace actually used the word 'opinion': 'What's the matter, you dissentious rogues,/That rubbing the poor itch of your opinion/Make yourselves scabs?' (*Coriolanus,* I, i, 164–6).

For him, as for Milton's Jesus, 'the people' is a 'miscellaneous rabble' with no true apprehension of fame or glory; that is why he finds it so painful to have to solicit their 'voices'. Here 'opinion' is opposed to knowledge. So too in Jonson's *Hymenaei* Opinion appears disguised as Truth, and conducts a debate with Truth herself. Sometimes the opponent of Opinion is Reason. Always it is a matter of what *appears* rather than what *is*. Greville, in his *Cleopatra*, makes the Chorus complain of Opinion as the 'Contriver of our greatest woes', as 'fed with shows', as judging all things in the world 'Not as they are but as they seem'. 'Opinion reigns without and truth within', he says elsewhere.[3] Behind Greville are the Stoic philosophers who enjoyed a revival of popularity at the time; and behind them is Plato.

But we need not confine ourselves to philosophy or philosophical poetry. Iconographically, Opinion was represented as gaudily dressed, 'a blindfolded goddess with the world in her lap and a chameleon on her wrist'.[4] The *OED* has a striking quotation, dated 1538: 'there is no difference between vice and virtue but strong opinion', which is close enough to Hamlet's 'There is nothing good or bad but thinking makes it so'. For Donne (if he wrote the Seventeenth Elegy), Opinion was the enemy of libertinism; it upholds the notion of women's honour:

167

> The golden laws of nature are repealed,
> Which our first Fathers in such reverence held;
> Our liberty's reversed, our charter's gone,
> And we made servants to Opinion,
> A monster in no certain shape attired ...

Opinion may, then, have its uses in the eyes of the law-abiding; it makes 'unnatural' habits such as chastity seem natural; it upholds authority. When Hamlet says that 'thinking makes it [seem] so' he might be exploring the transitive and intransitive senses of *dokeo* I mentioned earlier. Of course there were more neutral usages, and we can find them in Shakespeare – they are the ancestors of such living senses as are found in 'counsel's opinion' or 'a second opinion' or 'my opinion for what it's worth'. But it is fair to say that the word had, for Shakespeare, a larger element of the pejorative; it was much more firmly in opposition to 'truth' than it now is; it had to do with appearances rather than realities, with the outside rather than the inside, with what is said about the worth of an object or a person rather than with their intrinsic value.

Later, in *Timon of Athens*, Shakespeare will appear to be playing with the hero's name, which is related to words meaning 'honour', 'worth', 'price', 'estimate' (whether of the price of a jewel or the worth of a man). The courtesan's name 'Timandra' ('we'll do anything for gold') also suggests both 'price' and 'men' in appropriate combination. And the play is much concerned with worth, and estimates of worth in jewels, friendship, persons of authority. *Troilus* is likewise much concerned with the question of value. What confers value upon gold or jewels? Opinion: their value is the value men place upon them, having regard to their appearance. Men may call out values, as at an auction sale, and the value is whatever the last bidder says it is – his voice confers value. So Troilus says of Cressida:

> Her bed is India, there she lies, a pearl   [I, i, 104]

for which he is the questing merchant. And of Helen:

> Is she worth keeping? Why, she is a pearl,
> Whose price hath launch'd above a thousand ships,
> And turn'd crown'd kings to merchants   [II, ii, 81–3]

There is an implication that the value of a woman is appraised in the same way as that of a jewel; and Troilus, despite his conviction of Cressida's unique worth, will defend that view. Neither Helen nor Cressida was subsequently thought of as valuable or true, and it is appropriate that different valuations of them are offered in the course of the play: Diomedes says outright that Helen has *cost* too much: a Grecian life for every drop of her blood, a Trojan's 'for every scruple/Of her contaminated carrion weight' (IV, i, 69ff). Paris laughingly calls him a 'chapman' or dealer, who dispraises the the thing he desires to buy. Earlier Hector also emphasises what Helen has cost (II, ii, 18–20) and says flatly that 'she is not worth what she doth cost/The keeping' (II, ii, 51–2). Cressida is similarly disvalued by Diomedes and by Ulysses.

But these are only the most evident instances of the obsession with worth, value. Words such as 'worthy', 'glory', 'fame', 'merit', 'esteem', 'estimate', 'estimation', 'value', 'cost', 'honour', recur with extraordinary frequency. So does 'opinion' – ten times, in fact. Now it is fairly commonplace, as we have seen, that (earthly) reputation, honour, fame and all the rest depend on opinion. We know, too, that a man cannot have fame or glory by his own inward knowledge; it must come from what others say about him, from without not from within. So if he is to know himself famous it must be by looking in the mirror of opinion, or into the eyes of others; for his fame is to be found in the world's eyes, and in 'broad rumour'. We shall see that in *Troilus* much is made of this reflective property of fame, and much also of attempts to establish value from within, to practise self-evaluation. This results in a series of strange compounds: 'self-assumption', 'self-admission', 'self-breath', 'self-affected'. The dependence of fame on the eyes and mouths of others has another consequence. Glory, being thus dependent, is subject to time, for when the praise stops the fame stops, too. Hence the fact, so often noticed, that time is also a recurrent preoccupation of the text.

I'll return to the topics of reflection and time. First, though, I must mention the simpler and more primary matter of the opposition of opinion (which alone supports these valuations of fame and glory) and truth. We notice two slightly forced juxtapositions of the words. In the Trojan debate scene Hector, having convicted Troilus of being the slave of opinion, gives in to him suddenly – an unconvincing surrender, though the language is interesting:

> Thus to persist
> In doing wrong extenuates not wrong,
> But makes it much more heavy. Hector's opinion
> Is this in way of truth; yet ne'er the less,
> My spritely brethren, I propend to you
> In resolution to keep Helen still. . . .   [II, ii, 186ff]

Here he uses 'opinion' in a neutral way, but by associating it with the truth distinguishes it from the opinion (bad sense) which he is now willing to embrace; for his reason for keeping Helen is that it would detract from their 'joint and several dignities' to let her go. Later Troilus distinguishes himself from other men by saying that they 'fish with craft for great opinion' while he 'with great truth' catches 'mere simplicity' (IV, iv, 103–4) – a self-estimate by one who by word and deed has been the great upholder of opinion as the sole criterion of value.

Troilus, indeed, has, when it matters to him, a great regard for truth. 'I am as true as truth's simplicity,/And simpler than the infancy of truth' (III, ii, 169–70). The repetition of 'true' and 'truth' in the scene of his parting from Cressida (IV, iv) is very remarkable. We have earlier heard from him that in future fidelity in lovers will be measured by Troilus: 'True swains in love shall in the world to come/Approve their truth by Troilus' (III, ii, 173–4); and from Cressida, in the same scene, that if she is untrue she should for ever be the standard for falseness in women. Now they part.

> *Cres.* And is it true that I must go from Troy?
> *Tro.*   A hateful truth . . .
>   . . . Be thou but true of heart –
> *Cres.* I true? how now? . . .
> *Tro.*   I speak not 'be thou true' as fearing thee . . .
>   But 'be thou true' say I to fashion in
>   My sequent protestation: be thou true,
>   And I will see thee.
> *Cres.* . . . but I'll be true . . .
> *Tro.*   But yet be true.
> *Cres.*   O heavens, 'be true' again? . . .
> *Tro.*   I with great truth . . .
>   Fear not my truth: the moral of my wit
>   Is 'plain and true' . . .   [IV, iv, 30–108]

This scene surrounds 'true' and 'truth' (used mostly in the sense of 'faithful' and 'fidelity') with other words relevant to the investigation of opinion. Troilus has a remarkable speech on 'injurious time'; he represents the chance which will separate him from Cressida as an act of violence, then as an act of theft (contrasted with the honest mercantile deal done between him and Cressida):

> We two, that with so many thousand sighs
> Did buy each other, must poorly sell ourselves
> With the rude brevity and discharge of one.
> Injurious time now with a robber's haste
> Crams his rich thiev'ry up. . . .   [IV, iv, 39–43]

When Diomedes courteously praises Cressida, Troilus tells him her worth is beyond his praise, and calls the Greek 'unworthy to be call'd her servant' (IV, iv, 125). The reply of Diomedes: 'To her own worth/She shall be priz'd' (133–4).

We may notice also that the language of the lovers is a language of sense, of appetite, here as formerly. Cressida cannot make her 'palate [a recurring word] weak and cold to suffer grief' (7); Troilus says that time leaves them nothing but 'a single famish'd kiss,/Distasted with the salt of broken tears' (47–8). Troilus has always spoken so: 'Th'imaginary relish is so sweet/That it enchants my sens; what will it be/When that the wat'ry palates taste indeed/Love's thrice-repured nectar?' (III, ii, 19–22). This love, being a matter of opinion, is subject to time, indifferent to 'true merit or worth, and founded in the senses, known for their inadequacy, and for being, like the act of love itself, slaves to limit.

Perhaps we can best understand the critique of *doxa* by looking at the scene in which the leaders visit the tent of Achilles (II, iii). Agamemnon instructs Patroclus to inform Achilles that he must act or be rejected by the leaders.

> Much *attribute* he hath, and much the reason
> Why we *ascribe* it to him; yet all his virtues,
> Not virtuously on his own part *beheld*,
> Do in our *eyes* begin to lose their gloss,
> Yea, like fair fruit in an unwholesome dish,
> Are like to rot *untasted*. Go and tell him
> We come to speak with him, and you shall not sin
> If you do say we think him over-proud

> And under-honest, in *self-assumption* greater
> Than in the note of *judgment*. . . .
>   add,
> That if he overhold his *price* so much,
> We'll none of him. . . .
>   [II, iii, 116–34]

I have emphasised the words that belong to the critique of opinion. 'Attributes' (or in the common and telling Shakespearian word, 'additions') come from outside, and so do ascriptions. 'Beheld' here means 'retained, kept hold of'; but the word slips inevitably into the sense of 'observed', and here it suggests the 'eyes' of the next line: he does not 'behold' them virtuously, we shall behold them as having lost virtue ('gloss' may remind us of Milton's 'glistering foil' in the account of earthly fame). The fruit 'untasted' (remember the 'distasted' of Troilus) implies that the beholder, hearer, taster, cannot be compelled to endure what his palate rejects; yet on his acceptance honour and fame depend. 'Self-assumption', what he assumes himself to be worth, is a greater value than external judges endorse; he 'overholds his price'.

So, as Agamemnon later remarks (155ff), the proud man is his own glass, his own trumpet; he 'devours the deed in the praise'. Ulysses takes up the theme of Achilles' 'self-admission' (166), his 'self-breath' (172):

> Imagin'd worth
> Holds in his blood such swoll'n and hot discourse
> That 'twixt his mental and his active parts
> Kingdom'd Achilles in commotion rages,
> And batters down himself. What should I say?
> He is so plaguy proud that the death-tokens of it
> Cry 'No recovery'.
>   [II, iii, 172–8]

'Imagin'd worth' is pure *doxa*, and since *doxa* is of the senses and appetites Achilles is represented as in the grip of a fatal disease of the blood, exhibiting its terminal symptoms. The imagined worth of love, a subject on which Pandarus has so much to say, brings similar consequences, and we see him at the end of the play complaining of the terminal symptoms of syphilis. The association of self-glory, and of erotic fantasy, with the blood and the senses is very strong, and perhaps in the long run it derives from Plato.

Ajax, who 'drinks' applause (201) and is just as 'self-affected' (238), suffers more comically from these afflictions, but it is to Achilles that we are returned for the fullest study of the disease of glory. As part of his plot, Ulysses contrives that Agammemnon and the other leaders should pass Achilles' tent and 'Lay negligent and loose regard upon him' (III, iii, 41). Not to be respectfully *looked at* is fatal to fame, since fame arises from respectful attention. 'Unplausive eyes' (43) may cure the hero's disease; Ulysses speaks of the plan as a medicine to be *drunk* down, and introduces us to the figure of reflection: 'pride hath no other glass/To show itself but pride' (47–8). The trick seems to work, and Achilles speaks a perceptive meditation. 'What, am I poor of late?' (74). His price has already fallen, simply because the generals did not look on him 'plausively'.

> What the declin'd is,
> He shall as soon read in the eyes of others
> As feel in his own fall. . . .
> And not a man, for being simply man,
> Hath any honor, but honor for those honors
> That are without him, as places, riches, and favor –
> Prizes of accident as oft as merit . . . [III, iii, 77–83]

But he has not really learned the lesson that honour comes from without, and goes on to say he has lost nothing 'Save these men's *looks* – who do, methinks, find out/Something not *worth* in me such *rich beholding*/As they have often given' (90–2) – having already forgotten that on this account of honour those looks are its sole source; he has in fact lost everything. And at this point Ulysses joins him. There follows a superbly repetitive discussion of the nature of fame (*Troilus and Cressida* is remarkable for these sinewy set pieces). Ulysses pretends that the book in his hand contains a moral observation on the reflective nature of fame. A man, however handsomely endowed,

> Cannot make boast to have that which he hath,
> Nor feels not what he owes, but by reflection;
> As when his virtues, aiming upon others,
> Heat them, and they retort that heat again
> To the first giver. [III, iii, 97–101]

173

In fact, Ulysses has introduced a new idea: *virtue*, rather than a mere form, is what must be emitted if there is to be a satisfactory reflection. And virtue may mean primarily strength, courage, manliness or even 'essence', but it retains some ethical quality. Achilles in his very striking reply again reduces the notion to one of reflection and sensory experience:

> . . . nor does the eye itself,
> That most pure spirit of sense, behold itself,
> Not going from itself; but eye to eye opposed,
> Salutes each other with each other's form. . . .
>
> [III, iii, 105–8]

It is, surprisingly, Achilles who gives the idea its most philosophical formulation. The eye is traditionally the 'most pure spirit of sense', and in a familiar neo-Platonic scheme there is a choice to be made as to the use of what the eye receives. From it one may ascend through the higher powers of the mind towards the idea of beauty, or sink to the lower senses, touch and taste. To use it for glory, as we have seen, is to commit it to the service of the appetites and the disorders of the blood.

But Ulysses uses the discussion entirely in furtherance of his plot to regain the services of Achilles, and now insists on applying the point of his 'author' to that end: '. . . no man is the lord of anything . . Till he communicate his parts to others . . . Till he behold them formed in th'applause/Where th'are extended . . .' (115–20). He reinforces the idea of reflection: virtue is received again by the giver as an arch reverberates the voice or a steel gate the heat and light of the sun (121–3). And he reminds Achilles that things may be 'abject in regard and dear in use' or 'dear in the esteem/And poor in worth' (128–30). It depends entirely on how they are reflected, though to be reflected they must first be shown. Achilles remembers that the Greek leaders passed him by with neither 'Good word nor look. What, are my deeds forgot?' (144). And it is here that Ulysses introduces Time as the enemy of virtues not put forth:

> Let not virtue seek
> Remuneration for the thing it was; for beauty, wit,
> High birth, vigor of bone, desert in service,
> Love, friendship, charity, are subjects all

> To envious and calumniating Time. . . .
> The present eye praises the present object . . .
>
> [III, iii, 169–80]

'I see my reputation is at stake', says Achilles, 'My fame is shrowdly gor'd' (227–8), a curious blend of gaming and bear-baiting imagery not at all inappropriate: to have glory is to be engaged in an endless game from which one cannot withdraw; and Ulysses is 'baiting' Achilles.

So, in this remarkable scene, the figures of opinion are brought together, the enquiry into glory deepened, while at the same time Ulysses is engaged (unsuccessfully as it turns out) in a machiavellian attempt to exploit opinion on behalf of the state, itself an organisation dependent on opinion. We can never be certain, in this play, as to who is right. Ulysses fails. Patroclus guys the greatness of Agamemnon, which is only a matter of opinion, as the sarcastic courtesy of Aeneas also tells us; he cannot recognise the 'high and mighty Agamemnon' (I, iii, 232) by 'those most imperial looks' which should distinguish him from 'other mortals' (224–5). Thersites is always on hand to tell us that fame, chivalry, honour are only anger and cruelty and craftiness disguised by opinion, and that love is only lust similarly dressed up. The theme is a recurrent one in Shakespeare, and we remember it most poignantly from *Lear*, with its insistence that you convert the forked thing into an office-holder – a beadle, a courtier, a magistrate, a king – only by putting clothes on it, so that clothes, denoting office, confer power and authority, and are the emblems of opinion.

But Thersites in deriding, and Ulysses in exploiting, *doxa* are not themselves the agents of the truth; nor is the play, with all its conflicting valuations and futile strategies and its ending with instances of dishonour both military and erotic. Thersites says of opinion that 'a man may wear it on both sides like a leather jerkin' (III, iii, 264–5), and it is this ambivalence that is fully represented in the play; it is not making statements about honour or love, or the power use of authority; it is not placing opinion in respect of value or truth. It is instead giving, in extraordinary depth, the sense of them as they occur in language and action. (I have not, for example, fully developed the theme of taste and distaste,

175

palate and appetite, often grossly emphasised by Thersites but frequent also elsewhere.)

I have been talking about the Achilles-baiting scenes as set pieces. As part of the dramatic action they accomplish rather little; the politic plot of Ulysses fails, Achilles is not thus to be drawn back into the fighting. When he returns it is out of rage at the death of Patroclus, and his opinion of chivalry and honour is indicated by his slaughter of Hector. It is of course characteristic of this work that loquacious attempts to induce this or that course of action should end in failure. It is the talk that is important. That is why *Troilus* has two extraordinary scenes of debate, one in the Greek camp (I, iii) and the other in the Trojan (II, ii). In the first of these Ulysses explains the failure of the Greek campaign so far as a consequence of the neglect of 'degree'. His speech on the subject is too famous to need detailed exposition. But it should not be taken quite simply at its face value. As a politician Ulysses is a manipulator of opinion. What he is saying is that degree is necessary, but that degree is upheld by opinion. Agamemnon's 'place and sway' (I, iii, 60) depend upon their acceptance by opinion; they can be imitated, mimicked, instead of respected. Degree is the force of opinion that distinguishes one man, one place, from another.

> How could communities,
> Degrees in schools, and brotherhood in cities . . .
> The primogenity and due of birth,
> Prerogative of age, crowns, sceptres, laurels,
> But by degree stand in authentic place?   [I, iii, 103–8]

You can see the circularity in this: How could degrees . . . stand but by degree? Nothing gives efficacy to degree but the fact that it is taken to exist; remove it and the political order collapses, right and wrong 'lose their names' (118). 'There is no difference between vice and virtue but strong opinion'.

And Ulysses proceeds to give as an example Achilles, 'whom opinion crowns/The sinew and the forehand of our host,/Having his ear full of his airy fame' (142–4). 'Broad rumour' sustains Achilles, but not Agamemnon. Ulysses' failed plot is an attempt to alter the distribution of opinion.

The other debate, in the Trojan camp, deals squarely with the issue of opinion as the determinant of value. Why should Helen be kept? Her cost is high. Hector says she is not worth the keeping. Troilus, elsewhere self-proclaimed the very image of truth, is now the champion of opinion: 'Weigh you the worth and honor of a king/So great as our dread father's in a scale/Of common ounces?' (II, ii, 26–8). And this opinion, as Helenus points out, is contrary to *reason*, as it was for Plato. Troilus frankly accepts this opposition: 'Reason and respect/Make livers pale and lustihood deject' (49–50): which is to say that they are bad for lovers as well as soldiers; they reduce appetite. And Troilus, speaking for Opinion, asks: 'What's aught but as 'tis valued?' (52).

This exchange is the nub of the matter, a conflict between Truth and Opinion almost as formal as Johnson's in *Hymenaei*, though that is centred on a different topic, marriage and virginity. Hector states the case of Truth, which, if accepted, undermines all the martial and erotic valuations we have heard in the play.

> But value dwells not in particular will,
> It holds his estimate and dignity
> As well wherein 'tis precious of itself
> As in the prizer.   [II, ii, 53–6]

This denial of the power of opinion is challenged by Troilus: my senses guide my will, for instance when I choose a wife. I place a high value upon her, as we all did on Helen. If she later disgusts me I cannot reject her. The language here is of appetite: *distaste*, leftovers of food (which will be recalled when in disillusion he speaks of Cressida's love as 'the fragments, scraps, the bits and greasy relics/Of her o'ereaten faith' (V, ii, 158–60)), and the use of this figure undermines the argument. Yet it is true that the Trojans made a valuation: Paris' prize was 'worthy', they cried out 'Inestimable!' and ought not now to 'beggar the estimation which' they 'priz'd' and be 'thieves unworthy of a thing so stol'n' (II, ii, 86–94). The irruption of Cassandra prompts Hector to ask whether Troilus' blood is so distempered as to be beyond the reach of reason – the usual case with slaves of opinion, as we see also from Paris, 'besotted on' his 'sweet delights' (II, ii, 143). Indeed, Hector's final speech accuses them both of producing only the kind of reason that is dominated by 'the hot passion of distemp'red blood' (169). The law of nature is 'corrupted through affection' (i.e., passion) (177); the law of nations ought to 'curb those raging appetites' (181).

But honour, dignity, renown, fame, glory (all named in Troilus' next speech) prevail; opinion prevails, and the war will continue in a manner to justify the oversimplifications of Thersites. If you remove from the story all the mythology of valour, courtesy, beauty and merit, this is what becomes of it. And the great V, ii restates the conclusion as it affects the love of Troilus and Cressida. This is the real end of the Trojan debate. Troilus, as true as truth's simplicity, is so deluded by opinion that he cannot understand how Cressida could have betrayed his love. He wants there to be two Cressidas, one of 'truth' and one he can see and hear. Ulysses, reasonably, sees but one; he will not 'swagger himself out of his own eyes', as Thersites puts it (136). The 'true' Cressida is a product of opinion, of distempered blood, of taking seeming for being. One might be bold enough to say that the principal subject is indeed opinion arising from distemper of the blood; and Pandarus, in his epilogue, lends some force to the statement.

That would be a mistake, however. There is a great deal going on in the play that I haven't mentioned – I have stuck to my limited topic. And we should not imagine that a text of this degree of complexity can have or be a *message*. All attempts to simplify it by reducing it to some particular genre – satire, comedy, tragical satire – have failed. The Greeks proclaim barbarism; policy grows into an ill opinion; the great heroes, Achilles and Hector, feed their eyes upon each other in mutual contempt (IV, iv); promises, which bear a man's or a woman's truth, are repeatedly broken – by Achilles, Cressida, Diomedes. The famous turn out to be worthless, the true unfaithful. But none of that means that Hector was wrong in his argument against opinion, though he was presumably wrong to give in and lose truth in opinion ('Hector's opinion/Is this in way of truth . . .'). The semantic implications of *doxa* have, in the end, ethical implications. But we are not guided to some simple formulation of them. We should not, like Troilus, 'invert th'attest of eyes and ears' (V, ii, 122) in order to make a false play as he made a false Cressida; what we should do is to hold all the implications of opinion and truth, worth, estimate, fame and the rest, as far as possible in a single thought, a thought ordered by the play. Otherwise we shall find ourselves speaking of cynicism and the like; saying that Thersites is in the right, that valour is only anger plus opinion, that fair outsides, like the suit of armour peeled off by Hector, always contain rottenness within.

There is nothing good or bad but thinking makes it so; but *Troilus* will not yield a single ethical sense. To pursue the related words I have been discussing with a view to rearranging them into a simple sense would be to frustrate the unusually deliberate means Shakespeare took to leave them in the complex relations established by the set pieces, and by the gaps which open between the language of those set pieces and the action of the play – not only the futile politicking but also something I've had to leave out, the fun, the sense of erotic pleasure none the less pleasant for depending on the senses and on opinion. The truth is not a possession of Hector or of Troilus, Thersites or Ulysses, the critic or the director. All we can say is that in the long run, in the Platonic run, the existence of opinion implies truth, if only as the object of a kind of knowledge above that of the senses; and perhaps that is why Shakespeare felt he must write the Hector–Troilus dialogue on value, even though he could not allow Hector to win the argument without altering the whole matter of Troy, even though he would face the awkwardness of Hector recanting, having spoken the truth. Somewhere, if opinion were to be placed at all, the truth had to be spoken for.

NOTES

1 All Shakespeare references are to the Riverside edn, Boston, Massachusetts, Houghton Mifflin Company, 1974.
2 R.E. Brown, *The Gospel According to John, I–XII*, The Anchor Bible, vol. 29, New York, 1966, p. 223 and note, pp. 225–6.
3 For other examples of its use in philosophical poetry contemporary with Shakespeare, see P. Ure, 'A Notice on "Opinion" in Daniel, Greville and Chapman', *Modern Language Review*, 1951, vol. 46, pp. 331–8.
4 Ibid., p. 338.

11 Monologue in *Macbeth*

Raymond Williams

1

Reared on an idea of the soliloquy, we shall have difficulty in understanding the true varieties of dramatic monologue, and for that matter dialogue. To begin with, there is a divergence between dictionary definitions and current literary usage. Thus in *The Oxford Dictionary of English Etymology* (1966):

> *Monologue:* dramatic scene or composition in which a single actor speaks, XVII (Dryden). – F. *monologue* (XV), after *dialogue*; cf. late Gr. *monologos* speaking alone.
> *Soliloquy:* talking aloud to oneself. XVII. – late L. *soliloquium* (Augustine).

Or in Fowler's *Modern English Usage* (1926), under 'Technical Terms':

> *Monologue:* (lit.); 'sole speech'. This and *soliloquy* are precisely parallel terms of Greek, and Latin, origin; but usage tends to restrict *soliloquy* to talking to oneself or thinking aloud without consciousness of an audience whether one is in fact overheard or not, while *monologue*, though not conversely restricted to a single person's discourse that *is* meant to be heard, has that sense much more often than not, and is especially used of a talker who monopolizes conversation, or of a dramatic performance or recitation in which there is one actor only.

What then is usage? I can say only that in more than forty years, in

180

a relevant environment, I have never heard *soliloquy* and *soliloquise* used of 'talking to oneself', in any ordinary sense. Conversely, while I have heard *monologue* in Fowler's two senses, of monopolising conversation and of dramatic performance or recitation by a single actor, and in a third sense, of a kind of poem written as if spoken by a single character, I have regularly heard *soliloquy* in the sense of a 'dramatic scene or composition in which a single actor speaks' and especially in the sense of a speech in a play in which a 'character' is taken to be at least temporarily alone and in that sense (but there, as we shall see, all the difficulties begin) as 'talking to him or herself'.

The problem is much wider than one of technical terms. Yet their history has some significance. It is the shift in *soliloquy* that has most importance. The late *soliloquium* is commonly cited from the *Liber Soliloquiorum* of Augustine, which has the subtitles *Soliloquia animae ad Deum* and *Meditationes, soliloquia et manuali*. It was freely translated into Old English under Alfred in the late ninth century. Most medieval English references are to the Augustinian soliloquy. But then soliloquy, in this line, is not a matter of represented singular speech. Indeed, in Augustine it is often in dialogue form, as between the soul and God, or between different faculties of the mind. This sense of private meditation or prayer persisted as the primary meaning until at least the eighteenth century, though there is a recorded early seventeenth-century use as 'private talk'. There is a characteristic title from 1738: *Devout Exercises of the Heart in Meditation and Soliloquy*.

It is difficult to be certain when the sense of religious meditation went out or when the sense of a mode of composition in drama came in. Johnson, in his *Dictionary*, defined *soliloquy* as 'a discourse made by one in solitude to himself': the formal version of the twentieth century's 'talking to oneself'. He defined *monologue* as 'a scene in which a person of the drama speaks by himself, a soliloquy', where 'speaks *by*' (rather than *to*) may be important. The addition of *soliloquy*, in a dramatic context, is somewhere near the shift we are tracing, but not yet of it, since there is a citation of 'monologue, to which unnatural way of narration Terence is subject in all his plays', where the confusion between narrative and dramatic is historically significant, and where 'unnatural' is a key indicator of the problems of changing dramatic conventions.

181

The most interesting moment in the history comes in Shaftesbury's essay *Soliloquy, or Advice to an Author* (1710).[1] Shaftesbury is discussing the relations between experience and practice. Having insisted that we have ourselves to practise on, he supposes the objection:

> ... who can thus multiply himself into *two Persons*, and be *his own Subject*?

To this he replies:

> Go to the *Poets*, and they will present you with many Instances. Nothing is more common with them, than this sort of SOLILOQUY. A Person of profound parts, or perhaps of ordinary Capacity, happens, on some occasion, to commit a Fault. He is concern'd for it. He comes alone upon the Stage; looks about him, to see if any body be near; then takes himself to task, without sparing himself in the least. You wou'd wonder to hear how close he pushes matters, and how thorowly he carrys on the business of *Self-dissection*. By virtue of this SOLILOQUY he becomes two distinct *Persons*. He is Pupil and Preceptor. He teaches, and he learns. And in good earnest, had I nothing else to plead in behalf of the Morals of our modern Dramatick Poets, I shou'd defend 'em still against their Accusers for the sake of this very Practice, which they have taken care to keep up in its full force. For whether the Practice be *natural* or no, in respect of common Custom and Usage; I take upon me to assert, that it is an honest and laudable Practice; and that if already it be not natural to us, we ought however to make it so, by Study and Application.

This passage may be decisive for subsequent usage (though it seems not to have penetrated the dictionaries). Yet Shaftesbury is concerned with the dramatic method only as example. His central argument is that such private practice is necessary;

> ... 'tis a certain Observation in our Science, that they who are great Talkers *in Company*, have never been any Talkers *by themselves* ... For which reason their Froth abounds;

yet that at the same time it is

> very indecent for any one to publish his *Meditations, Occa-*

sional Reflections, Solitary Thoughts, or other such Exercises as come under the notion of this *self-discoursing Practice.*

A characteristic sense of decorum, with clearly distinguished rules for public and private behaviour, admitted one, but only one, written form of 'self-discoursing Practice', and even then, within the special case of dramatic speech 'by a character', only as private example. The full shift depended on a wide alteration of attitudes. It was above all in the Romantic movement, with its intense interest in new forms of subjectivity in verse, in its practice and popularisation of the relatively new form of the autobiography, and in its attachment to new forms of self-reflective fiction and to forms of internal analysis of private thought and feeling within more general fiction, that a new strong emphasis and interpretation of this already available and apparently subjective form in drama developed and eventually became dominant. The centre of interest was in Shakespeare and above all in what came to be generalised as 'the soliloquies': in practice the major set speeches in which so many leading actors specialised. The shift was congruent with an increasingly internal 'psychological' analysis of characters. Critical and academic practice followed this line. *Soliloquy* was preferred to *monologue* since all the previous associations of *soliloquy* with private meditation and reverie – in a more modern term, 'inner speech' – supported the selected emphasis. The more technical *monologue*, without such associations, was in effect crowded out.

Yet the actual difficulties persist. It is possible to take *soliloquy*, with these associations, as an appropriate term for one kind of dramatic speech, to which such characteristics are commonly assigned: the 'great soliloquies', as it is put, of Hamlet or Macbeth. Yet it is not only that there are other kinds of monologue, to which such characteristics need not or can not be assigned. Nor only that such characteristics can in fact be discovered in *dialogue*; some 'well remembered' soliloquies turn out, in the text, to be dialogic. It is also that certain major problems of convention and definition, centred in the problem of subject and object in writing, and very actively present in the texts of dramatic writing for speech of various kinds before actual and presumed audiences, inhere not only in these wider forms but within the 'soliloquies' themselves.

2

I want to begin some analysis of these difficulties from the text of *Macbeth*. But, because the terms and their implications have become so confused, I must first set out something like the actual range of monologue, and its relations with dialogue, not only for convenience in analysis, but as a deliberate break with what now increasingly seems to me the mystifying concept of *soliloquy* in current academic and critical usage.

It is necessary to begin rather far back, yet at a point so obvious that only conceptual mystification would obscure or marginalise it. The preposition in Johnson's definition can help us here. A person in a drama may indeed speak *by* him- or herself, but literally cannot speak *to* him- or herself, in the sense in which that description is used for 'talking to oneself in private'. Always, and obviously, there is an audience, to whom, in some manner, the words are by deliberation made available.

It is within that general description, 'by deliberation made available', that the true varieties of dramatic speech must be distinguished. The relations of any speech to an audience can be inscribed within particular forms of composition, and are in any case governed by wider dramatic conventions. Thus some relations are evident or can become evident only in analysis of the text within the dramatic conventions for which it was written. For a dramatic text, unlike texts written for silent reading (on which most studies of direction of address have been based), presumes both an inherent multivocal form – the composition is distributed between different speaking voices – and certain governing physical relations, in the relational presence of actors in a playing space and in the further (and often complex) relational presence of these actors with an audience.

These relations cannot be reduced to those of any particular dramatic convention. In the case of *soliloquy* there has been some unnecessary confusion because of an unnoticed assimilation, in the modern period, of the conventions of 'naturalist' drama. Here the relations between actors and audience are negatively defined. The audience is of course present, but the actors do not *dramatically* notice the audience; instead, they play out their action before it, in a space defined by the raising or lowering of curtains or lights. It usually follows from this that the actors are under-

stood as invariably *talking to each other*. When only one actor is on
the stage, that actor has then, within the convention, *nobody to
speak to but him- or herself*. Then, since 'talking to oneself' carries
certain habitual social and psychological implications, what had
once been the *soliloquy* is felt to be 'unnatural'. This is generally
known, but what is less often noticed is the common (retroactive)
conclusion that when an actor is alone on the stage and speaks, he
or she is 'talking to him- or herself', as in the dominant sense of
soliloquy. For who else, within the 'naturalist' convention, could he
or she be talking to? That an actor might be talking *to*, rather than
in the unnoticed presence of, an audience has been conventionally ruled out.

In fact, monologue within a multivocal dramatic form can
include, as we shall see, direct address to an audience. But there
are then more complex relations: some of them very indirect,
though not necessarily identical with the wholly enclosed and
internal speech relations of the 'naturalist' convention. Between
the explicitly direct and such indirect cases, there are intermediate cases, which we can properly call 'semi-direct', in which
speech is given in full consciousness of the audience but without
the marks of direct address. These three most general types, and
the main variations within them, can be set out as follows, with
brief examples from English Renaissance drama.

A Direct

(i) *Presentational*
The most easily recognised form of direct address, commonly in
Prologue and Epilogue of a certain type, preceding or succeeding
the full dramatic action and relying on direct relation between
performer and audience; e.g.,

> The general welcomes Tamburlaine receiv'd,
> When he arrived last upon our stage,
> Have made our poet pen his Second Part. . . .
> > [*Tamburlaine the Great, II*, Prologue]

Other examples: *2 Henry IV*, Epilogue ('If you be not too much
cloyed with fat meat, our humble author will continue the story
. . . and make you merry. . . .'); *Midsummer-Night's Dream*, Puck

epilogue ('If we shadows have offended. . . .'); *All's Well that Ends Well*, Epilogue ('The king's a beggar now the play is done . . .').

(ii) *Expository*
A different use of Prologue especially, though it can appear elsewhere; at times combined with (i), as in the later lines of the *Tamburlaine II* epilogue. E.g.,

> Two households, both alike in dignity,
> In fair Verona, where we lay our scene,
> From ancient grudge break to new mutiny. . . .
>
> [*Romeo and Juliet*, Prologue]

Other examples: *Henry V*, Prologue (includes elements of (i)); *Troilus and Cressida*, Prologue ('In Troy there lies the scene. From isles of Greece. . . .'); *Winter's Tale*, IV, i, spoken by Time; *2 Henry IV*, Induction, spoken by Rumour.

Though there is often combination of the expository with the presentational, the former function is typically more integrated with the dramatic action and the speaker then passes from performer to a certain kind of generalised character, often specified as Time, Rumour, Armed Chorus, etc. This mode is then close to certain kinds of expository self-introduction by a named character; cf. Machevill prologue, *Jew of Malta*; Gloucester, *Richard III*, I, i (cf. B (ii) below); Autolycus in *Winter's Tale*, IV, iii (cf. B (iii) below).

(iii) *Indicative or homiletic*
Common as direct homily in medieval drama, presenting the religious and moral significance of the action. More generally indicative in Renaissance drama, though the range can be illustrated even there; e.g.,

> Cut is the branch that might have grown full straight,
> And burned is Apollo's laurel bough,
> That sometime grew within this learned man.
> Faustus is gone. Regard his hellish fall. . . .
>
> (Homiletic)   [*Doctor Faustus*, Epilogue]

And my ending is despair,
Unless I be relieved by prayer,
Which pierces so that it assaults
Mercy itself, and frees all faults.
As you from crimes would pardon'd be,
Let your indulgence set me free.

[*The Tempest,* Epilogue]

(In this epilogue by Prospero the indicative is combined with and
qualified by the presentational.)

Till then I'll sweat, and seek about for eases;
And at that time bequeath you my diseases.

[*Troilus and Cressida,* V, x]

(Not formal epilogue, and the *you* specified to 'as many as be here
of pandar's hall'; this is the dramatically indicative at full development from the homiletic.)

B Semi-direct

(i) *Aside*
The most easily recognised form of semi-direct address, evidently
spoken 'to' the audience but qualified by its placing as a short
break within dialogue; e.g.,

I know them all, though they suppose me mad,
And will o'erreach them in their own devices;
A pair of cursed hell-hounds and their dam.

[*Titus Andronicus,* V, ii]

(ii) *Secretive/explanatory*
In some ways a relatively complex development of the aside, but
often tending towards the undifferentiated form of 'soliloquy',
from which, however, in that usual sense, it can be functionally
distinguished; e.g.,

A credulous father! and a brother noble
Whose nature is so far from doing harms
That he suspects none; on whose foolish honesty

> My practices ride easy! I see the business.
> Let me, if not by birth, have lands by wit;
> All with me's meet that I can fashion fit.
>
> [*Lear*, I, ii, 182–7]

This can be functionally distinguished, in this case formally by the characteristic concluding rhymed 'sentence', from Edmund's monologue in *Lear*, I ii, 1–22, which is relationally more indirect; cf. C (ii) and (iii) below. The point may be clearer in a comparison between Iago in *Othello*, I, iii ('Thus do I ever make my fool my purse') and in II, iii ('And what's he then that says I play the villain?'), where the matter is in both cases required to be secret, and is dramatically made so by the convention of monologue, but where the former more evidently includes necessary explanation of 'the business' in hand, so that the audience may understand its manoeuvres. This is the distinguishing element of conscious if semi-direct relation to an audience.

(iii) *Characteristic*
A very different kind of semi-direct monologue, with some functional relations to the indicative (A (iii) above). A certain type of self-introducing character functions, explicitly or implicitly, as a form of commentary upon the action, which within this formal mode is temporarily distanced; e.g.,

> Now they are clapper-clawing one another; I'll go look on. That dissembling abominable varlet, Diomed, has got that same scurvy doting foolish young knave's sleeve of Troy there in his helm. I would fain see them meet . . .
>
> [*Troilus and Cressida*, V, iv, 1–5]

Other monologue examples: *Cymbeline*, V, iv, end (First Gaoler: 'Unless a man would marry a gallows. . . .'); *Macbeth*, II, iii, 1–20. The linguistic markers on this type are especially evident: the composition is not only in 'prose', but is deliberately (and often in sharp contrast) popular (colloquial) in syntax and diction.

C Indirect

(i) *Rhetorical*

This type answers, in general, to the description of monologue/soliloquy as 'self-discoursing practice', but sets up specific linguistic relations between presumed subject and object. The type example is:

> Settle thy studies, Faustus, and begin
> To sound the depth of that thou wilt profess. . . .
> > [*Doctor Faustus*, I, i, 1–2]

This long opening monologue of Faustus is a form of 'self-discourse' predominantly written in a grammar of the self addresssing the self as if a second person. There are subordinate uses of the first-person pronoun in lines 6, 36, 56, and 62, but the second-person address controls the overall style. The effect can be seen by contrast with the first-person monologue that soon follows, lines 77–96, which is primarily B (ii). The contrast can be seen again in the remarkable final monologue of *Faustus*, V, ii, 143–200, which begins (143–54) in second-person address and then shifts dramatically to first-person:

> Oh, I'll leap up to my God: who pulls me down?

This continues to 168, and thereafter the monologue is a combination of first- and second-person pronouns and forms.

Other known rhetorical figures for this type were also used.

(ii) *Reflexive*

This is the type which has been most widely generalised as *soliloquy*, in which a self-discoursing practice is spoken, alone on the stage, in the first person. It is clearly an extremely important kind; e.g.,

> O, what a rogue and peasant slave am I. . . .
> > [*Hamlet*, II, ii, 553–609]

In this type example, there is deliberate notation –

> Ay, so, God bye to you! now I am alone.

Among numerous other examples, *Hamlet*, I, ii, 129–59 or IV, iv, 32–66.

It should be noted that the condition of being alone on the stage, though normal for this type, is not always fulfilled; there can be other forms of temporary isolation (see below).

(iii) *Generic*
This type is often, under the influence of general psychologising or characterising explanations of all monologue/soliloquy in terms of the private or the wholly subjective, reduced from its full function. It is usually apparently similar to the reflexive, but can often be linguistically distinguished by its use of the 'we' rather than the 'I' pronouns; e.g.,

> To be, or not to be . . .
> . . . and by a sleep to say we end . . .
> . . . When we have shuffled off this mortal coil
> Must give us pause . . .
> . . . And makes us rather bear those ills we have
> Than fly to others that we know not of?
> Thus conscience does make cowards of us all.
> [*Hamlet*, III, i, 56–88]

The need to distinguish the generic from the reflexive is more than formal. It is an indication of the true range and flexibility of this highly developed dramatic speech that there can be such transitions from the reflexive/subjective to the generic/objective. Whatever may be said of the reflexive, the generic is evidently not 'inner speech'. It is, rather, most notably through its selection of 'we', the realisation of a communal mode which is not (as in some other communal forms) opposed to subjectivity but is a deepening and then a transformation of it: a common 'individual' condition in the old sense of 'individual' as that which is specific but yet cannot be 'divided', that is, separated. It is essential that this type of indirect monologue should be distinguished from the post-Romantic version of 'soliloquy' as the 'private' or 'inner' (then 'deeper') self as distinct from 'public' and 'outer' identity.

This provisional classification of types of monologue requires two further notes: on the consequent relations to *dialogue*, and on staging.

Any full discussion of dialogue would go beyond the present scope, but it should already be evident that the variable modes of address in the full range of monologue make any simple contrast with dialogue, in the sense of the 'naturalist' convention, impossible. In particular, it cannot be assumed that dialogue occurs only when two or more people 'address each other', in the sense of an enclosed and internal exchange. Variably direct and indirect relations with an audience occur in dialogue as in monologue, and we can provisionally classify them as follows.

D Relations with the audience in dialogue

(i) *Formal exchange*
This occurs typically in certain socially marked situations – court, assembly, trial. The 'set' speeches (some, ironically, misremembered as 'soliloquies') are governed by the rules of formal exchange and are then often internally monologic in type. (This can include narrative report, as in *Macbeth*, I, ii, 7–23, 25–33, 35–43, 49–59, 60–4.) The audience in such scenes is in a *public* relation to the exchange. Examples include *Triolus and Cressida*, I, iii (with the typical markers 'Princes . . .', 'With due observance . . .', 'Speak, Prince of Ithaca'); *Henry V*, I, ii; etc. *Lear*, I, i, 36–265, and *Hamlet*, I, ii, 1–128, are especially interesting examples, since within this dominant mode of formal exchange the aside-monologue is used in an especially mature form, by Cordelia, 61, 75–7, and Hamlet, 65.

(ii) *Informal exchange*
Less conventionally marked than (i), but still a form in which persons speak 'with' and 'outward', rather than 'to' and 'inward'. The numerous examples include *Richard III*, I, iii; *Julius Caesar*, I, iii; *Anthony and Cleopatra*, II, ii; etc. This is an especially flexible type, and there can be shifts within scenes either way, to the more formal (including inset monologic) or to the more enclosed.

(iii) *Enclosed person-to-person*
This became so much the type of all dialogue, in most modern drama, that its assumptions are still often projected on to other dialogic modes. It is still very formal in its own terms in some of the best-known Renaissance examples – e.g., *Romeo and Juliet*, II, ii – but there are innumerable less formal cases: e.g., *Antony and Cleopatra*, III, iv; *Henry VIII*, V, i; *Merchant of Venice*, II, iii (before

brief monologue C (ii)), II, v; etc. Such scenes are also inset into other more complex modes.

The linguistic complexity of these types of monologue and dialogue, while usually distinguishable within the text, is complemented by a complexity of available stage positions, from which variable relations between speaker(s) and audience can be defined.[2] All that need be briefly indicated here is the continuity from direct address (centre downstage) positions, as in all types in A, to semi-direct and indirect address positions, typically involving a move downstage, B(ii), C(i) and usually C(ii) and (iii). Other moves include the turn towards the audience, B(i), and the move down and back again as in some forms of C(ii) and C(iii) – see below. B(iii) is more complex, since it is sometimes from the simple direct-address position but can be also from a downstage position while upstage is otherwise occupied in a different mode: e.g. Thersites in *Triolus and Cressida*, V, ii. Linguistic and positional markers, while typically corresponding, cannot always be read from the text alone, in its ordinary sense. Indeed, here as elsewhere, the text has to be read through the markers and, in the broadest sense, through both linguistic and playing conventions.

3

Macbeth[3] contains several well-remembered soliloquies, but we may now make some more precise descriptions and distinctions. Monologue in general, and the reflexive monologue in particular, are extensively used in the play; indeed, monologue comprises an unusually high proportion of it, at 15 per cent (see Tables 1 and 2 below). There is no monologue of the direct type, A, and the monologue aside, B(i), is very sparingly used; for one example see I, iii, 116–17. It should be noted here that there are cases of the 'dialogue aside' – a detached and inset break from general dialogue exchange, as in II, iii, 119–24, in which Malcolm and Donalbain would move downstage; in the subsequent 135–46 they are left alone.

B(iii) is well represented by the Porter's monologue, II, iii, 1–20. Often dismissed as 'comic relief', this is in fact a typical example of what has been called in recent linguistics 'anti-language' but can be better called 'counter-language', in which the evident linguistic shift, to a traditional colloquial mode, is not empty 'relief' but a deliberate shift of dramatic perspective: a connecting communal mode, played very close to the audience, in which the action is seen from a different base.

B(ii) is often difficult to distinguish from the more indirect types in C. In two examples in *Macbeth* there are useful linguistic markers: the secretive/explanatory function is marked by rhymed sentences. In I, iv, 48–53 Macbeth is not left alone but moves downstage to speak three rhymed couplets, ending:

> . . . Stars hide your fires
> Let not light see my black and deep desires:
> The eye wink at the hand; yet let that be
> Which the eye fears, when it is done, to see.

Duncan, still formally upstage, speaks to Banquo *after* this typical summary exit. The more usual case is in III, i, 140–1, in which Macbeth is left alone after speaking to the murderers:

> It is concluded: Banquo, thy soul's flight,
> If it find heaven, must find it out to-night.

On the other hand, there are cases which are clearly explanatory rather than self-discursive in function, without such evident markers; the best example is in II, ii, 1–13, notably in 'I have drugged their possets', though lines 12–13 ('Had he not resembled my father . . .') move towards the reflexive mode. Banquo's monologue in III, i, 1–10 seems to me also primarily explanatory, and therefore B(ii).

There are interesting examples of the rhetorical type of monologue, C(i). The most evident is in I, v, 1–29, where a mode of exchange, as in dialogue, is set up in Lady Macbeth's monologue by the device of her reading Macbeth's letter and then, in monologue, addressing him as if he were present:

> what thou wouldst highly,
> That wouldst thou holily.

A more arguable case is in III, iv, where Macbeth speaks in what is in effect inset monologue (50–1, 70–3, 93–6, 99–107) to the ghost of Banquo. It is not the ghost as such that makes this to some degree monologic; other ghosts, as in *Hamlet*, are both seen by others and themselves speak. Here it is only Macbeth *and the audience* who see the ghost, and it does not speak. The effect is very complex, but may be defined as speech without an object internal to the web of dramatic speech; hence (without the need for psychological explanation, though this may be added) as monologic projection of an object. But this has in turn, since the audience sees the ghost, to be distinguished from a related form, itself fully reflexive, in which Macbeth, but now only Macbeth, 'sees' (imagines) the dagger: II, i, 33 *et seq.* The linguistic forms overlap, in projection of an object –

> I see thee yet, in form as palpable

– but there is an easy transfer to the fully reflexive –

> It is the bloody business which informs.

Interestingly, however, this whole monologue is markedly projective –

> Thou sure and firm-set earth

– and indeed invocative, in the rhetorical form of the *apostrophe* –

> Hear not my steps.

It concludes with a summary rhymed sentence, in 63–4.

The fully reflexive is, as has been said, unusually frequent in *Macbeth*. Examples include, I, iii, 127–42, 143–5, 146–7; I, v, 37–53; I, vii, 1–28; II, i, 33–61; II, ii, 57–63; III, i, 47–71; IV, i, 144–55; IV, ii, 72–8; V, i, 31, 33–9, 41–4, 49–51, 61–3, 65–7; V, iii, 22–8; V, viii, 1–3. The mode, nevertheless, is sufficiently complex to include other functions; B(ii) is evident, for example, in IV, i, 150–4, again concluding with a summary rhymed sentence. The purest kind of reflexive, with the characteristics so often assigned to the 'soliloquy', is to be found in the longer monologues, e.g., I, vii, 1–28. What Shaftesbury had in mind as 'self-discoursing practice' is evidently exemplified in lines 12–28:

> He's here in double trust:
> First . . .
>> . . . then . . .
>> . . . Besides. . . .

This is argument in a single mind, spoken aloud. Another famous example is in I, iii, 130–42:

> If ill . . .
> If good . . .
> My thought . . .
> Shakes so my single state of man that function
> Is smothered in surmise . . ..

These last lines indeed express, precisely, this situation of agitated and as yet indecisive 'self-discourse'. Yet this sense of internal argument, which is clearly a major function of the reflexive, should not be taken as exclusive. The mode of argument, so clear in I, vii, 12–18, is surpassed, in lines 19–25, by a kind of speech which it would be seriously reductive to call argument. It is in this further mode that some of the most difficult questions arise.

Within the assumptions of 'soliloquy', and indeed within the categories of an older kind of literary linguistics, a relatively simple definition would be possible.

> And pity, like a naked new-born babe,
> Striding the blast. . . .

Is this not 'emotive' rather than 'referential' language? Is it not Macbeth 'overcome' by powerful feeling, which transforms and intensifies his 'argument'? But this is not 'private' or 'internal' meditation. It is dramatic monologue, spoken, to be sure indirectly, before an audience. While the mode is construed solely in terms of a character as subject, whose 'thoughts' and 'feelings' have only this isolated and enclosed reference, some of this writing can not be understood at all; can not, that is to say, be fully 'read', in its actual conventions and notations. For even in this monologue, of a classically reflexive type, more complex linguistic and (even within monologue) dramatic relations are in fact composed. Thus the full transition to the first-person pronoun as subject –

> First, as I am his kinsman. . . .

– does not occur until line 13. In the preceding lines, though the speech is of course directly relevant to Macbeth's own specific situation, there is the characteristic use of the plural pronoun, which in more integral cases can be seen as marking the important C(iii), the 'generic':

> But in these cases
> We still have judgement here – that we but teach
> Bloody instructions, which being taught return
> To plague th' inventor: this even-handed justice
> Commends th'ingredience of our poisoned chalice
> To our own lips.

It would be wrong to reduce this deliberately engaging argument, of a common condition and consequence, to a mere generalisation made by this isolated and agitated man. The relations implicit in such speech before an audience belong to an indirect communal mode rather than to the mode of expressive instances spoken by an isolated subject. Moreover, to put it another way, the relations compose the play – the action – rather than a set of 'characters'.

At this borderline between the reflexive and the generic we should however look at one very interesting example which, if I am reading it rightly, reminds us to retain the reflexive in its most evidently subjective cases. The case is also interesting as dramatic construction. It is significant at this stage of the development of monologue, even in a play which uses conventional monologue so freely, that elements of explanation are entered at some points. See, for example, 'Look how our partner's rapt' (I, iii, 142), pointing Macbeth's reflexive monologue in I, iii, and Macbeth's own explanatory and apologetic 'my dull brain was wrought/With things forgotten' (I, iii, 149–50). But there is a more remarkable case in V, i, where Lady Macbeth's reflexive monologue (as it must surely be defined) is dramatically controlled by the condition of sleepwalking: the true monologue but overheard within the play, as in other cases. Interestingly, her speech is predominantly projective and in its later parts a form of projected (but unanswered) dialogue with Macbeth:

> I tell you yet again. . . .

But this is, we could say, the most fully internal mode. It is private guilt – 'Yet here's a spot' – and only through overhearing, confession. This use of monologue, for the representation of mental *process* (either disordered, as here, or simply unarranged) as distinct from the articulation of mental *product* (fixed attitudes and beliefs, ordered stages of an argument or event, settled feelings), is of great importance in English Renaissance drama. It is this element which has helped to sustain the narrow sense of 'soliloquy'. Linguistically it is marked by strong uses of the dramatic present (as distinct from the historic present) tense, with relatively uncomposed – in fact often directly oral rather than 'written' – sentences:

> Whence is that knocking?
> How is't with me, when every noise appals me?
> What hands are here? ha! they pluck out mine eyes!
>
> [II, ii, 57–9]

Yet these same qualities of active presence and process are to be found also in dialogue:

> *M*:   What soldiers, whey-face?
> *S*: The English force, so please you.
> *M*: Take thy face hence. Seton! I am sick at heart,
>   When I behold – Seton, I say! – This push. . . .
>
> [V, iii, 17–20]

At the same time monologue, including reflexive monologue, can be quite differently composed, in weaker present or in perfect or past tenses:

> I have almost forgot the taste of fears:
> The time has been, my senses would have cooled
> To hear a night-shriek. . . .
>
> [V, v, 9–11]

Thus there is no formal equivalence between presumed psychological content, of a subjective kind, and a mode of writing centred on a single and isolated speaker. The 'soliloquy', to put it another way, is not 'inner speech' in any defining or exclusive sense. The degrees of address, over a range from 'self-discoursing practice' to indirect and direct monologue of more outward kinds, control much more variable and complex relations, which within the modern private/public dichotomy cannot be construed; indeed, often literally cannot be read.

It is on this basis that we can return to the relations between the reflexive and the generic. For the true generic is the completion of that common element of the reflexive which is not in any limiting sense 'inner speech' but is the engagement, often from within personal crisis, with a common condition. The most notable example in *Macbeth*, again linguistically marked by the plural pronoun, is the famous

> Tomorrow, and tomorrow, and tomorrow,
> Creeps in this petty pace from day to day,
> To the last syllable of recorded time;
> And all our yesterdays have lighted fools
> The way to dusty death. . . .
>
> [V, v, 19–23]

This should not be reduced to the speech of a subjective psychological condition, as can be seen from its evident formal difference from a closely related speech in the same Act:

> I have lived long enough: my way of life
> Is fall'n into the sere, the yellow leaf. . . .
>
> [V, iii, 22–3]

The latter is reflexive, within an individual condition; the former is generic, engaging a possible common response within a common condition. It is relevant to notice that the linguistic forms of the generic are often close to those of shared prayer, or prayer offered for sharing, within liturgy, though in the two most famous cases – this from *Macbeth* and 'To be or not to be' in *Hamlet* – the content has been transformed. The developed reflexive, in its more or less subjective forms, but also this dramatic rather than orthodox–liturgical generic, are then remarkable extensions of the range of public discourse, within the changing social and historical conditions of this secular drama.

4

The point of distinguishing and illustrating these types of monologue is not classification but an extension of vocabulary in the service of analytic rather than annotative ('critical') reading. There is room for argument about each of the types and their definitions, and of course for variation of judgment in the reading and assigning of any particular example. In my own analysis of *Macbeth* the distribution can be summarised in Table 1. Analysis of the variations of monologue leads necessarily into variations of dialogue and of the relations between monologue and dialogue. These, as has been argued, are especially complex in this unusually flexible dramatic form. Thus the generic quoted above occurs within very complex staging. Act V, scene v begins with Macbeth ordering his defences: therefore speaking to soldiers. There is a break at the 'cry within of women' and Macbeth's question to Seton, who has then perhaps been present from the beginning. Macbeth's reflexive 'I have almost forgot the taste of fears' is then not necessarily 'soliloquy' in the sense of being alone on the stage; it is, more strictly, inset indirect address. The next break is the question 'Wherefore was that cry?', which Seton answers. Has he left and returned? What matters more is the rapid and flexible shift between exchange, as in the question and answer, and both direct in-play ('Hang out our banners') and reflexive ('I have supped full with horrors') address. This kind of shift is especially notable in the movement from response (of its kind) to the news that the queen is dead – the reduced exchange – to the fully generic monologue, downstage but not necessarily 'alone', of 'Tomorrow, and tomorrow, and tomorrow', itself pointed by the next shift, with the certain entry of a messenger: 'Thou com'st to use thy tongue'.

Table 1

	A(i)	A(ii)	A(iii)	B(i)	B(ii)	B(iii)	C(i)	C(ii)	C(iii)	D(i)	D(ii)	D(iii)
% of text–	–	–	0.2	1.5	1	2.2	9	1.1	16.6	31	37.4

Such relations between monologue and dialogue, and more crucially between levels and types of address, are also evident, as was argued, within different kinds of dialogue where the object of address is also often variable and shifting. It may be possible to discern some relations between types and proportions of both monologue and dialogue and certain kinds of play. Some preliminary comparative analysis is summarised in Table 2. It should be clear, even from such preliminary comparisons (which, to bear further weight, need much more detailed collaborative work), that there is radical variation between plays (and not only by date) in the use of any monologue, and also of its types, and that there are possible relations between this and predominant types of

Table 2

Play	Total Monologue	A(i)	A(ii)	A(iii)	B(i)	B(ii)	B(iii)	C(i)	C(ii)	C(iii)	D(i)	D(ii)	D(iii)
						(Percentage of text)							
	%	%	%	%	%	%	%	%	%	%	%	%	%
Macbeth	15	–	–	–	0.2	1.5	1	2.2	9	1.1	16.6	31	37.4
Hamlet	7.6	–	–	–	0.1	0.4	–	1.4	4.8	0.9	8.6	43	40.8
Julius Caesar	5.9	–	–	–	0.2	2.4	–	1.1	1.5	0.7	21.5	42.3	30.3
Troilus and Cressida	5.2	0.3	0.7	0.5	0.3	0.5	2.3	–	0.4	0.2	19.5	22.3	53
Coriolanus	1.0	–	–	–	–	0.6	–	–	0.4	–	16.4	52.9	29.7

dialogue (as, for example, between the proportion of monologue and especially reflexive monologue and the enclosed 'private-exchange' dialogue of D(iii)).

More generally, we can urge the more vigorous inclusion of such analysis in the development of English studies. 'Practical criticism', in its reduced and residual forms, can at best read such 'words on the page' in an expressive sense: at times in itself relevant, and characteristically capable of literary analysis of a kind developed for other forms of writing, notably the short poem (thus theme, imagery, selected words, etc.). The decisive elements of verbal organisation which become evident in analysis of relation and address are easily missed in such reading, yet for dramatic texts especially – and for these as texts written for performance, in which relation and address are physically actualised – they are inescapably important. Any full reading, like any playing, centrally depends on them, yet it has been common to read Shakespeare as texts for silent reading, without theatre or performance, or to include such considerations as merely peripheral. As has been shown, and as indeed should be obvious, these fundamental conditions of production of the text are everywhere present in the verbal organisation itself.

This point bears more generally on the developing relations between linguistics and literary analysis. Problems of relation and address have been widely studied in prose narrative, but there has been comparative neglect of the more pressing problems and opportunities in the written relations and forms of address of this explicitly multivocal form. Certain tendencies in structuralist analysis, and in the development of the idea of 'fictionality', have both theoretically and practically obscured the inevitable relationships, including 'interpersonal' relationships, which texts of many kinds but especially and necessarily dramatic texts compose. At the same time, certain kinds of drama, and especially that of the English Renaissance, compose more complex forms of relationship than 'interpersonal' alone would suggest: not only A–B or A–B–C *exchanges*, but also widely variable (including and excluding) relationships not necessarily confined to 'exchange'. Moreover, when it is realised that these are not simply relations 'within a text' – that is to say, between voices composed by the text – but are also relations of a variable kind with both actual and presumed audiences, differently present as a fact of composition

201

from any silent reader, there are many opportunities to go beyond that enclosure of the text, or of the text-analyst, which has marked so much recent work. This is also one of the ways of defeating that abstraction of texts from society and from history which marked a powerful recent phase. For here the social presence – and then that presence as both historical and permanently available – is a function of the specific composition: that actual audience, of an historically specific kind, carrying the necessary conventions of relation and address; that required audience, in a necessarily multivocal form in which relations and objects of address are linguistically composed.

These wider matters, theoretical and as ground for new historical research and social analysis, belong to future work. Meanwhile it is possible that we have found some ways beyond the technical and ideological impasse of 'soliloquy'.

NOTES

1 Reprinted in Shaftesbury, *Characteristicks*, vol. 1, 1727, pp. 153ff.
2 For a fuller discussion of these, see Robert Weimann, *Shakespeare and the Popular Tradition of the Theater*, ed. Robert Schwartz, Baltimore, Johns Hopkins University Press, 1978, pp. 73–85 and 215–45.
3 All references are to the 'New Shakespeare' *Macbeth*, standard edn, Cambridge University Press, 1946, 1950.

12 *The Duchess of Malfi*: A case study in the literary representation of women

Lisa Jardine

The Jacobean drama has regularly attracted the attention of critics for its lively representation of women as strong, manipulative, self-willed, passionate and controlling of dramatic action. This 'masculine strength' wins the acclaim of the critic for its authenticity, and for its real insight into woman's character. It is the mark of the superior vision of the Jacobean dramatist: he sees beyond the contemporary stereotypes of meek and grieving womanhood to the 'true nature of woman' – to a full-bloodedly warrior-like femaleness to which the Renaissance for the first time gave a voice. And inevitably in the last decade both feminist critics and female actors have been drawn to the leading female roles in the plays of Webster and Middleton by their reputation for 'liberatedness'. The temptation to adopt these figures as role-models for our own period has proved irresistible. Helen Mirren, interviewed about her highly successful and critically acclaimed performance as the Duchess in Webster's *The Duchess of Malfi* in the 1981 Round House production, attributed her success with the role to the fact that it is 'very much a play for today': 'It is essentially a feminist play about a woman who is fighting for her autonomy.'[1]

The suggestion that the Duchess, Vittoria in Webster's *The White Devil* or Beatrice-Joanna in Middleton's *The Changeling* are faithful portraits of possible womanhood in the early seventeenth century, or even dramatic projections of a kind of female outlook lurking beneath the calm surface of the Jacobean world, is puzzling, and in my view misleading. The rapidly growing body of information we can gather from non-literary sources, both of woman's actual position in early modern society and of contemporary attitudes towards her, is striking for the consistent picture it gives of the *absence* of emancipation of women, both at a theoretical and at a practical level.[2] Where, then, do the strong female characters who wheel-and-deal their way through the drama come from? How are they related to their real-life sisters who were, it transpires, increasingly constrained by an ideology of duty and obedience which removed from them the most elementary possibilities for rebellion against traditional serving roles?

In this lecture I shall be looking at the impression of strength in the Jacobean female hero in one play, John Webster's *The Duchess of Malfi*, and offering tentative answers to these questions.[3] I shall be suggesting that the 'psychological insight' of the Jacobean dramatists' representations of women is related to actual seventeenth-century women and their roles in an unexpected way, and one which must give us pause for thought in our wider exploration of the literary representation of women. This is, if you like, a cautionary tale, and a direct challenge to those who suggest that the vision of the well-intentioned dramatist (be he Shakespeare or Webster or Middleton) can transcend the limits of his time and sex in the representation of women.

Let us begin by trying to identify some of the features of female characterisation which lead the critics to refer to them as 'strong' in the first place, and as admirable in that strength. Passion, sensuality, courage, intelligence, cunning, ambition are some of the attributes associated with female heroes like Bianca in Middleton's *Women Beware Women*, Beatrice-Joanna in *The Changeling*, Vittoria in Webster's *The White Devil*. All these qualities are at various times shown by the Duchess. They add up to such forcefulness and spirited independence that generations of audiences have been seduced into accepting them as part of a consistent and believable female heroic persona. And it is in the interests of that 'believableness', I think, that the critics are led to assert the correspondence between this 'strength' of character and emancipated possibilities for individual women of the period. A recent critic writes:

> One of John Webster's most original contributions to English tragedy consisted in his examination of the character-

istics which combine to produce a convincing tragic heroine.[4]

But as she pursues this 'convincingness' it emerges that the critic views this in a very particular sense; the 'convincing tragic heroine' is convincingly (and, the suggestion is, realistically) threatening to men:

> While providing a convincing answer to the question, 'What did this woman do to merit death?', the tragedy which successfully presents a sympathetic tragic heroine must also be concerned with the question, 'Can this woman be trusted?' It is not a matter of one woman being able to trust another . . . but it is a matter of whether one man or many men can trust one particular woman.[5]

'Can this woman be trusted?' is a peculiarly patriarchal question to ask. And indeed, our critic acknowledges this:

> In Webster's major tragedies this point is emphasised by the strange situation of his heroines. Both Vittoria and the Duchess of Malfi move in exclusively masculine worlds; both appear to be cut off from contact with other women; both are virtually isolated from the friendship or companionship of women of their own rank.[6]

The female hero moves in an exclusively masculine stage-world, in which it is the task of the male characters to 'read' her. Is she what she appears? 'Look to't: be not cunning:/For they whose faces do belie their hearts/Are witches, ere they arrive at twenty years – /Ay: and give the devil suck' (I, i, 308–11). Shakespeare's 'strong' women find themselves in a similarly male world: Gertrude in *Hamlet* (and her reflection in Ophelia), Desdemona in *Othello* (more manipulated than manipulating), Cleopatra in *Antony and Cleopatra*.

So when the critic tells us that the Jacobean dramatist shows peculiar insight into female character, and even into female psychology, what he or she means is that a convincing portrayal is given *from a distinctively male viewpoint* (even if this is not made explicit by the critic). Another female critic, apparently content that 'psychological insight' into female character be *male* insight, writes:

Middleton's capacity for tragedy is inseparable from his other supreme gift, his discernment of the minds of women; in this no dramatist of the period except Shakespeare is his equal at once for variety and for penetration [sic].[7]

The strength of the female protagonist is as seen through male eyes.

It is seen through male eyes, and as such it is dramatically compelling. But the female character traits to which the critics give this enthusiastic support are on inspection morally dubious: cunning, duplicity, sexual rapaciousness, 'changeableness', being other than they seem, untrustworthiness and general secretiveness. In *The Duchess of Malfi*, the first entrance of the Duchess is in an atmosphere fraught with explicitly offensive sexual innuendo, in which she is implicated, and which controls our assessment of her character:

Ferdinand: You are a widow:
You know already what man is, and therefore
Let not youth, high promotion, eloquence –
Cardinal: No, nor anything without the addition, honour,
Sway your high blood.
Ferdinand: Marry! they are most luxurious [lust-
ful]
Will wed twice.
. . .
Duchess: Will you hear me?
I'll never marry: –
Cardinal: So most widows say:
But commonly that motion lasts no longer
Than the turning of an hour-glass – the funeral sermon
And it, end both together. [I, i, 293–304]

A handful of speeches later the sexual innuendo comes to a climax, and the Duchess reveals the accuracy of her brothers' predictions (confirming their dark travesty of female lasciviousness and 'doubleness') simultaneously:

Ferdinand: You are my sister –
This was my father's poinard: do you see?
I'd be loth to see 't rusty, 'cause 'twas his: –
A visor and a mask are whispering-rooms

That were ne'er built for goodness: fare ye well: –
And women like that part which, like the lamprey
Hath ne'er a bone in't.
Duchess: Fie sir!
Ferdinand: Nay,

I mean the tongue: variety of courtship:. . . .
What cannot a neat knave with a smooth tale
Make a woman believe? Farewell lusty widow.   [*Exit.*]
Duchess: Shall this move me? If all my royal kindred
Lay in my way unto this marriage,
I'd make them my low footsteps.   [I, i, 330–43]

The picture of stereotyped female virtue painted in advance of
her appearance by the Duchess' infatuated servant (and subsequent husband) Antonio cannot compensate for the impact of
this initial encounter: 'I'll case the picture up. . . ./ All her particular worth grows to this sum: / She stains the time past, lights
the time to come' (I, i, 207–9). The Duchess' 'luxuriousness'
(lustfulness) drives her powerfully into secret marriage and flou-
ting of her brothers' wishes, just as Gertrude's sexuality, in
Hamlet, drives her into her dead husband's brother's bed. Lower
in her sexual drive than 'a beast that wants discourse of reason',[8]
the Duchess of Malfi steps out of the path of duty and marries for
lust. Thereafter she remains heroically determined to follow
through the consequences of her initial base action, until her
resoluteness is gradually commuted into the splendour of re-
signed passive acceptance of inevitable downfall:

Ferdinand: How doth our sister duchess bear herself
In her imprisonment?
Bosola: Nobly; I'll describe her:
She's sad, as one long us'd to't; and she seems
Rather to welcome the end of misery
Than shun it; – a behaviour so noble
As gives a majesty to adversity;
You may discern the shape of loveliness
More perfect in her tears, than in her smiles.
[IV, i, 1–8]

'Majesty' in the female hero is here at its most reassuring and
admirable when associated with patient suffering: Griselda, the

Virgin Mary, Hecuba prostrate with grief. A 'convincing' representation of the developing psychology of the female hero is apparently the transformation of lascivious waywardness into emblematic chaste resignation.[9]

The impulsive offer of love by a woman is most likely to be a sign of unreliableness and untrustworthiness, if the male characters are allowed to have the final say in 'reading' that offer. When Beatrice-Joanna, in *The Changeling*, takes the decision to follow her sensual desire and marry Alsemero, disposing of her husband-to-be, she is already embarked on the course which will lead to her obsessive sexual involvement with De Flores:

> *De Flores:*   If a woman
>   Fly from one point, from him she makes a husband,
>   She spreads and mounts then like arithmetic,
>   One, ten, a hundred, a thousand, ten thousand,
>   Proves in time sutler to an army royal. . . .
>   Methinks I feel her in mine arms already,
>   Her wanton fingers combing out this beard,
>   And being pleased, praising this bad face.
>   Hunger and pleasure, they'll commend sometimes
>   Slovenly dishes, and feed heartily on 'em,
>   Nay, which is stranger, refuse daintier for 'em.[10]

If we miss this patriarchal assumption in the drama we are bound to be bemused by subsequent developments. In *Othello*, Desdemona has amply demonstrated her driving sensuality and female unreliability by marrying for love, without parental consent:

> Look to her, Moor, if thou hast eyes to see;
> She has deceiv'd her father, and may thee. [I, iii, 292–3]

Such careful intrusions into the drama reminding the audience of the sensual strain in the central female character should, I think, alert us to the *guilt* which adheres to such characters. In the eyes of the Jacobean audience they are above all *culpable*, and their *strength* – the ways in which they direct the action, scheme and orchestrate, evade the consequences of their impulsive decisions, and ultimately face resolutely the final outcome – need to be seen in this context. Over the years critics have tended to attempt complicated exonerations of the female heroes of the Jacobean drama, to make them 'innocent' of the sexual slur. We should take another look at the case.

The acknowledged source for Webster's *The Duchess of Malfi* is William Painter's *The Palace of Pleasure* (1566/7), an extremely popular compendium of lively tales of domestic and court life, drawn from the ancient and European traditions. The twenty-third 'nouel' is entitled, 'The Duchess of Malfi, the infortunate marriage of a Gentleman, called Antonio Bologna, with the Duchess of Malfi, and the pitifull death of them both'. The moral message of this novella is unequivocal, from the opening paragraphs of the tale:

> Wherefore it behoueth the Noble, and such as haue charge of Common wealth, to liue an honest lyfe, and beare their port vpryght, that none haue cause to take ill example vpon dyscourse of their deedes and naughtie life. And aboue all, that modestie ought to be kept by women, whome as their race, Noble birth, authoritie and name, maketh them more famous, euen so their vertue, honestie, chastitie, and continencie more praiseworthy. And behouefull it is, that like as they wishe to be honoured aboue all other, so their life do make them worthy of that honour, without disgracing their name by deede or woorde, or blemishing that brightnesse which may commende the same. I greatly feare that all the Princely factes, the exploits and conquests done by the *Babylonian* Queene *Semyramis*, neuer was recommended with such praise, as hir vice had shame in records by those which left remembrance of ancient acts. Thus I say, bicause a woman being as it were the Image of sweetnesse, curtesie and shamefastnesse, so soone as she steppeth out of the right tracte, and leaueth the smel of hir duetie and modestie, bisides the denigration of hir honor, thrusteth hir self into infinite troubles and causeth the ruine of such which should be honored and praised, if womens allurement solicited them not to follie.[11]

The litany of conventional cautions against 'dishonest' behaviour sets the tone of the story. 'Woman being as it were the Image of sweetenesse, curtisie and shamefastnesse' has no alternative: any single act which does not square with this emblem of passive and dutiful behaviour condemns the individual as 'fallen' from the

209

pedestal. An entire glorious military career is blotted out when Semyramis seduces her son.

In the dramatic version of *The Duchess of Malfi*, active sexuality codes for female breach of decorum. In the moment of disobeying her brothers and remarrying (remarrying a social inferior, to emphasise that this is 'lust' not 'duty'), the Duchess of Malfi asserts her sexual self. In so doing she is metamorphosed from ideal mirror of virtue ('Let all sweet ladies break their flatt'ring glasses/ And dress themselves in her' (I, i, 203–4)) into lascivious whore. It is not simply that her brothers view her as such; the dominant strain in the subsequent representation of her *is* such. And we have to ask ourselves what it is about that knowing step she takes which is sufficient to rock the social system and warrant such ritualised condemnation. From the moment of her assertion of sexual independence, the Duchess moves with dignity but inexorably towards a ritual chastisement worthy of a flagrant breach of public order. Thereafter her strength lies in her fortitude in the face of a doom she has brought upon herself.

Yet the initial stand taken by the Duchess retains its dramatic power, despite the fact that success is apparently never a real possibility, the threat to patriarchal order never an actual one. I want now to suggest that there was an area of early modern social order in which *apparently*, although not actually, women had become frighteningly strong and independent, and one which maps plausibly on to the dominant preoccupations of the drama. This is the idea of property inheritance and Land Law.

The sixteenth century in England was a period of major and far-reaching change in inheritance practice. Unfortunately, these changes are masked from the student of literature by blanket references, whenever some comment on customary inheritance is called for, to a ubiquitous law of primogeniture (inheritance of the entire estate by the eldest male heir). Immediately he has introduced his bastard son, Edmund, to Kent, in *King Lear*, Gloucester specifies his family position:

> But I have a son, sir, by order of law, some year elder than this, who yet is no dearer in my account: though this knave came something saucily to the world before he was sent for, yet was his mother fair. [I, i, 17–20]

This we are told is to establish that Edgar is Gloucester's legitimate *heir* as well as his legitimate son, since either way he is *older* than Edmund. Lear himself, meanwhile, divides his kingdom by 'partible' inheritance (equal division) among his daughters, in the absence of a male heir. Certainly by the sixteenth century this was considered to be the ideal state of affairs, as codified in English Land Law, but as recent historians and historians of the Land Law themselves are quick to point out, inheritance *practice* never conformed with the ideal, and consisted in modifying and evading the most stringent requirements of lineal inheritance as codified, because of disastrous consequences this could in practice have in fragmenting individual estates.[12]

During the sixteenth and seventeenth centuries, great landowners, under direct threat from wealthy status-seeking burghers, tinkering energetically with legislation and precedent in a determined effort to keep their dwindling estates together. The issue, inevitably, came down to a head-on conflict between land (the nobleman's asset) and cash (the increasingly powerful asset of the expanding mercantile class). And at the heart of every 'tinkering' to be found in the meticulously drawn up wills of the nobility and gentry of the period, one is almost certain to find a woman.[13]

Even before demographic accident had produced a dangerous shortfall in male heirs, female kin had come to be seen as destructive of estate conservation. A daughter had to be provided with a dowry, part at least of which, in noble households, would be in the form of land. As soon as she produced an heir to her husband's line, that land became part of the alien line's permanent holdings (in the absence of an heir it would revert to her own family, either upon her death, or upon that of her husband). In the absence of any sons at all, the estate would be divided among the daughters – once again a catastrophe in terms of consolidation of power in the form of an intact estate. And finally, in the event of a nobleman's dying before his wife, one-third of all his lands passed not to his male heir, but to his dowager widow, for her use during her lifetime. This both imposed a considerable burden on the heir, and might, if she remarried, result once again in the partition of previously intact estates. One wonders whether the regular confusion of 'dowry' and 'dower' (entirely distinct in law) in popular parlance stemmed from the threat both represented to the continuity of male inheritance.

211

In their concern over the absence of male heirs, and over the damage being done to their estates by strict settlement and traditional patterns of inheritance, heads of household increasingly turned their attention to the settlements on daughters and on younger sons. Traditionally these had taken the form of 'portions' allocated in place of land at the time when the younger children left home. Increasingly landowners concentrated on these settlements to compensate for the erosion of the main estates: if a well-dowried girl could attract a good husband, or a younger son make a match with a wealthy heiress or widow on the strength of his portion, that might compensate for the initial outlay. Particularly important for the bargaining power of dowries was the fact that the daughter's dowry in goods was available to the *father* of the bridegroom to pay his debts in ready money (lands could not be easily 'alienated' – sold out of the inheritance pattern).

Portions for younger sons and marriageable daughters increase dramatically during the Elizabethan and Jacobean periods. 'Dowry inflation' was considered the curse of the age, decried by clergy and lawyers:

> The excesses of our times in giving great Dowries is growen to such a height, that it impoverisheth oftentimes the Parents; it seemeth a point worthy the consideration whether it were not expedient that the Parliament should limit the quantity of Dowries according to the State and Condition of every Man; which no doubt would greatly ease the Nobility and Gentry.[14]

The effectiveness of the strategy as a lure is evidenced by the fact that some sumptuary legislation (legislation controlling richness of dress according to rank and status) aligned the permitted richness of dress for a woman with the size of her marriage portion. In Thomas Heywood's *A Woman Killed with Kindness*, the shifting fortunes of Mountford are directly reflected on stage by the dress his sister wears, and this in turn decides her desirability as a bride:

> *Enter SIR CHARLES, gentlemanlike, and his Sister, gentle-womanlike.*
> *Susan*: Brother, why have you trick'd me like a bride?

Bought me this gay attire, these ornaments?
Forget you our estate, our poverty.[15]

The woman's dress defines her power as a magnet to attract wealth on behalf of the paternal line.

The prominent position occupied by female heirs in all this discussion of the complex tactical manoeuvres surrounding inheritance is in striking contrast to their enforced submissiveness elsewhere within the Elizabethan and Jacobean social systems. This fact is, of course, somewhat ironic. It was not the intention of lawyers and landowners preoccupied with patrilinear succession to involve their women as other than means to a patriarchal end. But it remains true that female nobles and gentry do obtrude during this period in their capacity as carriers of inheritance.

Not that this gave them any *actual* power, and this is really the point at issue. They are technically strong (or strong enough to cause patriarchal anxiety), but actually in thrall. In Middleton's *Women Beware Women*, the handsomely dowried Isabella bewails her lack of personal choice of a marriage partner whilst at the same time affirming her importance in the inheritance stakes:

Isabella: Oh the heart breakings
    Of miserable maids, where love's enforced!
    The best condition is but bad enough:
    When women have their choices, commonly
    They do but buy their thraldoms, and bring great
                                    portions
    To men to keep 'em in subjection –
    As if a fearful prisoner should bribe
    The keeper to be good to him, yet lies in still,
    And glad of a good usage, a good look sometimes.
    By 'r Lady, no misery surmounts a woman's:
    Men buy their slaves, but women buy their
                                    masters.[16]

Yet in *Women Beware Women* it is in fact the female characters who, while formally protesting their ineffectualness, weakness and submissiveness to men, wheel-and-deal their way through adultery, murder and incest. The alliance of the heart which Isabella would prefer to an arranged marriage with a wealthy ward is an incestuous relationship with her uncle: the female

213

drive towards independent choice leads to sexual licence. The shift from passivity to bravura activity is accompanied by a marked moral decline, apparent in her subsequent disparaging remarks on the indignity of being 'marketed' as an heiress:

> *Isabella: (aside)* But that I have th'advantage of the fool,
> As much as woman's heart can wish and joy at,
> What an infernal torment 'twere to be
> Thus bought and sold, and turned and pried into:
> when alas
> The worst bit is too good for him! And the comfort is
> 'Has but a cater's place on't, and provides
> All for another's table.[17]

With comparable bravado, the Duchess of Malfi resolutely identifies her elevated fiscal position (as a young widow to a large estate, and heiress in her own right) with her actual entitlement to act exactly as she chooses:

> *Duchess:* The misery of us that are born great –
> We are forc'd to woo, because none dare woo us:
> . . . .
> sir, be confident –
> What is't distracts you? This is flesh, and blood, sir;
> 'Tis not the figure cut in alabaster
> Kneels at my husband's tomb. Awake, awake, man!
> I do here put off all vain ceremony,
> And only do appear to you a young widow
> That claims you for her husband, and like a widow,
> I use but half a blush in't. [I, i, 441–59]

In both cases, I suggest, we are witness to the acting out of a taboo. As the loyal Cariola comments on the Duchess' behaviour:

> Whether the spirit of greatness or of woman
> Reign most in her, I know not, but it shows
> A fearful madness. [I, i, 504–6]

The Duchess acts out her remarriage and its consequences *as if* her forcefulness as royal heir, dowager of the Dukedom of Amalfi, carrier of a substantial dowry in movable goods (which she and Antonio take legitimately with them when they flee together), gave her *real* power. In this she is proved pathetically wrong. In a passage which modern producers prefer to omit as tedious, the patriarchy's retaliation for her behaviour is spelt out:

> *2nd Pilgrim:*   They are banish'd.
> *1st Pilgrim:* But I would ask what power hath this state
> Of Ancona to determine of a free prince?
> *2nd Pilgrim:* They are a free state sir, and her brother
>   show'd
> How that the Pope, fore-hearing of her looseness,
> Hath seiz'd into th' protection of the church
> The dukedom, which she held as a dowager.
>   [III, iv, 27–33]

The Duchess has lost her princely immunity through forfeiture of her dower – the forfeiture being because she has proved herself 'loose' by marrying, without her brothers' consent, 'so mean a person' as Antonio (who himself has his own lands confiscated for his 'felony'). From this moment she is not, despite her own protests to the contrary, 'Duchess of Malfi still':

> *Duchess:* Am I not thy duchess?
> *Bosola:* Thou art some great woman, sure, for riot
> begins to sit on thy forehead, clad in gray hairs,
> twenty years sooner than on a merry milkmaid's.
> Thou sleepest worse than if a mouse should be forced to
> take up her lodging in a cat's ear: a little infant that breeds
> its teeth, should it lie with thee, would cry out, as if thou
> were the more unquiet bedfellow.
> *Duchess:* I am Duchess of Malfi still.
> *Bosola:* That makes thy sleep so broken. [IV, ii, 134–43]

Proved pathetically wrong in her belief in emancipation through hereditary strength, the Duchess is reduced to the safe composite stereotype of penitent whore, Virgin majestic in grief, serving mother, and patient and true turtle dove mourning her one love. The Duchess acts out on stage her inheritance power which in real life was no power at all for the individual woman. In real life the verdict was decided upon in advance. As Painter put it:

> Behold here (O ye foolish louers) a Glasse of your lightnesse,

215

and ye women, the course of your fonde behauior. ....
Shall I be of opinion that a houshold seruaunt ought
to sollicite, nay rather suborne the daughter of his Lord
without punishment, or that a vile and abiect person dare to
mount vpon a Princes bed? No no, pollicie requireth order
in all, and eche wight ought to be matched according to their
qualitie, without making a pastime of it to couer our follies,
and know not of what force loue and desteny be, except the
same be resisted. A goodly thing it is to loue, but where
reason loseth his place, loue is without his effect, and the
sequele rage and madnesse.[18]

In Webster's play, the spectre of real female strength implicit
in the inheritance structure is ritually exorcised. Headstrong,
emancipated female love is chastened into figurative submission.

The general lesson to be learned from all this is, I hope, clear.
Whatever is to be discovered by considering women figures in
literature, it is unlikely to be a simple matter to read it out of
the text of novel or play. However much of an inspiration the
Duchess may appear to us – the strong woman challenging conventional attitudes – she is not a 'real' woman, neither is she a
direct reflection of individual women of her time. She is a transposition of a complex of attitudes towards women into a 'travesty'
(literally, a man in woman's clothes) of seventeenth-century
womanhood. The strength we enjoy in performance is her actual
weakness – perhaps that is what makes the Duchess of Malfi so
captivating and poignant a stage figure.

NOTES

1 *The Observer*, Review Section, 27 March 1981.
2 For a full documentation on this and all other historical
  material used in this lecture see L. Jardine, *Still Harping on
  Daughters: Women and Drama in the Age of Shakespeare*,
  Brighton, Harvester, 1983.
3 All references to *The Duchess of Malfi* are to the Revels edn, ed.
  J.R. Brown, London, Methuen, 1964.
4 E.M. Brennan (ed.), *The Devil's Law-Case*, New Mermaid,
  London, Ernest Benn, 1975, p. xvi.
5 Ibid., p. xvii.

6 Ibid.
7 U. Ellis-Fermor, *The Jacobean Drama*, London, Methuen, 1936, p. 149.
8 *Hamlet*, I, ii, 150.
9 On emblematic chastity see Marina Warner, *Alone of All Her Sex: The Myth and the Cult of the Virgin Mary*, London, Quartet Books, 1978, pp. 81–120.
10 N.W. Bawcutt (ed.), *The Changeling*, Revels edn, London, Methuen, 1958, II, ii, 60–152.
11 Reprinted in the Revels edition of *The Duchess of Malfi*, pp. 175–209, pp. 176–7.
12 For a lucid account of the history of the English Land Law and its modifications in practice see A.W.B. Simpson, *An Introduction to the History of the Land Law*, Oxford University Press, 1961. I am grateful to Professor Glanville Williams and Mr Peter Glazebrook for their advice on the history of the Land Law.
13 See J.P. Cooper, 'Patterns of Inheritance and Settlement by Great Landowners from the Fifteenth to the Eighteenth Centuries', in J. Goody, J. Thirsk and E.P. Thompson (eds), *Family and Inheritance*, Cambridge University Press, 1976, pp. 192–305. I am extremely grateful to Diane Owen Hughes for referring me to this article.
14 Cited in Cooper, op. cit., p. 222.
15 R.W. Van Fossen (ed.), *A Woman Killed with Kindness*, Revels edn, London, Methuen, 1961, scene xiv.
16 J.R. Mulryne (ed.), *Women Beware Women*, Revels edn, London, Methuen, 1975, I, ii, 166–76.
17 Ibid., III, iv, 33–9.
18 Painter, in the Revels edn, pp. 192–3.

Notes on Contributors

The positions listed are those which the contributor held during the teaching year 1980–1.

John Barrell: Fellow of King's College; university lecturer, Faculty of English, Cambridge

Norman Bryson: Fellow and assistant lecturer in English, King's College; lectured on American Literature to the Faculty of English, Cambridge

Stephen Heath: Fellow of Jesus College; university lecturer, Faculty of English, Cambridge

Lisa Jardine: Fellow of Jesus College; university lecturer, Faculty of English, Cambridge

Susanne Kappeler: Research Fellow in English, Jesus College; lectured on the Literary Representation of Women to the Faculty of English, Cambridge

Anita Kermode: Supervisor in English; lectured on American Literature to the Faculty of English, Cambridge

Frank Kermode: Fellow of King's College; King Edward VII Professor, Faculty of English, Cambridge

Colin MacCabe: Fellow of King's College; assistant lecturer, Faculty of English, Cambridge

Christopher Prendergast: Fellow of King's College; university lecturer, Faculty of Modern and Medieval Languages, Cambridge; contributor to a series of lectures on European literature for the Faculty of English, Cambridge

Joseph Peter Stern: Professor of German, University College,

218

London; contributor to a series of lectures on European literature for the Faculty of English, Cambridge

Tony Tanner: Fellow of King's College; Reader, Faculty of English, Cambridge.

Raymond Williams: Fellow of Jesus College; Professor of Drama, Faculty of English, Cambridge

Teaching the Text